WILEY BOOKS IN THE CERTMIKE SERIES

CompTIA ITF+ CertMike: *Prepare. Practice. Pass the Test! Get Certified! Exam FC0-U61*
by Mike Chapple
(ISBN 9781119897811)

CompTIA A+ CertMike: *Prepare. Practice. Pass the Test! Get Certified! Core 1 Exam 220-1101*
by Mike Chapple and Mark Soper
(ISBN 9781119898092)

CompTIA A+ CertMike: *Prepare. Practice. Pass the Test! Get Certified! Core 2 Exam 220-1102*
by Mike Chapple and Mark Soper
(ISBN 9781119898122)

CompTIA Network+ CertMike: *Prepare. Practice. Pass the Test! Get Certified! Exam N10-008*
by Mike Chapple and Craig Zacker
(ISBN 9781119898153)

CompTIA® Network+® CertMike

Prepare. Practice. Pass the Test! Get Certified!

CompTIA® Network+® CertMike

Prepare. Practice. Pass the Test! Get Certified!
Exam N10-008

Mike Chapple
Craig Zacker

SYBEX®
A Wiley Brand

ACKNOWLEDGMENTS

From Mike Chapple:

This book marks the start of a new series of CertMike Test Prep books, and I'd first like to thank the people who helped shape the vision for this series. The original idea was hatched over breakfast with two very supportive editors from the Wiley team: Ken Brown and Jim Minatel. I've worked with both Jim and Ken on many books over many years, and they're both insightful industry experts who know what it takes to produce a great book.

Craig Zacker did the heavy lifting of putting this book together, and I am grateful to him for lending this series his expertise on end-user support and the Network+ exam.

I'd also like to extend a special thank-you to my agent, Carole Jelen of Waterside Productions. Carole is also an experienced industry pro who can deftly navigate the murky waters of publishing. Carole is the one who pushed me to create my own series.

Of course, the creation of any book involves a tremendous amount of effort from many people other than the authors. I truly appreciate the work of Adaobi Obi Tulton, the project editor. Adaobi and I have now worked together on many books and she keeps the train on the tracks! I'd also like to thank Buzz Murphy, the technical editor, who provided insightful advice and gave wonderful feedback throughout the book, and Saravanan Dakshinamurthy, production editor, who guided me through layouts, formatting, and final cleanup to produce a great book. I would also like to thank the many behind-the-scenes contributors, including the graphics, production, and technical teams who make the book and companion materials into a finished product.

Finally, I would like to thank my family, who supported me through the late evenings, busy weekends, and long hours that a book like this requires to write, edit, and get to press.

About the Authors

Mike Chapple, PhD, is the author of the best-selling *CISSP (ISC)² Certified Information Systems Security Professional Official Study Guide* (Sybex, 2021) and the *CISSP (ISC)² Official Practice Tests* (Sybex, 2021). He is an information technology professional with two decades of experience in higher education, the private sector, and government.

Mike currently serves as Teaching Professor in the IT, Analytics, and Operations department at the University of Notre Dame's Mendoza College of Business, where he teaches undergraduate and graduate courses on cybersecurity, cloud computing, data management, and business analytics.

Before returning to Notre Dame, Mike served as executive vice president and chief information officer of the Brand Institute, a Miami-based marketing consultancy. Mike also spent four years in the information security research group at the National Security Agency and served as an active duty intelligence officer in the U.S. Air Force.

Mike has written more than 25 books. He earned both his B.S. and Ph.D. degrees from Notre Dame in computer science and engineering. Mike also holds an M.S. in computer science from the University of Idaho and an MBA from Auburn University. Mike holds the IT Fundamentals (ITF+), Cybersecurity Analyst+ (CySA+), Data+, Security+, Certified Information Security Manager (CISM), Certified Cloud Security Professional (CCSP), and Certified Information Systems Security Professional (CISSP) certifications.

Learn more about Mike and his other security certification materials at his website, CertMike.com.

Craig Zacker is the author or co-author of dozens of books, manuals, articles, and websites on computer and networking topics. He has also been an English professor, a technical and copy editor, a network administrator, a webmaster, a corporate trainer, a technical support engineer, a minicomputer operator, a literature and philosophy student, a library clerk, a photographic darkroom technician, a shipping clerk, and a newspaper boy.

ABOUT THE TECHNICAL EDITOR

George B. Murphy (Buzz), CISSP, CCSP, SSCP, CASP, CDWA, CISM, CRISC, CIPT, PCSA, ITIL, is a public speaker, corporate trainer, author, and CEO of CyberSpace Intelligence International who has consulted with cybersecurity professionals around the world over the past 25 years with training courses, seminars, and consulting presentations on a variety of technical and cybersecurity topics. A former Dell technology executive, he has addressed audiences at RSA, COMDEX, SecureWorld Conference, World Security Conference, NetWorld, and the National Computer Conference as well as major corporations and educational institutions such as Princeton University, Oak Ridge, CERN, and major U.S. government agencies. Buzz has earned more than 29 IT and cybersecurity certifications from such prestigious organizations as (ISC)^2, CompTIA, PMI, and Microsoft, and other industry certification organizations, and has authored 12 Cyber Security textbooks. He is an (ISC)^2 Authorized Instructor.

CONTENTS AT A GLANCE

Contents

INTRODUCTION

If you're preparing to take the Network+ exam, you might find yourself overwhelmed with information. This exam covers a very broad range of topics, and it's possible to spend weeks studying each one of them. Fortunately, that's not necessary!

As part of the CertMike Test Prep series, this book is designed to help you focus on the specific knowledge that you'll need to pass the exam. CompTIA publishes a detailed list of exam objectives, and this book is organized around those objectives. Each chapter clearly states the single objective that it covers and then concisely covers the material you need to know about that objective.

You'll find two important things at the end of each chapter: Exam Essentials and Practice Questions. The CertMike Exam Essentials distill the major points from the chapter into just a few bullet points. Reviewing the Exam Essentials is a great way to prepare yourself right before the exam. We've also recorded a free audio version of the Exam Essentials that you'll find on the book's companion website at www.wiley.com/go/sybextestprep. They're great listening when you're in the car, at the gym, or mowing the lawn!

Each chapter concludes with two Practice Questions that are designed to give you a taste of what it's like to take the exam. You'll find that they're written in the same style as the Network+ exam questions and have detailed explanations to help you understand the correct answer. Be sure to take your time and thoroughly read these questions.

Finally, the book's website includes a full-length practice exam that you can use to assess your knowledge when you're ready to take the test. Good luck on the Network+ exam!

> **NOTE**
>
> Don't just study the questions and answers! The questions on the actual exam will be different from the Practice Questions included in this book. The exam is designed to test your knowledge of a concept or objective, so use this book to learn the objectives behind the questions.

THE NETWORK+ CERTIFICATION

Network+ is designed to be a vendor-neutral certification for those seeking to demonstrate their networking expertise. CompTIA recommends this certification for individuals who want to develop careers in IT infrastructure, specifically in the areas of troubleshooting, configuring, and managing networks. Common job roles held by Network+ certified individuals include the following:

- ▶ Junior network administrator
- ▶ Network engineer
- ▶ NOC technician

► Cable technician
► Data center support technician
► System administrator
► Telecommunications technician

The exam covers five major domains of knowledge:

1. Networking Fundamentals
2. Network Implementations
3. Network Operations
4. Network Security
5. Network Troubleshooting

These five areas include a range of topics, from securing networks to configuring subnets, while focusing heavily on the core knowledge expected of all networking professionals.

The Network+ exam uses a combination of standard multiple-choice questions and performance-based questions that require you to manipulate objects on the screen. This exam is designed to be straightforward and not to trick you. If you know the material in this book, you will pass the exam.

The exam costs $348 in the United States, with roughly equivalent prices in other locations around the globe. You can find more details about the Network+ exam and how to take it at

www.comptia.org/certifications/network#examdetails

You'll have 90 minutes to take the exam and will be asked to answer up to 90 questions during that time period. Your exam will be scored on a scale ranging from 100 to 900, with a passing score of 720.

> **NOTE**
>
> CompTIA frequently does what is called *item seeding*, which is the practice of including unscored questions on exams. It does so to gather psychometric data, which is then used when developing new versions of the exam. Before you take the exam, you will be told that your exam may include these unscored questions. So, if you come across a question that does not appear to map to any of the exam objectives—or for that matter, does not appear to belong in the exam—it is likely a seeded question. You never really know whether or not a question is seeded, however, so always make your best effort to answer every question.

Taking the Exam

Once you are fully prepared to take the exam, you can visit the CompTIA website to purchase your exam voucher:

https://store.comptia.org

Currently, CompTIA offers two options for taking the exam: an in-person exam at a testing center and an at-home exam that you take on your own computer.

> **TIP**
> This book includes a coupon that you may use to save 10 percent on your Comp-TIA exam registration.

In-Person Exams

CompTIA partners with Pearson VUE's testing centers, so your next step will be to locate a testing center near you. In the United States, you can do this based on your address or your zip code, while non-U.S. test takers may find it easier to enter their city and country. You can search for a test center near you at the Pearson Vue website, where you will need to navigate to "Find a test center."

`www.pearsonvue.com/comptia`

Now that you know where you'd like to take the exam, simply set up a Pearson VUE testing account and schedule an exam on their site.

On the day of the test, take two forms of identification, and be sure to show up with plenty of time before the exam starts. Remember that you will not be able to take your notes, electronic devices (including smartphones and watches), or other materials in with you.

At-Home Exams

CompTIA began offering online exam proctoring in 2020 in response to the coronavirus pandemic. As of this writing, the at-home testing option was still available and appears likely to continue. Candidates using this approach will take the exam at their home or office and be proctored over a webcam by a remote proctor.

Due to the rapidly changing nature of the at-home testing experience, candidates wishing to pursue this option should check the CompTIA website for the latest details.

After the Exam

Once you have taken the exam, you will be notified of your score immediately, so you'll know if you passed the test right away. You should keep track of your score report with your exam registration records and the email address you used to register for the exam.

After you earn the Network+ certification, you're required to renew your certification every three years by either earning an advanced certification, completing a CertMaster continuing education program, or earning 20 continuing education units over a three-year period.

Many people who earn the Network+ credential use it as a stepping stone to earning other certifications in their areas of interest. Those interested in end-user support work toward the A+ credential, data analytics professionals might go on to earn the Data+ certification, and the Security+ program is a gateway to a career in cybersecurity.

WHAT DOES THIS BOOK COVER?

This book covers everything you need to know to pass the Network+ exam. It is organized into five parts, each corresponding to one of the five Network+ domains.

Part I: Domain 1.0: Networking Fundamentals

Chapter 1: OSI Model
Chapter 2: Network Topologies
Chapter 3: Cables and Connectors
Chapter 4: IP Addressing
Chapter 5: Ports and Protocols
Chapter 6: Network Services
Chapter 7: Network Architecture
Chapter 8: Cloud Computing

Part II: Domain 2.0: Network Implementations

Chapter 9: Network Devices
Chapter 10: Routing and Bandwidth Management
Chapter 11: Switching
Chapter 12: Wireless Standards

Part III: Domain 3.0: Network Operations

Chapter 13: Network Availability
Chapter 14: Organizational Documents and Policies
Chapter 15: High Availability and Disaster Recovery

Part IV: Domain 4.0: Network Security

Chapter 16: Security Concepts
Chapter 17: Network Attacks
Chapter 18: Network Hardening
Chapter 19: Remote Access
Chapter 20: Physical Security

Part V: Domain 5.0: Network Troubleshooting

Chapter 21: Network Troubleshooting Methodology
Chapter 22: Troubleshooting Cable Connectivity
Chapter 23: Network Software Tools and Commands
Chapter 24: Troubleshooting Wireless Connectivity
Chapter 25: Troubleshooting Network Issues

Study Guide Elements

This study guide uses a number of common elements to help you prepare. These include the following:

Exam Tips   Throughout each chapter, we've sprinkled practical exam tips that help focus your reading on items that are particularly confusing or important for the exam.

CertMike Exam Essentials   The Exam Essentials focus on major exam topics and critical knowledge that you should take into the test. The Exam Essentials focus on the exam objectives provided by CompTIA.

Practice Questions   Two questions at the end of each chapter will help you assess your knowledge and if you are ready to take the exam based on your knowledge of that chapter's topics.

Additional Study Tools

This book comes with a number of additional study tools to help you prepare for the exam. They include the following:

> **NOTE**
>
> Go to www.wiley.com/go/sybextestprep to register and gain access to this interactive online learning environment and test bank with study tools.

Sybex Test Preparation Software

Sybex's test preparation software lets you prepare with electronic test versions of the Practice Questions from each chapter and the Practice Exam that is included in this book. You can build and take tests on specific domains or by chapter, or cover the entire set of Network+ exam objectives using randomized tests.

Audio Review

I've (Mike) recorded an audio review where I read each of the sets of chapter Exam Essentials. This provides a helpful recap of the main material covered on the exam that you can use while you're commuting, working out, or relaxing.

> **NOTE**
>
> Like all exams, the Network+ certification from CompTIA is updated periodically and may eventually be retired or replaced. At some point after CompTIA is no longer offering this exam, the old editions of our books and online tools will be retired. If you have purchased this book after the exam was retired, or are attempting to register in the Sybex online learning environment after the exam was retired, please know that we make no guarantees that this exam's online Sybex tools will be available once the exam is no longer available.

EXAM N10-008 EXAM OBJECTIVES

CompTIA goes to great lengths to ensure that its certification programs accurately reflect the IT industry's best practices. They do this by establishing committees for each of its exam programs. Each committee consists of a small group of IT professionals, training providers, and publishers who are responsible for establishing the exam's baseline competency level and who determine the appropriate target-audience level.

Once these factors are determined, CompTIA shares this information with a group of hand-selected subject matter experts (SMEs). These folks are the true brainpower behind the certification program. The SMEs review the committee's findings, refine them, and shape them into the objectives that follow this section. CompTIA calls this process a job-task analysis.

Finally, CompTIA conducts a survey to ensure that the objectives and weightings truly reflect job requirements. Only then can the SMEs go to work writing the hundreds of questions needed for the exam. Even so, they have to go back to the drawing board for further refinements in many cases before the exam is ready to go live in its final state. Rest assured that the content you're about to learn will serve you long after you take the exam.

CompTIA also publishes relative weightings for each of the exam's objectives. The following table lists the five Network+ objective domains and the extent to which they are represented on the exam.

Domain	% of Exam
1.0 Networking Fundamentals	24%
2.0 Network Implementations	19%
3.0 Network Operations	16%
4.0 Network Security	19%
5.0 Network Troubleshooting	22%

N10-008 CERTIFICATION EXAM OBJECTIVE MAP

Objective	Chapter
1.0 Networking Fundamentals	
1.1 Compare and contrast the Open Systems Interconnection (OSI) model layers and encapsulation concepts	1
1.2 Explain the characteristics of network topologies and network types	2
1.3 Summarize the types of cables and connectors and explain which is the appropriate type for a solution	3
1.4 Given a scenario, configure a subnet and use appropriate IP addressing schemes	4
1.5 Explain common ports and protocols, their application, and encrypted alternatives	5
1.6 Explain the use and purpose of network services	6
1.7 Explain basic corporate and datacenter network architecture	7
1.8 Summarize cloud concepts and connectivity options	8
2.0 Network Implementations	
2.1 Compare and contrast various devices, their features, and their appropriate placement on the network	9
2.2 Compare and contrast routing technologies and bandwidth management concepts	10
2.3 Given a scenario, configure and deploy common Ethernet switching features	11
2.4 Given a scenario, install and configure the appropriate wireless standards and technologies	12

NOTE

Exam objectives are subject to change at any time without prior notice and at CompTIA's discretion. Please visit CompTIA's website (www.comptia.org) for the most current listing of exam objectives.

HOW TO CONTACT THE PUBLISHER

If you believe you have found a mistake in this book, please bring it to our attention. At John Wiley & Sons, we understand how important it is to provide our customers with accurate content, but even with our best efforts an error may occur.

In order to submit your possible errata, please email it to our Customer Service Team at wileysupport@wiley.com with the subject line "Possible Book Errata Submission."

CompTIA® Network+® CertMike

Prepare. Practice. Pass the Test! Get Certified!

Domain 1.0: Networking Fundamentals

Networking Fundamentals is the first domain of CompTIA's Network+ exam. It provides the foundational knowledge that IT professionals need to work with common network devices and technologies. This domain has eight objectives:

1.1 **Compare and contrast the Open Systems Interconnection (OSI) model layers and encapsulation concepts.**

1.2 **Explain the characteristics of network topologies and network types.**

1.3 **Summarize the types of cables and connectors and explain which is the appropriate type for a solution.**

1.4 **Given a scenario, configure a subnet and use appropriate IP addressing schemes.**

1.5 **Explain common ports and protocols, their application, and encrypted alternatives.**

1.6 **Explain the use and purpose of network services.**

1.7 **Explain basic corporate and datacenter network architecture.**

1.8 **Summarize cloud concepts and connectivity options.**

Questions from this domain make up 24% of the questions on the Network+ exam, so you should expect to see approximately 22 questions on your test covering the material in this part.

CHAPTER 1

OSI Model

Objective 1.1: Compare and contrast the Open Systems Interconnection (OSI) model layers and encapsulation concepts.

The OSI reference model can serve as a roadmap to many of the other concepts covered on the Network+ exam, providing a common lexicon that enables people working with these processes to communicate more easily.

In this chapter, you'll learn everything you need to know about Network+ Objective 1.1, including the following topics:

▶ OSI model
▶ Data encapsulation and decapsulation within the OSI model context

OSI MODEL

The *Open Systems Interconnection (OSI) reference model* is an architectural diagram of network communications. The model defines a highly complex process by dividing it into its component elements, in this case seven discrete layers, as shown in Figure 1.1.

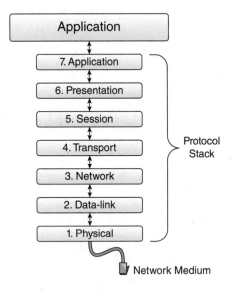

FIGURE 1.1 **The seven layers of the OSI reference model**

The seven layers of the model correspond to various network communications processes (called protocols) running on a computer. Table 1.1 lists the model layers, their functions, and the protocols that implement them. These protocols are covered in more detail throughout this book.

EXAM TIP

Memorizing this table is a good idea, as many Network+ exam questions reference the various layers of the OSI model, their functions, and their protocols. An easy way to remember the order of the layers is with the mnemonic "Please Do Not Throw Sausage Pizza Away."

TABLE 1.1 **OSI reference model layers**

Number	Layer	Main functions	Protocols
7	Application	File, print, messaging, and other services	DNS, FTP, HTTP, POP3, SMTP, SNMP, DHCP
6	Presentation	Syntax translation	
5	Session	Dialog control, dialog separation	

Number	Layer	Main functions	Protocols
4	Transport	Data segmentation, packet acknowledgment, error detection and correction, flow control, port identification	TCP, UDP
3	Network	Addressing, routing, error detection, protocol identification	IP, IPv4, IPv6, ICMP
2	Data Link	Framing, media access control, protocol identification	IEEE 802.3 (Ethernet), IEEE 802.11 (Wi-Fi)
1	Physical	Network interface hardware, binary signaling	Twisted pair, fiber-optic, Wi-Fi

EXAM TIP

The layers of the OSI model are numbered from the bottom of the stack to the top. The physical layer at the bottom is designated as layer 1 and the application layer at the top as layer 7. In some reference works and product documentation, the model layers are referenced by number instead of name.

A *protocol* is a language that computers use to communicate with each other. Collectively, the processes running on the seven layers of the model are called the *protocol stack*. The network medium (whether a copper cable, fiber-optic cable, or wireless) connects to the physical layer at the bottom of the stack, and the signals entering at this layer travel up through the layers of the stack to the top. In the same way, data being sent over the network by software running at the top of the stack travel down through the layers and out to the network using the connected medium.

This vertical communication between the layers of the protocol stack takes the form of services that each layer provides for the layer above and requests from the layer below. For example, when an email client application sends a message, it typically generates a request for the services of the Simple Mail Transfer Protocol (SMTP), running at the application layer. SMTP then passes the request down to the next lower layer, which hands it off to the next layer, and so forth, until it reaches the bottom layer and is transmitted over the network.

The server receiving the transmission over the network then begins the same process in reverse, passing the message up through the layers of its own protocol stack until it reaches a mail server application running on the computer. The protocols running at specific layers of the OSI model have complementary functions that make network communication possible. The protocols at the individual layers of the model can therefore be said to communicate virtually with their counterparts on other systems.

One of the objectives of the OSI model was to define a networking architecture that enables manufacturers to create products that communicate readily with those of other manufacturers. As long as two computers are running compatible protocols at each layer of the OSI model, communication between them is theoretically possible, even if they are using different hardware and software.

While there have been other protocols over the years, LANs today nearly always run Ethernet or Wi-Fi at the physical and data link layers, *Internet Protocol (IP)* at the network layer, *Transmission Control Protocol (TCP)* and *User Datagram Protocol (UDP)* at the transport layer, and a collection of *Transmission Control Protocol/Internet Protocol (TCP/IP)* protocols and services at the application layer.

This TCP/IP protocol suite has a layered architecture similar to that of the OSI model, but it has only four layers, as shown in Table 1.2, and the layers do not correspond exactly to those of the OSI model. Some documents, such as the Requests for Comments (RFCs) that define the various TCP/IP protocols, reference the layers of the TCP/IP model instead of the OSI model layers.

TABLE 1.2 Corresponding OSI model and TCP/IP layers

OSI model layers	TCP/IP layers
Application	Application
Presentation	
Session	
Transport	Transport
Network	Internet
Data Link	Link
Physical	

The seven layers of the OSI reference model are described in more detail in the following sections.

Layer 1: The Physical Layer

The physical layer, as the name implies, provides the actual physical connection between the computer and the network. The hardware implementing the physical layer in a computer—called a *network interface adapter*—typically includes either a connector for a network cable or a transceiver that provides wireless connectivity. In the network communications architecture, the physical layer specification is responsible for providing the following elements:

Network Medium   The technology that carries signals from one computer to another, such as copper-based cable, fiber-optic cable, or radio transmissions

Network Interface   The connection between the computer and the network medium, such as a cable connector or a radio transceiver

Network Topology   The arrangement of the network medium in the work site, such as the star topology typically used by cabled networks today

Network Installation   The guidelines for the installation of the network medium, such as radio frequencies, maximum cable lengths, number of devices permitted, and proximity to other equipment

Network Signaling   Specifies the nature of the signals: electrical, optical, or radio, which the devices use to transmit binary data over the network medium.

Computers communicate at the physical layer by generating signals and transmitting them over a network medium. For outgoing communications, the physical layer receives data from a protocol running on the layer above it (the data link layer), converts the data into a binary code appropriate for the medium, and transmits it over the network. In the same way, the physical layer receives incoming signals from the network and converts them into an appropriate form for the data link layer protocol.

These elements—the network medium, interface, topology, installation, and signaling scheme—are all typically defined by a single protocol specification. For example, a typical Ethernet physical layer specification might call for unshielded twisted pair (UTP) cable, installed in a star topology, with a maximum segment length of 100 meters, using RJ-45 connectors and an encoding scheme called Differential Manchester. Other Ethernet specifications call for fiber-optic or other network media, each with its own interface, topology, installation, and signaling characteristics. For more information on physical layer hardware, see Chapter 2, "Network Topologies and Types," and Chapter 3, "Cables and Connectors."

EXAM TIP

When preparing for the Network+ exam, it can be easy to get lost in details that are unlikely to appear in exam questions. It's only important to know the basic functions associated with each layer of the model and how those functions fit into the network communications process.

Layer 2: The Data Link Layer

The data link layer, layer 2 of the OSI model, is closely associated with the physical layer. The two together implement the computer's connection to and communication with the local area network (LAN) to which the device is attached. Selecting a protocol for the data link layer also dictates the network medium options that are available at the physical layer. For more information on Ethernet variants and their supported cable types, see Chapter 3.

The functions that data link layer protocols typically perform include the following:

Frame Format   The data link layer protocol packages the data passed down to it from the network layer in a protocol data unit called a frame. A *frame* consists of a header and a footer generated by the data link layer protocol, with the network layer data as the payload in between.

Addressing   Every network interface adapter has a unique 6-byte identifier assigned to it by the manufacturer called a *media access control (MAC) address*. Data link layer frames use these addresses in their headers to identify the sender and recipient of each packet.

Protocol Identification   Data link layer headers include a code that indicates which network layer protocol generated the data in each packet. This enables the data link layer protocol on the receiving system to pass incoming traffic up to the correct network layer process.

Error Detection   The frame footer contains the result of a cyclical redundancy check (CRC) calculation performed on the frame's data payload by the sending system. The receiving system performs the same calculation and, if the results do not match, discards the packet.

Media Access Control (MAC)   When a LAN has devices connected to a shared network medium, the data link layer protocol uses a media access control mechanism to prevent two devices from transmitting simultaneously and causing a data collision.

Physical Layer Specifications   The data link layer protocol also includes specifications for the physical layer options associated with the protocol.

Most cabled LANs run the Ethernet protocol at the data link layer, the actual name for which is IEEE 802.3, after the standards published by the Institute of Electrical and Electronics Engineers. The functions just listed are all implemented as part of the Ethernet frame.

Layer 3: The Network Layer

The protocols running at the physical and data link layers of the OSI model are dedicated to local network communications only. For example, Ethernet is capable of transmitting frames to another computer or router on the LAN; it is not concerned with the delivery of the data to its final destination. That is the responsibility of the network layer protocol.

Network layer devices called routers connect individual networks together, forming an *internetwork*, or network of networks. A *router* is an intermediate system that only processes incoming packets as high as the network layer, as shown in Figure 1.2.

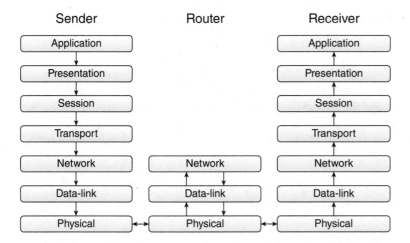

FIGURE 1.2   **Network traffic processed by an intermediate router**

The functions of a network layer protocol are as follows:

End-to-End Addressing   The network layer protocol header contains the addresses of both the sending system and its final destination. Data link layer MAC addresses change for each leg of an internetwork journey, but network layer addresses always reflect a packet's starting point and its final destination.

Routing   Routers are intermediate network layer devices that forward packets to other networks. Network layer protocols use routing tables to look up the addresses of other networks, so the router can forward packets to the correct destinations.

Fragmentation   Networks can have different frame size limits, based on their *maximum transmission unit (MTU)* values, so if a single frame is too large to transmit over another network, the network layer protocol splits it into smaller fragments and transmits each fragment in a separate frame. The network layer protocol reassembles the fragments when they reach their final destination.

Protocol Identification   Just as a data link layer protocol header contains a code to identify the network layer protocol that generated the data in the packet, the network layer protocol contains a code identifying the transport layer protocol that generated the data.

On TCP/IP networks, the primary protocol at the network layer is the *Internet Protocol (IP)*. IP exists in two versions: *IPv4*, with a 32-bit address space, which is the standard Internet protocol at the network layer, and *IPv6*, which is a newer version with a 128-bit address space. IPv6 has not yet been widely adopted for public Internet communications. For more information on the Internet Protocol, see Chapter 4, "IP Addressing."

IP functions are implemented in the header, which the protocol applies to the data it receives from the transport layer. This forms a unit called a *datagram*.

Layer 4: The Transport Layer

The term *TCP/IP* refers to the two protocols operating at the transport and network layers. The protocols at these two layers function together to provide a unified quality of service. IP, as noted earlier, provides addressing and routing services. The protocols at the transport layer of the OSI model provide additional end-to-end communication services, such as guaranteed delivery and flow control, to the adjacent layers, as needed.

Connection-Oriented and Connectionless Protocols

The OSI model standard recognizes two basic types of end-to-end protocol at the transport layer:

Connection-Oriented   A connection-oriented protocol always establishes a connection between the sending and receiving systems before it transmits any application data. The systems do this by exchanging messages (called a *handshake*) containing *TCP flags* that confirm that both systems are available to send and receive data. After the transmission, another handshake terminates the connection. These additional messages (and a connection-oriented protocol's larger header) cause a significant increase in bandwidth overhead for this type of protocol. On most networks, the primary connection-oriented protocol at the transport layer is the *Transmission Control Protocol (TCP)*.

Connectionless   A connectionless protocol provides no additional services other than the basic transmission of data, so there is no need for handshake messages and the header can be much smaller. This reduces the protocol's bandwidth overhead significantly. On most networks the primary connectionless protocol at the transport layer is the *User Datagram Protocol (UDP)*. The Internet Protocol (IP) running at the network layer is also connectionless.

Transport Layer Functions

The transport layer provides a variety of services for data transmissions. Most of the functions in the following list are provided by connection-oriented protocols such as TCP only. Only the protocol identification function is required for all protocols at the transport layer.

Data Segmentation   A connection-oriented protocol accepts data from upper-layer application processes and splits it into segments of appropriate size for the network. Each segment is numbered so that they can be reassembled by the receiving system, even if they arrive out of order.

Packet Acknowledgment   Connection-oriented protocols provide a *guaranteed delivery* service. The receiving system generates messages that acknowledge the successful receipt of packets from the sender.

Flow Control   A connection-oriented mechanism to regulate the speed at which a sending system transmits data. The responses returned to the sender by the receiving system specify the size of a *sliding window*—that is, a buffer that holds incoming data. When the sliding window gets smaller, the sending system reduces its transmission speed to avoid overwhelming the receiver.

Signaled Error Correction   A *signaled error* is a packet that has been discarded by the network layer protocol due to a CRC failure. The network layer protocol cannot correct errors, so it signals the transport layer protocol to retransmit the lost packets.

Unsignaled Error Detection and Correction   The transport layer provides the only end-to-end error detection and correction mechanism for the entire packet. The transport layer protocol on the sending system performs a CRC calculation and includes the results in its header. The receiving system then performs the same calculation and compares the results. For any lost packets, the receiver alters the packet acknowledgment value in its header, causing the sender to retransmit the unacknowledged packets.

Port Identification   Transport layer protocol headers always contain a code (called a *port*) identifying the application layer protocol that generated or will receive the packet's data.

The transport layer functions are implemented in headers applied by each protocol. Because it is a connection-oriented protocol with many functions, TCP has a large 20-byte header. UDP is connectionless and therefore needs only a comparatively small 8-byte header.

Layer 5: The Session Layer

The boundary between the transport layer and the session layer marks an important change in the functioning of the protocol stack. All of the communication functions, both end-to-end and local, that are needed to transmit data from one system to another over a TCP/IP network are handled by the bottom four layers of the OSI model. The session, presentation, and application layers assume that the communication services are functional and that any messages they need to send or receive will be handled correctly.

The top three layers of the OSI model do not have separate protocols to implement their functions in the TCP/IP suite. Instead, the session layer functions as something of a toolbox; the OSI model standard lists 22 functions performed at the session layer, but on a TCP/IP network, those functions are usually integrated into an application layer protocol. It is for this reason that the session, presentation, and application layers are often referenced collectively as the *upper layers*.

The functions associated with the session layer are mostly concerned with the establishment, maintenance, and termination of communications during a connection between two end systems, called a *session*. The maintenance of a session can be a complicated business requiring various session layer functions to initiate the dialog, maintain orderly communication, and then terminate it.

Two of the important functions used to manage a session include the following:

► **Dialog control:** Specifies the mode in which the systems communicate. *Simplex* mode is when only one of the computers is transmitting. In *half duplex*, also called *two-way alternate (TWA)* mode, the systems exchange a token, and only the computer with the token can transmit. In *full duplex*, also called *two-way simultaneous (TWS)* mode, there is no token, and the computers can transmit any time.
► **Dialog separation:** Calls for the creation of checkpoints in the data stream to separate functions.

Layer 6: The Presentation Layer

As noted earlier, each OSI model layer provides services to the layer above and requests services from the layer below. In the case of the presentation layer, its primary function is to provide pass-through services that enable application layer protocols to request session layer services. For each of the services at the session layer, there is a corresponding pass-through service at the presentation layer. This enables the upper layers to function as a single entity.

The presentation layer also includes a syntax translation service that enables two end systems to communicate, despite their use of data compression, encryption, or different bit-encoding algorithms.

Layer 7: The Application Layer

The application layer is the entrance point to the protocol stack for applications running on the computer. In some cases, the application is separate from the application layer protocol, but in others, the application and the application layer protocol are the same.

There are hundreds of application layer protocols, many more than at any of the other layers. This is because there are so many applications that require a variety of highly specific networking services.

DATA ENCAPSULATION

As outgoing data travels down through the protocol stack to the network medium, it undergoes a process called *data encapsulation*, which is the functional equivalent of putting a letter into an envelope for mailing. When an application produces data that needs to be transmitted over the network, it generates a request for one of the application layer protocols. This protocol generates a message, properly formatted for the application, and passes it down through the layers of the stack. The protocols at the lower layers then add their own data, such as addresses and codes, to implement their functions.

For example, when the application layer data reaches the transport layer, the protocol there generates a *Transmission Control Protocol (TCP) or User Datagram Protocol (UDP) header* and adds it to the data. The TCP header includes *TCP flags* that the protocol uses to establish a connection between the sending and receiving systems and then break down the connection after the data transmission. The application layer request then becomes the *payload* in the transport layer segment or datagram, as shown in Figure 1.3.

The transport layer protocol then passes the data down to the network layer, which adds its own *Internet Protocol (IP) header*. The *maximum transmission unit (MTU)* value for the interface specifies the size of the largest IP datagram that can be transmitted over the network. Datagrams that are larger than the MTU are split into fragments for transmission. Finally, at the data link layer, all of the data from the layers above becomes the payload in a data link layer frame. The data link layer protocol typically adds both an *Ethernet header* and a footer to the payload, resulting in a packet that is ready for transmission.

For packets arriving at the destination system, the process occurs in reverse, with the data passed up through the OSI model layers, a process called *decapsulation*. Each layer processes the incoming packet by reading and stripping off the header and then passing the payload up to the correct protocol at the next higher layer.

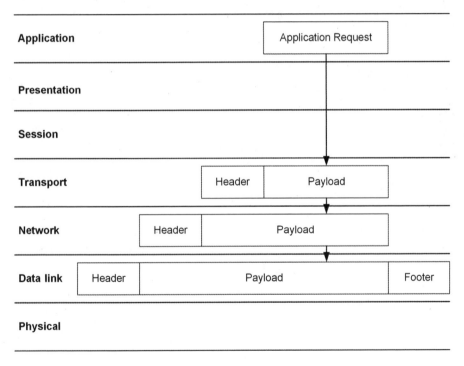

FIGURE 1.3 The data encapsulation process

CERTMIKE EXAM ESSENTIALS

▶ The OSI reference model divides the network communications process into seven layers. In order from the first layer to the seventh layer, these are the physical layer, the data link layer, the network layer, the transport layer, the session layer, the presentation layer, and the application layer. You can remember them in order using the mnemonic "Please Do Not Throw Sausage Pizza Away."

▶ Data encapsulation is the process by which the data generated by an application is packaged for transmission over the network through the application of headers by the protocols at the transport, network, and data link layers. When packets arrive at their destination, a decapsulation process occurs in which the protocols at each layer strip off their respective headers and pass the payload data up to the next layer.

Practice Question 1

There are several OSI model layers that provide error detection services, but only one that provides error correction as well. At which layer of the OSI model is there a protocol that provides both end-to-end error detection and correction?

A. Physical
B. Data link
C. Network
D. Transport

Practice Question 2

Which of the following OSI model layers specifies the address of each packet's sender and its ultimate recipient?

A. Data link
B. Network
C. Transport
D. Session

Practice Question 1 Explanation

A. is incorrect because the physical layer provides the connection to the network and implements the signaling algorithm that converts the packet data into the electrical, optical, or radio signals necessary for transmission. This layer does not manipulate or evaluate the data in any way, so it performs no error correction.

B. is incorrect because the data link layer is concerned only with local network communication. The data link layer performs a CRC calculation on each frame and includes the results in a frame check sequence field, but it cannot perform end-to-end error detection and has no error correction capability.

C. is incorrect because as a connectionless protocol, it has no packet acknowledgment capability and therefore no means of error correction. The network layer performs error detection by including a CRC code in its header. If a packet fails the CRC test, the network layer discards it and signals the loss to the transport layer.

D. is correct because TCP, a connection-oriented transport layer protocol, performs its own error detection, but it also includes a packet acknowledgment service. The segments transmitted during a TCP connection are numbered, so the acknowledgment messages generated by the receiver can specify the number of the last packet received correctly. The sender processes these messages and automatically retransmits any unacknowledged packets.

Correct Answer: D, Transport

Practice Question 2 Explanation

A. is incorrect because the data link layer is only concerned with local network communications. The frame's destination address does not identify the ultimate recipient of the packet, only the next recipient on the LAN.

B. is correct because IP, at the network layer, is the protocol responsible for end-to-end transmissions between the packet's sender and its ultimate recipient. The IP header therefore contains IP addresses that identify the two end systems.

C. is incorrect because the transport layer headers do not contain addresses for the end systems. The transport layer protocols, TCP and UDP, provide services that support the end-to-end network communication process, but they rely on the network layer for addressing.

D. is incorrect because the session layer provides functions that manage connections between end systems once they are established, but it does not have a dedicated protocol and has no addressing functionality.

Correct Answer: B, Network

CHAPTER 2

Network Topologies

Objective 1.2: Explain the characteristics of network topologies and network types.

This chapter examines the various types of networks that technicians encounter in their work, as well as the basic physical topologies that these networks use. These are fundamental networking concepts mentioned in many questions on the Network+ exam.

In this chapter, you'll learn everything you need to know about Network+ Objective 1.2, including the following topics:

▶ **Mesh**
▶ **Star/hub-and-spoke**
▶ **Bus**
▶ **Ring**
▶ **Hybrid**
▶ **Network types and characteristics**
▶ **Service-related entry points**
▶ **Virtual network concepts**
▶ **Provider links**

NETWORK TOPOLOGIES

In networking terminology, a *topology* is a definition of the manner in which a network medium is installed. Originally coined to describe cable installations, the topology of a network specifies how the cables are installed and how the computers and other devices are connected to each other.

For example, the most commonly used topology in cabled local area networks (LANs) today is the *star topology* (see Figure 2.1), sometimes called a *hub-and-spoke topology* because of the diagram's resemblance to a wheel.

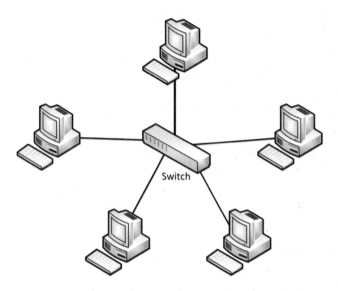

FIGURE 2.1   **A cabled local area network using a star topology**

In a star topology, each computer or other device has its own dedicated connection to a central cabling nexus called a *switch*. The switch relays the traffic it receives from each computer to the appropriate recipient on the network by transmitting it out through one of its other ports. Older star networks might use a hub instead of a switch. A hub is a physical layer device that forwards incoming traffic out through all of its ports instead of just one, forming a true shared network medium.

Virtually all cabled LANs installed today use the Ethernet protocol with unshielded twisted pair cable in a star topology. To build larger networks, it is possible to cable switches together, forming a hierarchical star topology in which the computers on all of the switches can communicate with each other.

Before the star topology became ubiquitous for cabled LANs, there were other topologies in use, including the following:

Bus   Early Ethernet networks used coaxial cable in a *bus topology*, in which each device is connected to the next device, forming a chain. The bus topology is no longer used primarily because of its lack of fault tolerance. A cable break or a malfunctioning network interface adapter in one of the computers splits the network in two, with the devices on one segment unable to communicate with the other segment.

Ring   A *ring topology* is essentially a bus with the two ends of the chain connected together so that traffic can circulate around the whole network. An early protocol called Token Ring used a ring topology in which the computers passed a small token frame from system to system around the ring. This functioned as a media access control mechanism because only the device in possession of the token was permitted to transmit its data. Another obsolete protocol called Fiber Distributed Data Interface (FDDI) called for fiber-optic cable in a physical ring topology, or a double ring for fault tolerance.

Hybrid   A *hybrid topology* is a network that uses elements of two or more topologies on one network. For example, the ring topology of a Token Ring network was virtual in most instances; the physical network was a star, with all of the devices cabled to a central hub called a multistation access unit (MAU). The signals, however, traveled in a ring, with the MAU sending each packet out to one computer at a time and waiting for its return before sending it to the next computer. This arrangement was sometimes called a star ring topology. Another hybrid topology was the star bus, in which multiple star networks were connected to a backbone that used a bus topology.

Mesh   A *mesh topology*, theoretically, describes a network in which each computer has a separate connection to every other computer, providing full redundancy and fault tolerance. For a cabled LAN, a mesh topology would in most cases be impossible, or at least wildly impractical. However, wide area network (WAN) connections between remote offices can conceivably use any topology, including a mesh. A WAN topology in which each site is connected to two or more other sites is called a partial mesh. In a full mesh topology, each site has a separate WAN connection to every other site. This arrangement provides fault tolerance in the case of a WAN link failure, but it is also extremely expensive.

NETWORK TYPES AND CHARACTERISTICS

The word *network* has different meanings in different contexts, even within the IT field. Technically, any group of computers that are connected together so that they can share data is a network. However, networking has evolved rapidly over the decades, and so has the definition of a network. The Network+ exam expects candidates to be familiar with the following network types:

Local Area Network (LAN)   A collection of computers and other devices in the same geographic area, such as a room, floor, or building, connected using cables or a wireless medium so they can share data. To connect a LAN to another network, a router is necessary. This creates a network of networks, also known as an internetwork.

Wireless Local Area Network (WLAN)   A collection of computers in a limited geographic area that are connected using a wireless network medium, such as Wi-Fi, the radio-based technology defined in the IEEE 802.11 standards.

Wide Area Network (WAN)   A point-to-point link between two remote locations, typically provided by a third-party carrier. WANs are generally slower than LANs, but they can span much longer distances. A WAN link can connect a single user to a remote LAN or connect two LANs together, enabling users at each site to access resources at the other site.

Metropolitan Area Network (MAN)   A collection of computers in a larger geographic area than a LAN, such as a neighborhood, district, or city. A MAN is essentially a group of LANs connected together using WAN technology, such as fiber-optic links, to form an internetwork.

Personal Area Network (PAN)   A collection of devices, such as smartphones, tablets, and laptops, that are in close proximity and usually belong to a single person. A PAN is typically wireless, connecting the devices together using a short-range medium such as infrared or Bluetooth, but it can also use cabled connections, such as Universal Serial Bus (USB).

Campus Area Network (CAN)   Larger than a LAN, but usually smaller than a MAN or WAN, a CAN is a group of LANs connected together using WAN links to service a school, enterprise, housing, or government campus. Unlike MANs or WANs, which typically rely on third-party service providers for their WAN connections, the CAN networking equipment is usually owned by the campus tenant.

Storage Area Network (SAN)   A collection of storage devices, such as disk arrays or *network attached storage (NAS)* units, connected to a network that provides servers with either direct block-level access or filesystem access to the devices. The servers can access the storage as though it was installed locally. High-end SANs are typically fiber-optic networks dedicated to storage traffic, with block-level storage devices running a specialized protocol such as Fibre Channel. However, there are lower-cost alternatives, such as iSCSI, which enables storage traffic to coexist with TCP/IP traffic on a standard Ethernet network.

> **EXAM TIP**
> Objective 1.2 for the Network+ exam introduces some concepts that are explored further in later objectives. For example, SANs receive only the most rudimentary coverage here but are examined further in Objective 1.7. Exam candidates should be conscious of these scattered topics so as to best evaluate how much time and preparation they deserve.

Software-Defined Wide Area Network (SDWAN)   A type of wide area network in which the hardware providing the WAN connectivity is separated from the mechanism that controls the traffic. This enables the network to combine various WAN technologies and dynamically route traffic by selecting the link that is most appropriate for the data being transmitted and the most efficient, based on current network conditions. The concept is similar to that of *software-defined networking (SDN)*, which separates the network control function from the network forwarding function. Instead of both functions being performed by individual routers, in SDN the routers still do the packet forwarding, but control of the routing process for the entire network is located in a centralized control unit.

Multiprotocol Label Switching (MPLS)   A packet routing technique that applies labels to packets and routes them based solely on the path information in the label, rather than using the packet's destination address. An MPLS network adds a 32-bit MPLS header to each packet, making it possible to route the traffic without consulting the data link and network headers. MPLS can therefore handle multiple protocols, including Frame Relay and Asynchronous Transfer Mode (ATM), as well as IP and Ethernet. Because its functionality spans the data link and network layers, MPLS is sometimes referred to as a layer 2.5 protocol.

Multipoint Generic Routing Encapsulation (mGRE)   Generic Routing Encapsulation (GRE) is a tunneling protocol that encapsulates network layer data and transmits it over an established point-to-point link, such as a virtual private network (VPN). Multipoint Generic Routing Encapsulation (mGRE) expands on that principle by dynamically creating new tunnels between points as needed. This eliminates the need for administrators to create individual tunnel mappings between sites.

> **EXAM TIP**
>
> The objectives for the Network+ exam sometimes include elements that seem out of place, such as the inclusion of MPLS and mGRE in a list of network types. Both of these are protocols that run on networks and provide traffic handling alternatives to the usual LAN and WAN technologies, but they are not network types in the sense that you might have an MPLS instead of a LAN. However, exam candidates should still have a basic familiarity with these technologies.

NETWORK ROLES

The roles of the computers on a network can vary depending on the operating systems (OSs) they are running and the hardware used to construct them. Network communication frequently involves two roles: the server and the client. A *server* is a computer that provides services to other computers. A *client* is a computer that generates requests for services and sends them to servers.

For example, a web server listens for incoming requests from the network and responds to them by supplying web content. Client computers running a web browser generate the requests when a user types a web address or clicks a hyperlink.

There are two basic network role configurations, as follows:

▶ **Client/server:** Describes a network that uses dedicated server and client computers. Novell NetWare, for example, was the server OS for a client/server network that possessed virtually no client capabilities. The server had a rudimentary character-based interface and could not run client applications. Client computers ran the client applications that sent requests to the server.

▶ **Peer-to-peer:** Describes a network on which the computers are capable of functioning both as clients and servers. Today's OSs, such as Windows and Unix/Linux, include both server and client capabilities. On a network that consists only of Windows workstations, for example, any computer can function as a server for the other computers and can also run client applications. Even a computer running a Windows Server operating system has full client capabilities.

SERVICE-RELATED ENTRY POINTS

While it is possible for a LAN or an internetwork to operate independently from all outside services, most networks do have connections with third-party providers. Nearly all networks today have a connection to an *Internet service provider (ISP)*, but businesses often have additional connections, such as those to telephone carriers and WAN service providers.

These connections to outside services require an entry point, a physical interface where the client's internal equipment meets the service provider's equipment. This is often referred to as a *demarcation point* (or *demarc*) because it specifies the place where the client's responsibility for the connection ends and the provider's responsibility begins. Any technical issues occurring outside the demarc are the provider's responsibility; for issues inside the demarc, the client is responsible.

The demarcation point takes the form of a network interface device (NID), a box containing the connection—electrical or optical—between the two networks. In its most basic form, an NID is purely a physical layer device. However, for some connections, additional equipment is needed. For example, a leased line requires a *channel service unit (CSU)* and a *data service unit (DSU)*, usually packaged in one device called a *CSU/DSU*. In some cases, the service provider might choose to install an NID with additional capabilities called a *smartjack*. A smartjack might have to amplify or recode signals, and it usually includes various types of diagnostics, such as a switchable loopback function and alarm notification capabilities. These diagnostics enable the service provider to monitor the connection remotely and perform rudimentary tests without having to send a technician to the site.

VIRTUAL NETWORK CONCEPTS

Virtualization has become a standard part of enterprise networking for most people working in IT. In its most basic form, a virtualization server running a software component called a hypervisor hosts multiple virtual machines (VMs). Each VM has its own virtualized hardware environment, so an administrator can install a standard operating system and applications on it.

Like a physical computer, for a VM to function on a network, it must have the standard networking hardware devices, such as a network interface adapter and access to a switch. As part of its virtualized hardware configuration, a VM includes software-based, virtualized versions of these devices, some of which are described in this section.

Hypervisor

The *hypervisor* is the software component that abstracts the physical hardware in the host computer and supplies a virtualized version of that hardware to each VM. There are two types of hypervisors currently in use, based on where the software runs in relation to the operating system, as follows:

- ▶ **Type 1:** Usually implemented as part of an operating system product, the Type 1 hypervisor loads before the OS and exists as an abstraction layer between the VMs and the physical hardware. The hypervisor creates partitions, the first of which is the parent partition and the others child partitions. The child partitions become the VMs, whereas the parent partition contains the host OS, which manages the physical hardware and runs the virtualization stack that creates the child partitions. In this arrangement, there is no underlying host operating system splitting resources with the hypervisor.
- ▶ **Type 2:** Implemented as a stand-alone product that runs on top of an existing operating system, the Type 2 hypervisor must share processor resources with the host OS and then divide its allocation of resources among the guest VMs. Used in workstation-based virtualization products, Type 2 hypervisors typically do not provide the VM performance needed to host production servers.

Virtual Network Interface Card (vNIC)

Every computer, even a virtual one, needs a network interface adapter to connect to the local network. In a virtualized environment, therefore, to connect a VM to a network, it must have a *virtual network interface card (vNIC)*.

A vNIC performs many of the same functions as a physical network interface adapter, such as implementing a data link layer protocol and generating packets for transmission to the network. With some virtualization products, it is even possible to install more than one vNIC in a single VM and create multiple networks within the virtualized environment.

vSwitch

In a virtualized environment, a *vSwitch* performs the same role as a physical switch on a LAN. A switch is a data link layer device that functions as the communications nexus for a LAN. Each computer connected to one of the switch's ports can communicate with the other connected computers by sending traffic through the switch.

Virtualization server administrators can create and configure vSwitches as needed, even creating vSwitches that are shared by multiple virtualization servers. The vNICs in the virtual machines connect to a vSwitch, which creates a virtual network internal to the computer. The VMs can all communicate with each other by sending traffic through the vSwitch.

For this internal, virtual network to communicate with the physical network outside, the vSwitch must connect to the physical network interface adapter in the computer. The physical adapter has a connection to a physical switch, which provides the virtualization server—and all the virtual machines running on it—with access to the physical network.

Network Function Virtualization (NFV)

Network function virtualization (NFV) is a type of network architecture in which specific networking devices are implemented in a logical form called a virtualized network function (VNF). VNFs can provide the functionality of firewalls, load balancers, intrusion detection systems (IDSs), and other devices. Administrators can then deploy the VNFs as needed around the enterprise using standard hypervisor-based virtualization servers.

PROVIDER LINKS

Most networks have a link to an ISP, providing users with access to the Internet. There are several technologies that a network can use for this access. The selection of an appropriate connection type is a decision based on cost, transmission speed, synchronicity, and product availability. The most commonly used ISP links are as follows:

Cable   Most cable television providers can supply Internet access as well to residential as well as business customers. In most cases, the Internet access is asymmetrical, meaning that the downstream speed (from the provider to the customer) is faster than the upstream speed. However, some providers have business-oriented services with more upstream bandwidth.

Digital Subscriber Line (DSL)   Asymmetric digital subscriber line (ADSL) is a telecommunications technology that splits the bandwidth of a standard voice carrier line and dedicates part of that bandwidth to network data, while leaving the voice service intact. Because ADSL is asymmetric, downstream traffic is much faster than upstream. Primarily intended for residential or *SOHO (small office, home office)* Internet connections, ADSL is less popular today than other types of provider links. However, it is the only practical alternative for some customers. For business customers, carriers might provide other DSL technologies with symmetrical speeds and greater bandwidth, such as a high-rate digital subscriber line (HDSL).

Satellite   Uses a dish installed by a satellite ISP at the client's location to access a communications satellite and connect to the Internet through it. There are two types of satellite service. In the *one-way service*, the customer receives downstream traffic through the satellite at high speed, whereas upstream traffic uses a slower land-based connection.

In the *two-way service*, both downstream and upstream traffic go through the satellite. Satellite service is expensive compared to other types of provider links, but for some customers in remote locations, it is the only solution.

Leased Line   A dedicated and permanent telecommunications connection between two points, installed by a telephone service provider and reserved for the exclusive use of the client. Providers can supply leased lines running at various speeds, and clients can use the bandwidth however they wish.

Metro-Optical   MANs typically use fiber-optic links to integrate the various LANs in a metropolitan area into one internetwork. The installation of a community fiber-optic network for use as a MAN is sometimes called a metro-optical network.

CERTMIKE EXAM ESSENTIALS

▶ Most LANs today use a star topology with devices plugged into a common switch. Other LAN topologies used in the past include the bus, the ring, and various hybrids, such as a star ring. The mesh topology is not generally used for LANs, but WAN connections can use it for redundancy.

▶ The "area network" terminology used for the acronym LAN has been adopted for other networking technologies as well. Wide area networks (WANs) are long-distance connections between networks. Other network types of various sizes include metropolitan area networks (MANs), campus area networks (CANs), and personal area networks (PANs).

▶ Virtual networking has become a major part of IT. A software component running on a server called a hypervisor enables administrators to create logical implementations of servers, NICs, switches, and other network components. These virtualized components function just as their physical counterparts do, by sharing in the hardware resources of the server.

▶ Residential and business customers can connect to ISPs using a variety of provider links with similar levels of performance. Home users typically opt for broadband access using a cable TV connection; DSL, which shares a voice telephone line; or a satellite dish. Most of these ISPs can provide business accounts as well, with additional services.

Practice Question 1

Ralph is consulting at a site with mixed networking technologies accumulated over many years. An assistant electrician working in the drop ceiling has informed Ralph that he accidentally severed one of the network cables running through the ceiling space. The electrician didn't know what kind of network cable it was, which concerned Ralph because the site had installations using coaxial, fiber optic, and twisted pair. The use of various topologies at the site meant that the effect of a single cable break could vary. With which topology would the severed cable cause the greatest amount of disturbance to the network?

A. Mesh
B. Logical ring
C. Bus
D. Star

Practice Question 2

Ralph is planning on a career in IT, and he wants to build a home LAN for learning purposes. Ralph has purchased three used PCs, and he has installed an Ethernet network interface adapter in each. He has also purchased three CAT 6 UTP patch cables. Ralph wants to use the star topology for his network, but he is unsure about what device to purchase for his cabling nexus, the center of the star. Which of the following components will result in a LAN when Ralph plugs his three computers into it? (Select all correct answers.)

A. Hub
B. MAU
C. Switch
D. Router

Practice Question 1 Explanation

A. is incorrect because although the mesh topology is not typically used for LAN installations, its redundant connections between nodes would enable it to function normally despite a severed cable.

B. is incorrect because a cable break in a star topology would only affect the network communication of a single node.

C. is correct because a severed cable in a bus topology would split the network into two halves. This would prevent the nodes on one side of the break from communicating with those on the other side. Both halves of the network would also have one cable end without a terminator, which could inhibit communication among the computers on the same side of the break.

D. is incorrect because a logical ring topology is physically implemented as a star, and a severed cable in a star topology would only affect the network communication of a single node.

Correct Answer: C

Practice Question 2 Explanation

A. is correct because a hub can function as the cabling nexus at the center of an Ethernet star topology. Each of the devices on the network is plugged into the hub, resulting in a LAN.

B. is incorrect because a multistation access unit (MAU) is only used on Token Ring networks, not on Ethernet LANs.

C. is correct because a switch can function as the cabling nexus at the center of an Ethernet star topology. Each of the devices on the network is plugged into the switch, resulting in a LAN.

D. is incorrect because routers are used to connect networks together; they cannot function as the cabling nexus for a star topology.

Correct Answer: A and C

CHAPTER 3

Cables and Connectors

Objective 1.3: Summarize the types of cables and connectors and explain which is the appropriate type for a solution.

This chapter examines the various types of cables and connectors technicians encounter in their work, as well as the standards that dictate how to install them. These are fundamental networking concepts mentioned in many questions on the Network+ exam.

In this chapter, you'll learn everything you need to know about Network+ Objective 1.3, including the following topics:

▶ **Copper**
▶ **Fiber**
▶ **Connector types**
▶ **Cable management**
▶ **Ethernet standards**

CABLE TYPES

Wireless local area networking is enormously popular today, especially in residential installations, but cabled LANs are still an essential element of business networking. There are two basic types of cable used in data networking: copper and fiber-optic, as discussed in this section.

Copper Cables

The original local area networking standards called for cables with copper conductors that carry signals in the form of electrical voltages. Copper cables are still the most common network medium in use today, largely because they are relatively inexpensive and easy to install. The first Ethernet LANs used coaxial cable, but today the most popular cable type for networking use is twisted pair.

Coaxial Cable

In a *coaxial* cable, the conductor carrying the signals is a copper core at the center of the cable. There is insulation around the core, and then a layer of braided metal mesh that shields the core and functions as a ground. A sheath around the layers protects the whole assembly from damage. The construction of the cable and the shielding around the core make coaxial cable resistant to electromagnetic interference (EMI).

Coaxial cables are almost never used for LANs anymore, although some legacy installations still exist. The Institute of Electrical and Electronics Engineers (IEEE) 802.3 standards that define Ethernet networks have deprecated the 10Base5 and 10Base2 coaxial specifications since 2011. However, coaxial cable is still used widely for cable television installations. Table 3.1 lists the main coaxial cable types and their properties, using their *Radio Guide (RG)* designations.

TABLE 3.1 Coaxial cable types

Cable type	Diameter	Impedance	Application	Notes
RG-8	9.5 mm	50 ohms	10Base5	▶ Thick Ethernet/Thicknet
RG-58	4.95 mm	50 ohms	10Base2	▶ Thin Ethernet/Thinnet
RG-59	6.15 mm	75 ohms	Video/cable TV	▶ Shorter distances ▶ Less expensive
RG-6	6.9 mm	75 ohms	Video/cable TV	▶ Longer distances

There is also a variant of coaxial cable called *twinaxial* that uses the same basic construction except that there are two copper conductors at the core of the cable instead of just one. Used primarily in data centers for short-range, high-speed links, twinaxial is less expensive to purchase and easier to install than fiber-optic cable.

Twisted Pair Cable

The copper cable that is most prevalent in local area networking today is *twisted pair*. Available as *unshielded twisted pair (UTP)* and shielded twisted pair (STP), the cable consists of eight wires in four pairs. Each pair of wires, a signal wire and a ground, is twisted together at a different rate than the other three, to help prevent crosstalk and other forms of interference. The four pairs are then enclosed in a sheath for protection.

Table 3.2 lists the graded categories of twisted pair cable currently in use.

TABLE 3.2 Twisted pair cable categories

Category	Bandwidth	Transmission speeds	Max length	Application	Notes
CAT 5	100 MHz	10/100 Mbps	100 meters	10BASE-T 100BASE-TX	
CAT 5e	100 MHz	10/100/1000 Mbps	100 meters	10BASE-T 100BASE-TX 1000BASE-T	▶ Enhanced to support 1000 Mbps
CAT 6	250 MHz	10/100/1000 Mbps	100 meters	10BASE-T 100BASE-TX 1000BASE-T	
CAT 6	250 MHz	10 Gbps	55 meters	10GBASE-T	▶ Supports 10 Gbps only at reduced length
CAT 6a	500 MHz	10/100/ 1000/ 10000 Mbps	100 meters	10BASE-T 100BASE-TX 1000BASE-T 10GBASE-T	▶ Enhanced to support 10 Gbps over 100 meters
CAT 7	600 MHz	10/100/1000/ 10000 Mbps	100 meters	10GBASE-T	▶ Shielded twisted pair ▶ Requires GG45 or TERA connectors ▶ Not recognized by the EIA/TIA
CAT 8	2 GHz	40 Gbps	30 meters	40GBASE-T	▶ Shielded twisted pair ▶ Short-range use in data centers

Twisted pair cable installations should conform to the standards published by the American National Standards Institute (ANSI) and the Telecommunications Industry Association (TIA). The current version of the standard is called *ANSI/TIA-568-D: Commercial Building Telecommunications Cabling Standard*. This standard specifies cable types, connector types, maximum cable lengths, testing methodologies, and other installation requirements for twisted pair as well as coaxial and fiber-optic cables.

EXAM TIP

The ANSI/TIA-568-D standard has undergone several name changes. The TIA was formerly a division of the Electronic Industries Alliance (EIA), which was once called the Electronic Industries Association (EIA). Many published references to the standard still use older designations, such as EIA/TIA-568 or TIA/EIA-568. Network+ exam candidates should be aware that these various names all refer to revisions of the same document.

The Network+ objectives cite the termination standards for twisted pair cables as *TIA/EIA-568A* and *TIA/EIA-568B*. These refer to the pinouts that cable installers use when attaching RJ45 connectors to UTP or STP cables. The wires inside the cable are color-coded orange, green, brown, and blue, with one solid and one striped wire for each color. The 568A and 568B pinouts refer to the order of the colored wires in the connectors, as shown in Figure 3.1.

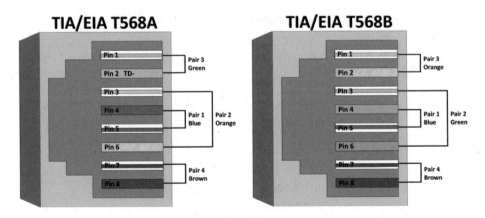

FIGURE 3.1   The TIA/EIA T568A and T568B pinouts for twisted pair cables

The only difference between the T568A and T568B pinouts is the reversal of the orange and green wire pairs. There is no difference in performance between the two, but it is critical for cable installers to use the same pinout at both ends of a cable run.

Fiber-Optic Cables

The primary alternative to copper-based cables for networking is fiber optic. Fiber-optic cables carry signals in the form of optical impulses generated by a laser or light-emitting diode (LED). A fiber-optic cable consists of a glass or plastic core that is the signal conductor, surrounded by layers of reflective cladding, buffering, and a protective sheath.

Compared to copper cables, fiber optic is much more efficient. It can span long distances, up to 120 kilometers, and it is completely resistant to EMI, crosstalk, and many other types of interference. However, fiber-optic cable is also much more expensive than UTP and more difficult to install, and requires specialized tools and training to maintain and troubleshoot.

There are many different types of fiber-optic cable, but they fall into two main categories, as follows:

Single-mode   Uses a laser light source to generate a single beam of light. Single-mode fiber can span distances up to 120 kilometers and achieves higher speeds than multimode.

Multimode   Uses an LED light source to generate multiple light impulses that travel through the core and reflect off the cladding to propagate the signal. Multimode fiber is relatively inexpensive compared to single-mode, but it only spans distances up to one kilometer and at lower speeds.

CONNECTOR TYPES

Network cables require connectors at both ends to plug into computers, patch panels, and other devices. Patch cables are available with connectors already attached, but for permanent cable installations, technicians pull bulk cable to the required locations and attach the connectors to both ends.

Copper Cable Connectors

The RG-59 and RG-6 coaxial cables used for cable television installations, cable modem connections, and other video applications use *F-type connectors*, which are screw-on connectors with the core protruding from the end. The IEEE 802.3 (Ethernet) standards and the Network+ exam objectives no longer include coaxial-based Ethernet specifications, so the *Bayonet Neill–Concelman (BNC)* and N-type connectors that RG-58 and RG-8 cables use are no longer covered.

Most twisted pair networks use *registered jack (RJ)* connectors, which are the standard snap-in modular connectors used by telephones and desktop computers. *RJ11* is the six-pin modular jack found in most telephones, although standard telephone connections only use two of the pins.

Internal LANs constructed with UTP and STP cables typically use the RJ45 connector to attach computers to wall plates and switch ports to patch panels. The *RJ45* connector is slightly larger than the RJ11 and has eight pins to accommodate standard four-pair cabling. Both the RJ11 and RJ45 connectors have a latch to hold them in place in the socket.

EXAM TIP

8P8C is the actual name of the four-pair connector intended for data networking. However, the term RJ45—intended for telephone installations—is much more prevalent, even on the Network+ exam.

Fiber-Optic Cable Connectors

Unlike the connectors for copper cables, which are generally standardized, fiber-optic cables can use several different types of connectors, including the following:

Straight Tip (ST)   A bayonet-type connector that locks into the socket with a half-twist

Subscriber Connector (SC)   A push-pull connector with a key to prevent twisting in the socket, and in some cases, a locking latch

Local Connector (LC)   A small form-factor connector similar to the SC connector but approximately half the size, with a latch to lock the male connector securely in the socket

Mechanical Transfer-Registered Jack (MT-RJ)   A small form-factor connector with duplex cores that is similar in size to an RJ45 connector

The ST and SC connectors are traditionally the most popular choices for fiber-optic cables, but the smaller form factors, such as MT-RJ and LC, have become more common, because they conserve space on switches and patch panels.

The interface between the fiber core in the cable and that in the socket is an important part of achieving a good-quality fiber-optic connection. Fiber-optic connectors are generally available in two interface formats, as follows:

Ultra-Physical Contact (UPC)   The fiber core is polished to a zero-degree (flat) surface. The join between the cores can therefore cause some light to be reflected back along the cable, causing return loss. However, the join between the flat surfaces reduces the amount of insertion loss caused by attenuation.

Angled Physical Contact (APC)   The fiber core is polished to an eight-degree angle so that reflected light is diverted to the cable cladding to reduce return loss. However, the amount of insertion loss is greater than in a UPC connection. APC connectors are distinguished by a green body or boot and must only be joined to other APC connectors; joining an APC to a UPC connector results in extremely high insertion loss.

Transceivers and Media Converters

A *transceiver* is a device that both transmits and receives signals. Network interface adapters (NICs) in computers generally have a built-in transceiver suitable for use with a given network medium, usually twisted pair. However, some devices, such as switches and routers, are equipped with small form-factor pluggable (SFP) slots that allow administrators to insert transceivers for any network type and medium. This is particularly useful for fiber-optic networks because the media and connector choices are so varied.

Since the introduction of the SFP slot, the transceiver technology has advanced through several iterations, with accompanying increases in speed, as shown in Table 3.3.

T A B L E 3 . 3 **SFP transceiver technologies**

Name	Date	Speed	Channels
Small form-factor pluggable (SFP)	2001	100 Mbps	1
Enhanced form-factor pluggable (SFP+)	2009	10 Gbps	1
Quad small form-factor pluggable (QSFP)	2006	4 Gbps	4
Enhanced quad small form-factor pluggable (QSFP+)	2012	40 Gbps	4

EXAM TIP

There are many other transceiver designations representing subsequent increases in transmission speed for each technology, such as QSFP28 and QSFP56, but the Network+ exam objectives only specify the four in Table 3.3.

There is a different type of external transceiver—called a *media converter* or sometimes a coupler—that exists only to connect network segments that use different media. The most common situation requiring a media converter is the need to connect an Ethernet UTP segment to a fiber-optic segment or single-mode fiber to multimode. A media converter can be a box with two network interfaces, or it could be a small connector barely larger than the cables themselves.

CABLE MANAGEMENT

A network installation can have hundreds of internal cable runs, all leading to a data center. To terminate those cable runs in the data center, it is common practice to use patch panels. A *patch panel* (or patch bay) is a physical layer device, mounted on the wall or in a rack, with rows of female RJ45 (or other) connectors on the front. The cable runs leading to the wall plates all over the site meet at the patch panel, where administrators punch them down into the backs of the connectors.

Many cable installations use specialized bulk cable types to provide service to distant locations, such as UTP cables containing 25 or more wire pairs in a single sheath. To make the wire connections for these cables, it is common practice to use a *punchdown block* that has connection points for all of the wires in one place.

Telephone service installations historically used a type of punchdown block called a *66 block*, which has rows of clips to which the individual wire pairs are connected. The 66 block is old technology that is still found in some telephone installations and was sometimes used for early 10BaseT Ethernet connections running at 10 Mbps, but it is not suitable for faster data networks.

The *110* block is a more modern version of a patch panel that is used for both telephone and data networking installations. Typically certified for use with specific UTP cable categories, often up to CAT 6a, 110 blocks can support the higher speeds of today's networks.

There are other types of punchdown blocks in use, such as the *Krone* block, which is popular in Europe. It's functionally similar to a 110 block, but it requires a special punchdown tool to fit its slightly larger connectors. The *Building Industry Cross-connect (BIX)* block has been in use since the 1970s, and it now supports CAT 5e and 6 cables. The BIX block also requires a proprietary punchdown tool.

As with UTP, some fiber-optic installations use cables with up to 24 fiber strands in a single sheath. To terminate those strands, a *fiber distribution panel* accepts the cable and allows administrators to splice each separate optical filament to a standard fiber-optic connector on the front of the box.

ETHERNET STANDARDS

The latest Network+ exam objectives cover only the Ethernet specifications that are currently in general use. There are many other designations in the IEEE 802.3 standards, some obsolete and others that never gained popularity. Table 3.4 lists the Ethernet specifications for copper-based UTP and STP cables.

T A B L E 3 . 4 Ethernet copper cable specifications

Designation/standard	Speed	Cable	Maximum segment length	Name
10BASE-T IEEE 802.3i	10 MHz	CAT 5 or higher	100 meters	Ethernet
100BASE-TX IEEE 802.3u	10/100 MHz	CAT 5 or higher	100 meters	Fast Ethernet
1000BASE-T IEEE 802.3ab	10/100/1000 MHz	CAT 5e or higher	100 meters	Gigabit Ethernet

Designation/standard	Speed	Cable	Maximum segment length	Name
10GBASE-T IEEE 802.3an	Up to 10 GHz	CAT 6 or higher	55 meters (CAT 6) 100 meters (CAT 6a)	10 Gigabit Ethernet
40GBASE-T IEEE 802.3bq	Up to 40 GHz	CAT 8 STP	30 meters	40 Gigabit Ethernet

In Ethernet designations such as 10Base-T, the first number indicates the transmission speed, BASE specifies that the network uses baseband transmissions, and the last initials represent the network medium. T is twisted pair, and in the fiber-optic designations, the letters S and L specify whether a specification is intended for short- or long-distance connections. Table 3.5 lists the Ethernet fiber-optic specifications currently in use.

TABLE 3.5 Ethernet fiber-optic specifications

Designation/standard	Speed	Cable	Light source	Maximum segment length	Notes
100BASE-FX IEEE 802.3u	100 Mbps	50 micron single-mode	1300 nm laser	2 kilometers	
100BASE-SX IEEE 802.3u	100 Mbps	62.5/50 micron multimode	850 nm LED	220/550 meters	Short haul
1000BASE-SX IEEE 802.3z	1000 Mbps	62.5/50 micron multimode	850 nm laser	220/550 meters	Short haul
1000BASE-LX IEEE 802.3z	1000 Mbps	9 micron single-mode	1300 nm laser	10 kilometers	Long haul
10GBASE-SR IEEE 802.3ae	10 Gbps	Various multimode	850 nm laser	400 meters	Short range
10GBASE-LR IEEE 802.3ae	10 Gbps	Various single-mode	1310 nm laser	10 kilometers	Long range

In addition to these standard Ethernet specifications, other technologies allow networks to make better use of the fiber-optic medium. *Bidirectional wavelength division multiplexing (WDM)* is a transmission technique that enables a single fiber to carry multiple signals simultaneously by assigning them to different wavelengths. *Coarse wavelength division multiplexing (CWDM)*, used by cable television networks, can transmit up to 18 signals in separate channels, upstream and downstream. *Dense wavelength division multiplexing (DWDM)* is a more advanced technique that can isolate up to 80 separate wavelengths. It was used in the replacement for the optical regenerators that synchronous optical networking (SONET) and synchronous digital hierarchy (SDH) networks once employed to amplify their signals.

Another Ethernet-based technology, called HDMI Ethernet Channel (HEC), adds a high-speed data channel to the HDMI interface. *High-Definition Multimedia Interface (HDMI)* is a cabled connection that is typically used to attach TV monitors to other home entertainment equipment. Adding the data channel eliminates the need to have a separate cabled network interface in each device. There are even protocols for transmitting Ethernet frames over *Universal Serial Bus (USB)* cables, such as Microsoft's Remote Network Driver Interface Specification (RNDIS).

CERTMIKE EXAM ESSENTIALS

▶ Cabled networks can use a variety of cable types, including coaxial, shielded and unshielded twisted pair, and single-mode and multimode fiber-optic.

▶ Twisted pair LANs nearly always use modular RJ45 connectors, but fiber-optic cables can use several different connector types, including ST, SC, LC, and MT-RJ.

▶ Data centers can have cable management devices, such as patch panels and punchdown blocks of several types. The 66 block is obsolete and was used mainly for telephone connections. The 110 block is currently in use for both telephone and data connections.

▶ The Ethernet standards currently include physical layer specifications for five copper cable options and six fiber-optic cable options.

Practice Question 1

Your company has just purchased an office building that stands 300 meters away from the current building, and the IT director has assigned you the task of joining together the networks in the two buildings. The connection must support at least Gigabit Ethernet speed and be resistant to the electromagnetic interference generated by manufacturing equipment in the area. The director also wants the solution to be as inexpensive as possible. Which of the following cable types should you use to connect the buildings?

A. RG-58 coaxial cable
B. CAT 6 unshielded twisted pair (UTP)
C. CAT 8 shielded twisted pair (STP)
D. Multimode fiber-optic
E. Single-mode fiber-optic

Practice Question 2

Which of the following IEEE twisted pair cable categories calls for shielded twisted pair (STP) instead of unshielded twisted pair (UTP) cable?

A. CAT 5e
B. CAT 6
C. CAT 6a
D. CAT 8

Practice Question 1 Explanation

A. is incorrect because coaxial cable is no longer used for data networking and only supports 10 Mbps transmission speeds and 185 meter cable segments.
B. is incorrect because although CAT 6 UTP can support Gigabit Ethernet transmission speeds, it can span distances no more than 100 meters.
C. is incorrect because CAT 8 cable is intended for short runs of 30 meters or less, usually within data centers, and cannot span 300 meters.
D. is correct because multimode fiber-optic cable can support both the 300 meter distance and the Gigabit Ethernet speed and is the most inexpensive option that meets both requirements.
E. Is incorrect because although single-mode fiber-optic cable can meet the distance and speed requirements, it is far more expensive than multimode cable.

Correct Answer: D, Multimode fiber-optic

Practice Question 2 Explanation

A. is incorrect because although the CAT 5e specification enhanced the cable to support Gigabit Ethernet, there were no significant interference issues that called for shielding.
B. is incorrect because although CAT 6 cable is rated for speeds up to 10 Gbps, that top speed is achievable only over reduced distances, so it is primarily intended for Gigabit Ethernet use. Shielding would also add significantly to the cost of the cable.
C. is incorrect because CAT 6a was enhanced by enlarging the cable's diameter and adding a separator to keep the pairs apart from each other, not by adding shielding to the wire pairs. This allows the cable to run at 10 Gbps over the full 100 meter distance.
D. is correct because achieving the extremely high transmission speeds of 40GBase-T, even over short distances, required shielding around the individual wire pairs and around the whole bundle, to provide additional protection against crosstalk and other types of interference.

Correct Answer: D, CAT 8

CHAPTER 4

IP Addressing

Objective 1.4: Given a scenario, configure a subnet and use appropriate IP addressing schemes.

This chapter examines the Internet Protocol (IP) addresses that devices on a TCP/IP network use to specify the sources and destinations of their network traffic. This is a fundamental concept in computer networking that is always covered in the Network+ exam and that is also a basic skill needed for network support and troubleshooting.

In this chapter, you'll learn everything you need to know about Network+ Objective 1.4, including the following topics:

▶ Public vs. private
▶ IPv4 vs. IPv6
▶ IPv4 subnetting
▶ IPv6 concepts
▶ Virtual IP (VIP)
▶ Subinterfaces

IP ADDRESSES

The Internet Protocol (IP), operating at the network layer of the OSI reference model, has its own addressing mechanism that it uses to specify the source and destination for each packet it transmits over the network. IP addressing is an essential element of the TCP/IP protocol suite that enables systems to forward packets to any location on the network.

IP exists in two versions—IPv4 and IPv6—and each of the two versions has its own addressing system. IPv4 uses addresses that are 32 bits long, and the rapid growth of the Internet over the years has threatened to deplete the IPv4 address space. Therefore, the IPv6 version expands the address size to 128 bits, providing an address space sufficiently large to support many years of network growth. The transition between IPv4 and IPv6 has been going on for years, but the Internet and most local networks still use IPv4.

IPv4 Addressing

IPv4 addresses are notated using a dotted-decimal format, in which an address consists of four 8-bit decimal values (called *octets*) separated by periods, as in the following example:

```
192.168.45.250
```

Because each of the decimals is 8 bits long, the range of possible values for each one is 0 to 255. It is important to note that, although an IPv4 address is notated using decimal values, the addressing process is sometimes easier to understand when you see the binary equivalent, which takes the form of 32 zeroes or ones. The address 192.168.45.250 in binary form is as follows:

```
11000000.10101000.00101101.11111010
```

An IP address has two elements: a network identifier and a host identifier. The network identifier specifies the network on which the system is located, and the host identifier specifies an individual computer or other device on that network. When a sending system transmits a packet, it passes through routers on the way to its destination. Routers use the network identifier in the destination IP address to forward the packet to the destination network. Then, the router on the destination network uses the host identifier to send the packet to its final recipient.

EXAM TIP

While Ethernet and other data link layer protocols also have an addressing system, they use a different type of address called a *media access control (MAC)* address. Data link layer protocols, because they are devoted to local network communications, use physical addresses called MAC addresses to identify each packet's next destination on the LAN. Therefore, a packet's destination MAC address in a packet might identify a different system than its destination IP address, which always identifies the ultimate recipient of the packet.

Every device on a TCP/IP network must have a unique IP address. Administrators can conceivably assign an address to each device manually, often referred to as a static address, but it is more common for them to use an automated addressing mechanism, such as the Dynamic Host Configuration Protocol (DHCP). When a computer on a TCP/IP network has no IP address assigned to it, most operating systems include a mechanism called *Automatic Private IP Addressing (APIPA)*, which generates a non-routable address on the 169.254.0.0/16 network that enables the system to communicate with the local network.

To communicate on the Internet, a device must use an IP address registered with the Internet Assigned Numbers Authority (IANA) through an official registrar, usually provided by an Internet service provider (ISP). The registrar assigns a network address to an applicant, and the applicant is responsible for creating subnets out of it and assigning a unique host address to each device.

IPv4 Subnetting

The most complicated aspect of IPv4 addressing is that the division between the network identifier and the host identifier in an address is not always in the same place. This is to provide support for networks of different sizes. The more bits assigned to the host identifier, the greater the number of unique IP addresses the administrators can create.

Classful Addressing

The Internet Protocol Version 4 standard, published by the Internet Engineering Task Force (IETF) as *Request for Comments (RFC)* 791, defines three IP address classes, as shown in Figure 4.1. Each class divides the 32 bits of the address into different-sized network and host identifiers.

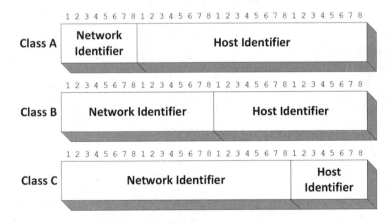

FIGURE 4.1 IP address classes

The characteristics of each address class are listed in Table 4.1. A Class A address can support the creation of up to 126 networks, each of which can have over 16 million hosts.

(The network address 127.0.0.0 is reserved for use as a loopback address.) Class C addresses support over 2 million networks, but each network can have no more than 254 hosts. Assigning IP addresses based on these classes is known as *classful addressing*.

TABLE 4.1   IP address classes and their characteristics

IP address class	Class A	Class B	Class C
First bit values (binary)	0	10	110
First byte value (decimal)	0–127	128–191	192–223
Number of network identifier bits	8	16	24
Number of host identifier bits	24	16	8
Number of possible networks	126	16,384	2,097,152
Number of possible hosts	16,777,214	65,534	254

In addition to Classes A, B, and C, the RFC 791 standard defines two additional classes, which are not used for host assignments, as follows:

▶ **Class D:** Beginning with 1110, Class D addresses are designated as multicast identifiers, which identify groups of hosts.

▶ **Class E:** Beginning with 11110, Class E addresses are reserved for experimental use.

To use classful addressing, a network administrator is assigned a network address, usually by an ISP. For example, 192.168.156.0 is a valid Class C network address. The administrator can take that network address, assign host values using the last octet, and create up to 254 IP addresses beginning as follows:

```
192.168.156.1
192.168.156.2
192.168.156.3
```

EXAM TIP

It is common for the Network+ exam to test the candidate's understanding of IPv4 addressing by offering some answers containing invalid IP addresses. Any octet with a value outside the range 0 to 255 is invalid. Host identifier values of 0 and 255 are also invalid because 0 identifies a network, not a host, and 255 is reserved for use as a broadcast address. Thus, the formula for determining the number host addresses for a given number of bits (n) is 2^n-2.

Public vs. Private Addresses

While communication on the Internet requires registered IP addresses, private networks nearly always use unregistered addresses for their internal communications. An IETF standard document called *RFC 1918*, "Address Allocation for Private Internets," defines three ranges of addresses that are allocated for private network use, one for each address class, as shown in Table 4.2.

TABLE 4.2 Private IP address ranges

Class	Address range	Subnet mask
Class A	10.0.0.0 to 10.255.255.255	255.0.0.0
Class B	172.16.0.0 to 172.31.255.255	255.255.0.0
Class C	192.168.0.0 to 192.168.255.255	255.255.255.0

A device that is assigned an address in one of these ranges can communicate with the other hosts on the same private network, but it cannot communicate on the Internet because the addresses are not routable. To make Internet access possible, most networks use a technique that substitutes a registered address for the private addresses, such as the following:

Network Address Translation (NAT)   A mechanism, usually built into a router, that dynamically modifies the addresses of IP packets destined for the Internet that the router receives from hosts on the internal network. The NAT router modifies outgoing packets by replacing their original private IP addresses with a registered public address, called a *virtual IP address*, which enables the router to transmit the packets over the Internet. The NAT router maintains a table of the address substitutions it makes so that when it receives an incoming reply from the Internet, it can again modify the packet, this time to restore the original unregistered address and forward the packet to the originating host.

Port Address Translation (PAT)   A variation of NAT that uses a single registered IP address for all the private hosts on the internal network. To distinguish one host from another, PAT also assigns each host a unique port number.

Subnet Masking

When configuring the IPv4 address settings for a computer or other device, in addition to the 32-bit address value, there is a second 32-bit value called a subnet mask. The *subnet mask* indicates which of the 32 bits in the address form the network identifier and which form the host identifier. For example, the subnet masks for the classful IPv4 addresses are as follows:

- ▶ **Class A:** 255.0.0.0
- ▶ **Class B:** 255.255.0.0
- ▶ **Class C:** 255.255.255.0

Although they are notated in decimal form, the subnet masks are based on the use of binary values; network identifier bits have a value of 1, and host identifier bits are 0s. There-fore, the Class B subnet mask in binary form is as follows:

```
11111111 11111111 00000000 00000000
```

The settings also call for a *default gateway* value, which is the IP address of a router on the local network that the system should use to access other networks. In a routing table, the default gateway entry uses 0.0.0.0 as its network destination address.

Creating Subnets

Classful addressing allows network administrators to modify the subnetting strategy for a given network address to accommodate the needs of the network. They do this by borrow-ing some of the host identifier bits from the network address and using them to create a subnet identifier. For example, a Class B network address has 16 host identifier bits, allow-ing the administrator to create addresses for 65,534 hosts. Few networks need this many host addresses, so the administrator can borrow some of the host bits to create subnets.

By using the 8 bits of the third octet as a subnet identifier, as shown in Figure 4.2, the administrator can create up to 256 subnets, each of which has up to 254 hosts.

FIGURE 4.2 Subnetting a Class B address

To indicate that the network address has been subnetted, the administrator changes the subnet mask for each of the host addresses. The subnet identifier in the third octet is now considered part of the network address, so the subnet mask in binary form substitutes 1s for 0s in that third octet, as follows:

```
11111111 11111111 11111111 00000000
```

In decimal form, therefore, the subnet mask for each of the host addresses becomes 255.255.255.0.

Classless Addressing

Subnetting along octet boundaries is easy but not always practical for every network. To provide greater flexibility, it is also possible to subnet a network address anywhere, not just between octets. To illustrate, an administrator can take the same network address from the previous example and borrow only 4 bits for the subnet identifier instead of 8. This leaves 12 bits for the host identifier, so the resulting network can have up to 16 subnets, each with up to 4,094 hosts. This process is called *classless addressing*.

In this case, the addresses use a technique called *variable length subnet masking (VLSM)* because the boundary between the network and host bits falls within an octet. Therefore, the subnet mask for this address with 20 network bits and 12 host bits, in binary form, is as follows:

```
11111111 11111111 11110000 00000000
```

In decimal form, the subnet mask that administrators must use for the host addresses they create is 255.255.240.0.

Classless Inter-Domain Routing (CIDR)

Classless addressing has largely overtaken classful addressing because it enables administrators to utilize the addresses allotted to them more efficiently. To simplify the notation of classless addresses, it is more common today to use *Classless Inter-Domain Routing (CIDR)*. In CIDR notation, the subnet mask for an address is written by appending a slash to the end of the address and specifying the number of network identifier bits, as in the following example: 172.16.20.0/22.

This example describes a Class B address with a 22-bit network identifier, 6 bits of which function as a subnet identifier, as shown in Figure 4.3. This subnet identifier allows administrators to create up to 64 (2^6) subnets, leaving the 10 remaining bits for the host identifier, which supports up to 1,022 ($2^{10}-2$) hosts per subnet. This is the CIDR equivalent to the network address 172.16.20.0 with a subnet mask of 255.255.252.0.

```
1 2 3 4 5 6 7 8 1 2 3 4 5 6 7 8 1 2 3 4 5 6 7 8 1 2 3 4 5 6 7 8
```

Network Identifier	Subnet Identifier	Host Identifier

FIGURE 4.3 Identifiers in the 172.16.20.0/22 CIDR address

Because the third octet in this example is partially allocated to the subnet identifier and partially to the host identifier, it is necessary to increment both parts separately when calculating the IP addresses for each subnet. Table 4.3 lists the values for the first three and the last of the 64 subnets.

TABLE 4.3 CIDR subnet addresses

Subnet	Network address	First IP address	Third octet binary value	Last IP address	Third octet binary value
1	172.16.0.0/22	172.16.0.1	000000 00	172.16.3.254	000000 11
2	172.16.4.0/22	172.16.4.1	000001 00	172.16.7.254	000001 11
3	172.16.8.0/22	172.16.8.1	000010 00	172.16.11.254	000010 11
64	172.16.252.0/22	172.16.252.1	111111 00	172.16.255.254	111111 11

Converting Binaries and Decimals

The Network+ exam typically includes questions on subnetting that require students to calculate IP addresses. When calculating addresses manually, the biggest problem is often converting between decimal and binary values. To convert a binary value into a decimal, assign decimal values to each of the binary bits, incrementing them from right to left and doubling them, as follows:

0	0	0	0	0	0	0	0
128	64	32	16	8	4	2	1

Then, plug in the bits of the binary value to be converted, in this case 10101100, and add the decimals for each of the 1 bits together, resulting in 172, as follows:

1	0	1	0	1	1	0	0
128	64	32	16	8	4	2	1

128 + 32 + 8 + 4 = 172

To convert a decimal into binary, subtract each of the incremented decimals, from left to right, from the number to be converted. For each of the incremented values it is possible to subtract, assign a binary value of 1. For all of the other values, assign a 0. Thus, starting with 172, it is possible to subtract 128, 32, 8, and 4, resulting in a binary value of 10101100, as shown here:

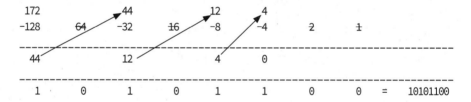

IPv4 VS. IPv6

Internet Protocol version 6 expands the IP address space from 32 to 128 bits, which increases the number of possible IP addresses from 2^{32} (or 4.2 billion) to 2^{128} (or 3.4×10^{38} or 340 undecillion, a 39-digit number). The notation of IPv6 addresses is also completely different from that of IPv4. Instead of decimal numbers, an IPv6 address consists of eight 16-bit hexadecimal numbers, separated by colons, as follows:

`XX:XX:XX:XX:XX:XX:XX:XX`

Each of the Xs represents 1 byte (8 bits), which in hexadecimal notation requires two characters. Therefore, a typical IPv6 address looks like the following:

`21cd:0053:0000:0000:e8bb:04f2:003c:c394`

IPv6 supports a *shorthand notation*, in which it is permitted to replace consecutive blocks of 0s with a double colon, as follows:

```
21cd:0053::e8bb:04f2:003c:c394
```

It is also permitted to omit any leading 0s in a block, as follows:

```
21cd:53::e8bb:4f2:3c:c394
```

IPv6 uses the same CIDR notation as IPv4 for network addresses. The network address for this example therefore looks like this:

```
21cd:53::/64
```

IPv6 Address Types

IPv4 uses three types of addresses: unicasts, multicasts, and *broadcasts*, which address a single recipient, a group of recipients, and all of the recipients on the local network, respectively. IPv6 does not use broadcast transmissions, but it introduces several new types of unicast addresses, retains the multicast addresses from IPv4, and adds a new anycast address. The IPv6 address types are as follows:

Unicast   An address resolving as a single host for one-to-one transmissions. IPv6 supports the following unicast address formats, each of which is identified by its own prefix.

> **Global Unicast (001 + 45-Bit Global Routing Prefix)**   A fully routable address identifying a single device that is the functional equivalent of a registered public IPv4 address.

> **Link local (fe80::/64)**   A stateless, non-routable address automatically generated on every IPv6 device; the link local address is the equivalent of an IPv4 APIPA address.

> **Multicast**   Unchanged in function from IPv4, multicast addresses represent a group of devices, registered using the Internet Group Management Protocol (IGMP), allowing one-to-many transmissions.

Anycast   As with multicasts, anycast addresses represent a group of recipients, such as all of the routers on the network, but the sender transmits packets to only one of the group members. The most common application for anycasts is to locate the nearest router.

Loopback   An address that causes the transmitting system to divert the outgoing packet to the network interface's input buffer. IPv4 reserves 127.0.0.1 for use as its loopback address, while IPv6 reserves the 0:0:0:0:0:0:0:0 and 0:0:0:0:0:0:0:1 addresses.

IPv6 Autoconfiguration

All IPv6 systems assign themselves a link local address, which, like all IP addresses, requires a network identifier and a host identifier. To determine the address of the network on which it is located, the system generates a *router solicitation (RS)* message, which it transmits as a multicast to all routers. The router on the local network responds with a *router advertisement (RA)* message that contains the network identifier.

To generate the host identifier for its link local address, the IPv6 system uses a process called *stateless address autoconfiguration (SLAAC)*, in which it takes the 48-bit MAC address of the network interface, splits it into 24-bit halves, and inserts the 16-bit value 0xFFFE between the two. This forms a 64-bit value called an *Extended Unique Identifier-64 (EUI-64)*, which the system uses as the host identifier portion of the address.

Transitioning to IPv6

IPv6 has existed for more than 20 years, but the Internet and many private networks still use IPv4 primarily. To provide support for both protocols during the process of transitioning from IPv4 to IPv6, several mechanisms are available.

Dual Stack

A *dual stack* system is one that has both IPv4 and IPv6 protocol stacks, both of which interface with the data link layer protocol the system uses. This enables the device to communicate with both IPv4 and IPv6 devices on the network. To communicate with other networks, however, all of the intervening systems between a source and a destination, including routers and Domain Name System (DNS) servers, must support dual stacks as well. Routers do this by using *subinterfaces*, logical network interfaces created from a single physical interface, which each have their own *virtual IP (VIP)* addresses.

Tunneling

Another method that allows IPv6 devices to communicate on IPv4 networks is called tunneling. *Tunneling* is the process of encapsulating one entire packet inside another to facilitate its transmission over the network. It is common to use tunneling for security purposes, but in this case, encapsulating an IPv6 datagram within an IPv4 packet allows IPv6 systems to communicate, even if some or all of the intervening networks only support IPv4. Some of the common tunneling protocols used for IPv6 transitioning include 6to4, Intra-Site Automatic Tunnel Addressing Protocol (ISATAP), and Teredo, all of which use some means to establish IPv4 tunnel endpoints that can carry IPv6 traffic between them.

CERTMIKE EXAM ESSENTIALS

▶ IP has its own addressing system in two versions. IPv4 uses 32-bit addresses written in dotted decimal notation, whereas IPv6 uses 128-bit hexadecimal addresses that greatly expand IP address space.

▶ IPv4 addresses were first defined using five classes, A through E, to support networks of various sizes. Later, Classless Inter-Domain Routing (CIDR) provided greater flexibility by allowing the address space to be divided within classes, instead of just between them.

▶ Both IPv4 and IPv6 systems can assign addresses to themselves, with IPv4 using Automatic Private IP Addressing (APIPA) and IPv6 using router advertisements (RAs) and stateless address autoconfiguration (SLAAC).

▶ Transitioning between IPv4 and IPv6 is possible using techniques such as dual stacks, in which a device has separate network layer protocol implementations supporting both IP versions, and tunneling, which encapsulates IPv6 in IPv4 packets, for transmission over an IPv4 network.

Practice Question 1

Alice has been directed by her supervisor to take a Class B network address and devise a plan to subnet it by creating 60 subnets supporting up to 1,000 hosts on each one. Alice has calculated that she needs 6 address bits to support 60 subnets and 10 bits to support 1,000 hosts, but she is unsure about how to go about allocating the bits. Which of the following best describes how Alice should manipulate the address she has been given to create a subnet identifier?

A. Extend the network identifier by 6 bits and the host identifier by 10 bits.
B. Borrow 6 bits from the existing host identifier.
C. Borrow 6 bits from the existing network identifier.
D. Borrow 6 bits from the existing network identifier and 10 bits from the host identifier.

Practice Question 2

Ralph has been asked to design an IPv4 network on which he can create 10 subnets supporting up to 2,000 hosts on each. Which of the following network addresses could Ralph use to create such a network?

A. 192.168.43.0/27
B. 172.16.96.0/21
C. 10.128.0.0/10
D. 127.223.0.0/16

Practice Question 1 Explanation

A. is incorrect because IPv4 addresses can only be exactly 32 bits long, so it is not possible to extend them.
B. is correct because borrowing 6 bits from the network identifier for a subnet identifier allows the creation of up to 64 subnets and leaves 10 bits for a host identifier, which can support up to 1,024 hosts.
C. is incorrect because borrowing 6 bits from the network identifier would change its value and interrupt network communications.
D. is incorrect for the same reason as answer (C). While borrowing 3 bits from the host identifier is permissible, changing the network identifier value would interrupt network communications.

Correct Answer: B, Borrow 6 bits from the existing host identifier

Practice Question 2 Explanation

A. is incorrect because a 3-bit subnet identifier supports only 8 subnets, not 10, and the remaining 5 host identifier bits can only support 32 hosts, not 2,000.
B. is correct because the network address has a 5-bit subnet identifier, supporting up to 32 subnets, leaving 11 bits for the host identifier, which can support up to 2,046 hosts.
C. is incorrect because, although the 22-bit host identifier can support up to 4,194,302 hosts per subnet, the 2-bit subnet mask can only support 4 subnets, not 10.
D. is incorrect because, although the network address can support up to 256 subnets and up to 4,194,302 hosts per subnet, the entire 127.0.0.1 network is reserved for use as a loopback address.

Correct Answer: B, 172.16.96.0/21

CHAPTER 5

Ports and Protocols

Objective 1.5: Explain common ports and protocols, their application, and encrypted alternatives.

This chapter examines the protocols commonly used on TCP/IP networks and the port numbers assigned to them. The Network+ exam expects candidates to be familiar with these protocols, their basic functions, and the port numbers used to identify them in transport layer protocol headers.

In this chapter, you'll learn everything you need to know about Network+ Objective 1.5, including the following topics:

▶ **Protocols**
▶ **Ports**
▶ **IP protocol types**
▶ **Connectionless vs. connection-oriented**

IP PROTOCOL TYPES

The TCP/IP suite is a collection of protocols, mostly running at the network, transport, and application layers of the OSI reference model. Systems use various combinations of protocols at the different layers depending on the amount and nature of the data to be transmitted over the network. Table 5.1 lists some of the most common protocols used at these three layers. The abbreviation TCP/IP, which gives the protocol suite its name, refers to the combination of the Transmission Control Protocol (TCP) at the transport layer and Internet Protocol (IP) at the network layer, which is one of the most commonly used combinations at those layers.

TABLE 5.1 TCP/IP protocols

Layer	Protocols
Application	FTP, SSH, SFTP, IMAP, POP3, SMTP, SNMP, DNS, DHCP, HTTP, HTTPS, TFTP, LDAP, SMB, NTP, Syslog, Telnet
Transport	TCP, UDP
Network	IP, ICMP

Connectionless vs. Connection-Oriented Protocols

The primary network and transport layer protocols of the TCP/IP suite fall into two basic categories: connectionless and connection-oriented. IP, at the network layer, and the User Datagram Protocol (UDP), at the transport layer, are both connectionless protocols. TCP, also at the transport layer, is a connection-oriented protocol.

Connectionless protocols are relatively simple because they are limited to best-effort delivery. This means that connectionless protocols transmit data, but they have no mechanism to guarantee its intact delivery. For IP, this is because it relies on TCP at the transport layer when guaranteed delivery or other services are needed. For UDP, at the transport layer, this is because the protocol is used primarily for brief transactions that consist of a single request and a single reply. Because they do not include guaranteed delivery and other complex features, connectionless protocols have a very low bandwidth overhead.

Connection-oriented protocols are designed for use when the data to be transmitted requires guaranteed delivery or other additional services. Before a connection-oriented protocol, such as TCP, transmits any data to a recipient, the two systems exchange messages to establish a connection. With the connection established, the sender's transmission of data packets can begin. As the data packets arrive, the receiver sends back periodic acknowledgment messages to confirm their receipt. If any packets go unacknowledged, the sender automatically retransmits them. When the data transmission is completed, the systems exchange messages to terminate the connection.

Connection-oriented protocols typically include other services in addition to guaranteed delivery. All of these services incur additional bandwidth overhead, both in the form of a larger protocol header and in the additional connection establishment and termination messages.

Internet Protocol (IP)

The *Internet Protocol (IP)*, as described in Chapter 4, "IP Addressing," is a network layer protocol that is the primary end-to-end carrier on all TCP/IP networks. IP is essentially the sealed envelope that carries upper-layer data all the way to its final destination. IP is responsible for addressing data packets, routing data through networks to its final destination, and fragmenting packets when necessary to transmit them over networks with smaller maximum transmission unit (MTU) sizes.

For incoming traffic, IP packet headers include a code that specifies which transport layer protocol, , TCP or UDP, should receive the data. For outgoing traffic, both TCP and UDP at the transport layer pass their data down to IP at the network layer.

Transmission Control Protocol (TCP)

Transmission Control Protocol (TCP) is a connection-oriented transport layer protocol that, in combination with IP at the network layer, is responsible for a large part of the traffic on any TCP/IP network. To establish a connection between the source and the destination, TCP systems perform a message transaction called a three-way handshake. Then, the sending system encapsulates the data it receives from the application layer by applying a 20-byte header and passes the resulting packet down to IP at the network layer.

The TCP header implements a variety of functions, including the following:

Packet Acknowledgment   Receiving systems acknowledge incoming packets by specifying in the header the number of the next packet expected.

Flow Control   Receiving systems specify in their acknowledgments how many bytes they can receive without dropping packets. The sending system adjusts its transmission rate accordingly.

Data Segmentation   TCP can handle large amounts of data, which has to be split into segments and transmitted in separate packets. The header for each packet includes a number that identifies its place in the packet sequence.

Error Detection   Each TCP packet includes a checksum calculated on the TCP header, the payload data, and an IP pseudo-header. Receiving systems perform the same calculation to confirm error-free delivery.

Port Identification   The TCP header specifies the port numbers of the source and destination application layer protocols.

User Datagram Protocol (UDP)

Compared to TCP, *User Datagram Protocol (UDP)* is a simple connectionless protocol with minimal overhead. There is no three-way handshake with UDP, and its header is only 8 bytes long, compared to TCP's 20 bytes, as shown in Figure 5.1. There is no guaranteed delivery with UDP, nor does it have any of the other TCP functions, except for an error detection checksum and source and destination port identification fields.

TCP Header

1 2 3 4 5 6 7 8	1 2 3 4 5 6 7 8	1 2 3 4 5 6 7 8	1 2 3 4 5 6 7 8
Source Port		Destination Port	
Sequence Number			
Acknowledgment Number			
Data Offset	Reserved	Control Bits	Window
Checksum		Urgent Pointer	
Options			
Data			

UDP Header

1 2 3 4 5 6 7 8	1 2 3 4 5 6 7 8	1 2 3 4 5 6 7 8	1 2 3 4 5 6 7 8
Source Port		Destination Port	
Length		Checksum	
Data			

FIGURE 5.1 TCP and UDP header sizes

Most UDP transactions consist of a single request message and a single reply, which eliminates the need for those advanced TCP functions. For example, in a typical DNS name resolution transaction, the client sends a single request message to a DNS server using the UDP and IP protocols. If the server receives the request, it transmits a reply, and this serves as acknowledgment of the transmission. If the client receives no response to its request, it can simply retransmit it until it receives a reply. There is no need for separate acknowledgment messages, nor is there a long data sequence to be segmented or any need for flow control.

Internet Control Message Protocol (ICMP)

Internet Control Message Protocol (ICMP) is a network layer protocol like IP, but it does not carry upper-layer data. Instead, ICMP performs a series of informational functions, including the transmission of error messages and diagnostic queries and responses. Unusually, ICMP messages are encapsulated within IP datagrams.

For example, the well-known ping utility works by transmitting ICMP Echo Request messages to the designated recipient, which then responds with Echo Reply messages. In the same way, error messages such as Destination Host Unknown that appear when a data transmission fails are carried by ICMP.

> **EXAM TIP**
>
> The original version of ICMP, designed for use with IPv4, is now known as ICMPv4. ICMPv6 is a new version designed for use with IPv6. The message formats for the two ICMP versions are the same, but ICMPv6 includes some new message types that do not exist in ICMPv4. Network+ candidates should be prepared to see any of the terms ICMP, ICMPv4, and ICMPv6 on the exam.

IPsec

IPsec is a series of standards that define a security architecture for IP traffic as it travels over a network. Operating at the network layer, the IPsec protocols can digitally sign or encrypt the data in a packet containing an IP datagram. The data remains secured for the packet's entire route through the network until it is finally read or decrypted by the destination end system.

IPsec consists of two primary protocols, as follows:

Authentication Header (AH)   Digitally signs IP datagrams by inserting an AH header after the IP header. The AH header includes fields that provide mutual authentication, so both parties are assured of the other's identity; anti-replay, so attackers cannot reuse all or part of the data; and data integrity, so the contents of the datagram cannot be modified in transit.

Encapsulating Security Payload (ESP)   Encrypts the data in an IP datagram by adding an ESP header and trailer surrounding the datagram's payload. Everything between the header and trailer is encrypted. ESP can also provide mutual authentication, anti-replay, and data integrity services.

It is possible to use each of the protocols individually or both together, for maximum protection. When protected by IPsec, it is possible for attackers to intercept packets in transit using a sniffer or network monitor, but they cannot read, modify, or reuse the contents of the datagram inside to discover passwords, spoof the recipients, or assume the sender's identity.

IPsec supports two modes: transport mode and tunnel mode. Transport mode, as described thus far in this section, provides protection between end systems, regardless of the number and type of routers between the source and the destination. Tunnel mode is designed to secure a wide area network (WAN) by creating an encrypted link between two routers. The packet structure is different in tunnel mode, and data is not encrypted or decrypted until it reaches one of the routers at each end of the tunnel.

Generic Routing Encapsulation (GRE)

Generic Routing Encapsulation (GRE) is a network layer tunneling protocol that encapsulates a whole IP datagram within another datagram to create point-to-point links and virtual private networks (VPN) over the Internet. A GRE tunnel connecting routers at two different sites appears to the routers at either end of the tunnel to be a direct link between them, even though the encapsulated traffic might pass through many other routers on the way. This makes it possible for the routers at different sites to exchange routing table information using a protocol such as Open Shortest Path First (OSPF), which would not be possible over a standard Internet connection in which the packets have to be processed by many intermediate routers.

By carrying IP datagrams within other IP datagrams, GRE technically violates the rules of the encapsulation process. However, unlike IPsec, which can also encapsulate datagrams, GRE provides no encryption for the encapsulated data. The original datagram, inside the GRE datagram, is transmitted in clear text.

APPLICATION LAYER PROTOCOLS

The TCP/IP suite includes a great many application layer protocols, which typically work together with applications or services running on a system to generate data for transmission over the network. The protocol then passes the data down through the OSI model layers for encapsulation, starting with either TCP or UDP at the transport layer.

Application layer protocols are identified by the ports they use, which are given numbers by the Internet Assigned Numbers Authority (IANA). The TCP and UDP headers both contain 16-bit fields for the port numbers of the application layer protocols that are the source and destination of the data. This allows the transport layer protocols on receiving systems to pass incoming data to the correct protocol at the application layer.

Because of the 16-bit Source Port and Destination Port fields in the TCP and UDP headers, there are 2^{16}, or 65,536, possible port numbers available. The IANA has defined three types of port numbers and has assigned them the ranges of values shown in Table 5.2.

T A B L E   5 . 2 TCP/IP port number ranges

Port number range	Port type	Description
0 to 1,023	Well-known	Permanently assigned to commonly used network services
1,024 to 49,151	Registered	Assigned to specific services on request by their developers
49,152 to 65,535	Dynamic, private, or ephemeral	Unregistered ports that can be used for private or temporary purposes, such as port numbers self-assigned by clients for a single network transaction

The Network+ exam calls for candidates to be familiar with the protocols shown in Table 5.3, their basic functions, and the port numbers they use. Note, however, that these are default port number values that can sometimes be modified by administrators. Web servers, for example, use port 80 for HTTP traffic by default, but administrators often assign servers alternative port numbers for security purposes.

EXAM TIP

Network+ questions sometimes test the candidate's familiarity with port number assignments by using them as part of IP addresses or *uniform resource locators (URLs)*. The combination of an IP address and a port number is called a *socket*; it is notated by appending the port number to the address, separated by a colon, as follows: 192.168.45.96:80. To specify the URL for a web server that uses a non-default port, you append the port number in the same way, as follows: `http://www.contoso.com:49853`.

TABLE 5.3 Application layer protocols and their port numbers

Protocol	Description	Port
File Transfer Protocol (FTP)	Transfers files between clients and servers using two ports, one for control traffic and one for data	20/21
Secure Shell (SSH)	Provides a secured command-line interface to remote systems	22
Secure File Transfer Protocol (SFTP)	Securely transfers files between clients and servers	22
Telnet	Provides an unsecured command-line interface to remote systems	23
Simple Mail Transfer Protocol (SMTP)	Transmits mail traffic between servers and between server and client	25
Domain Name System (DNS)	Resolves host and domain names into IP addresses	53
Dynamic Host Configuration Protocol (DHCP)	Assigns IP addresses to TCP/IP clients	67/68
Trivial File Transfer Protocol (TFTP)	Transfers files between clients and servers without authentication	69
Hypertext Transfer Protocol (HTTP)	Carries web page content from servers to browsers	80
Post Office Protocol v3 (POP3)	Retrieves user mail from a mail server	110
Network Time Protocol (NTP)	Carries time signals to remote computers for clock synchronization	123
Internet Message Access Protocol (IMAP)	Provides online access to user mail	143
Simple Network Management Protocol (SNMP)	Transmits network management information from agents to a central console	161/162
Lightweight Directory Access Protocol (LDAP)	Carries directory service information between domain controllers	389

Protocol	Description	Port
Hypertext Transfer Protocol Secure (HTTPS)/Secure Sockets Layer (SSL)	Carries web page content using a connection secured with SSL	443
HTTPS/Transport Layer Security (TLS)	Carries web page content using a connection secured with TLS	443
Server Message Block (SMB)	Provides file and printer sharing services on Windows networks	445
Syslog	Manages and transmits logging information	514
Real-Time Streaming Protocol (RTSP)	Carries multiplexed multimedia content between clients and servers	554
SMTP TLS	Transmits mail traffic server-to-server and server-to-client using TLS for secured authentication and data integrity	587
Lightweight Directory Access Protocol (over SSL) (LDAPS)	Securely carries directory service information between domain controllers	636
IMAP over SSL	Provides secured online access to user mail	993
POP3 over SSL	Securely retrieves user mail from a mail server	995
Structured Query Language (SQL) Server	Provides client/server communication for the SQL Server relational database management system	1433
SQLnet	Provides client/server communication for the SQLnet relational database management system	1521
MySQL	Provides client/server communication for the open source MySQL relational database management system	3306

Protocol	Description	Port
Remote Desktop Protocol (RDP)	Carries keystrokes, mouse movements, and display video between host and remote systems	3389
Session Initiation Protocol (SIP)	Creates and maintains audio/video connections for Voice over IP (VoIP), videoconferencing, and other multimedia applications	5060/5061

CERTMIKE EXAM ESSENTIALS

▶ Connection-oriented protocols require end systems to establish a connection before they can transmit data. They also have larger headers compared to connectionless protocols, which do not perform a connection establishment process.

▶ IP is the primary network layer protocol responsible for addressing data packets, routing data through networks, and fragmenting packets when necessary.

▶ TCP and UDP are transport layer protocols, connection-oriented, and connectionless, respectively. TCP provides packet acknowledgment, flow control, data segmentation, error detection, and port identification services. UDP provides only error detection and identification, but it has a much lower bandwidth overhead than TCP.

▶ Many application layer protocols have well-known port numbers assigned to them. Transport layer protocols use the port numbers to identify the process that should receive the data in a particular packet. Network+ exam candidates should be familiar with the protocols listed in the table and their port numbers.

Practice Question 1

Alice has been asked to examine a captured network traffic sample and identify the application layer protocols that are responsible for the most network traffic. The network monitor software Alice is using only identifies the application layer protocols by their port numbers. For each of the following port numbers, select the protocol from the list below that uses that port.

1. 53
2. 69
3. 161
4. 80
5. 443
6. 20
7. 25
8. 143
9. 68
10. 110

a. SMTP
b. FTP
c. HTTP
d. SNMP
e. TFTP
f. DNS
g. DHCP
h. HTTPS
i. IMAP
j. POP3

Practice Question 2

At the transport layer of the OSI model, all application traffic is handled by two protocols: TCP and UDP. Of the two, UDP is understood to have a significantly smaller bandwidth overhead than TCP. Which of the following factors in UDP contribute to its reduced overhead? (Choose all correct answers.)

A. No checksum

B. No three-way handshake

C. Lower port numbers

D. Smaller header

Practice Question 1 Correct Answers and Explanations

1. f. The Domain Name System (DNS) uses port number 53 for its client server communications.
2. e. Trivial File Transfer Protocol (TFTP) uses port number 69.
3. d. Simple Network Management Protocol (SNMP) uses port number 161.
4. c. Hypertext Transfer Protocol (HTTP) uses port 80 by default.
5. h. Hypertext Transfer Protocol Secure (HTTPS) uses port 443 by default.
6. b. File Transfer Protocol (FTP) uses two ports for its client/server communications, port 20 for control traffic and port 21 for data.
7. a. Simple Mail Transfer Protocol (SMTP) uses port number 25.
8. i. Internet Message Access Protocol (IMAP) uses port number 143.
9. g. Dynamic Host Configuration Protocol (DHCP) uses two ports, 67 and 68.
10. j. Post Office Protocol 3 (POP3) uses port number 110.

Practice Question 2 Explanation

A. is incorrect because TCP and UDP both include checksum fields in their headers.
B. is correct because TCP, a connected-oriented protocol, requires additional messages for connection establishment, whereas UDP, a connectionless protocol, does not.
C. is incorrect because both TCP and UDP have identically sized port number fields in their headers, so the number of bits transmitted is the same, whatever the port number values.
D. is correct because the header that UDP applies to each packet is only 8 bytes long, whereas the TCP header is 20 bytes.

Correct Answers, B, No three-way handshake, and D, Smaller header

CHAPTER 6

Network Services

Objective 1.6: Explain the use and purpose of network services.

This chapter examines some of the important services used on TCP/IP networks. All of them are virtually invisible to the average end user, but they provide administrative services that are vital to network communications and that save administrators a great deal of work. The Network+ exam expects candidates to be familiar with these services and their basic functions.

In this chapter, you'll learn everything you need to know about Network+ Objective 1.6, including the following topics:

▶ DHCP
▶ DNS
▶ NTP

DHCP

Every device on a TCP/IP network needs an IP address, but the task of configuring them manually and individually—called *static assignment*—is time-consuming and difficult for administrators. *Dynamic Host Configuration Protocol (DHCP)* is a combination of a service and a protocol that enables clients to request IP address assignments from a DHCP server. The server assigns each client a unique address from a pool—called a *scope*—along with other TCP/IP configuration settings, called *scope options*, such as subnet masks and default gateway addresses.

Three types of IP address assignments are defined in the DHCP standards, as follows:

Dynamic Allocation   The server leases an address from a pool to each device for a specified duration called the *lease time*. When the lease expires, either the client renews the address for another lease period or the server reclaims the address and returns it to the pool for reassignment.

Automatic Allocation   The server assigns an address from a pool to each device permanently, without a lease expiration or a renewal.

Manual Allocation   In the manual process, also called *reservations*, the server assigns a specific address to each device permanently, without a lease or renewal. This method is typically used for servers and other systems that require a permanent, unchanging IP address.

> **EXAM TIP**
>
> The terms *dynamic*, *automatic*, and *manual* are used by the DHCP standards to define the types of address allocation, but not all DHCP implementations use these terms. The Network+ objectives use the term *dynamic assignment*, but they describe manual address allocations as reservations.

The address assignment process occurs automatically when a device with a DHCP client starts, and proceeds as follows:

1. The DHCP client transmits a series of address request messages as broadcasts, using User Datagram Protocol (UDP) port 67.
2. Any DHCP servers on the local network with *available leases* that receive the broadcasts must reply with an offer of an IP address.
3. The DHCP client accepts one of the offered addresses by generating a request message containing the chosen server's IP address.
4. The chosen DHCP server replies to the request message with a positive or negative acknowledgment message, indicating either its confirmation of the address assignment or that the offered address is no longer available.
5. On receipt of a positive acknowledgment message, the client configures its own TCP/IP settings using the offered address and options. If the client receives a negative acknowledgment, the entire name resolution process begins again.

The DHCP server keeps track of the addresses it assigns, so there is no chance of IP address duplication on the network. In dynamic allocation, when the IP address lease reaches 50 percent of its lease time, and again when it reaches 87.5 percent, the client sends lease renewal requests to the DHCP server, which usually responds with a new lease for the same address. If the server does not receive renewal messages from the client, it reclaims the IP address it assigned previously and returns it to the scope for reassignment.

DHCP on IPv6

The original DHCP standards call for DHCP client/server communications to use UDP traffic on port 67 for clients and port 68 for servers, which remain the ports used for IPv4 address assignments. This original DHCP version is now commonly known as DHCPv4. There are now also standards defining the use of DHCP on IPv6 networks, referred to as DHCPv6.

IPv6 networks do not support broadcast transmissions, so the DHCPv6 address assignment process uses a multicast address for the initial requests sent by clients. DHCPv6 also uses different ports for its traffic: 546 and 547 for the client and server, respectively. The basic architecture is the same in DHCPv6 as it is in DHCPv4, but the message types and their formats are changed.

All IPv6 devices use stateless address autoconfiguration (SLAAC) to assign themselves a link local address, as described in Chapter 4, "IP Addressing," so many of them have no need for DHCP addresses, but DHCPv6 provides a stateful alternative to the stateless self-assignment process.

Creating a Scope

Although the term does not appear in the DHCP standards, a *scope* is a pool of IP addresses that a DHCP administrator has designated for assignment to clients. Usually, the scope is a range of addresses, which might include some or all of the addresses available on the local subnet. If there are addresses within a given range that the administrator does not want assigned, it is possible to create an exclusion range within the scope.

For example, the administrator might create a scope containing all of the addresses for a subnet, such as 192.168.54.1/24 to 192.168.54.255/24. However, if there are some servers on the network that already have static address assignments in that range, the administrator can designate 192.168.54.101/24 to 192.168.54.110/24 as an *exclusion range*, so those 10 addresses will never be assigned to DHCP clients.

In addition to the IP addresses themselves, a DHCP scope can have *scope options* defined, which specify the other settings needed by the TCP/IP clients on that network, including a subnet mask, a DNS server address, and a default gateway, which specifies the address of a router on the local network. The DHCP standards also support a large set of other options that administrators can configure to be included with IP address assignments from a particular scope or as server options for the clients on all of the server's scopes.

> **EXAM TIP**
> In TCP/IP terminology, the term *gateway* is synonymous with *router*, but it also has other meanings, such as a device that converts data from one protocol format into another. Network+ exam candidates should be conscious of the distinction and be sure which meaning is implied by a particular context.

DHCP Relays

Because they rely on broadcast messages as part of the address assignment process, DHCPv4 traffic is limited to the local network. For a large network with multiple subnets, this would ordinarily mean that there must be a DHCP server on each subnet, which would in most cases be impractical. However, there is a solution for this problem in the form of DHCP relay agents.

A *DHCP relay agent* is a software component, typically built into a router or server, which allows DHCP clients to obtain IP addresses from a DHCP server on another network. The address assignment procedure with an intervening relay agent is as follows:

1. The relay agent listens on UDP port 67 for address request messages sent as broadcasts by DHCP clients on the local network.
2. When it receives a broadcast, the relay agent inserts its own IP address into the client's request message and forwards it to a DHCP server on another network.
3. The DHCP server responds to the request by offering an IP address, but it sends its messages to the relay agent instead of to the client.
4. The relay agent forwards the server's replies to the client, which can then accept the offered address and configure its TCP/IP settings.

There are other protocols and services that have difficulties due to the limitations of broadcasts. There are products called *IP helpers* that can forward DHCP traffic like a relay agent, but can also forward traffic generated by other protocols, such as DNS, TFTP, NTP, and NetBIOS. Some implementations also call this *UDP forwarding*.

DNS

TCP/IP networks identify systems by their IP addresses, but people are more comfortable working with names. *Domain Name System (DNS)* is a service and protocol that implement a means of assigning names to TCP/IP systems and resolving the names to IP addresses on request.

When a user types a URL into a web browser, the browser sends a request containing the server name to the system's designated DNS server. The DNS server then replies with the IP address corresponding to the name, and the browser can then begin to communicate directly with the web server using its address. This process is called *name resolution*.

The transaction seems simple from the client side, but at the server end, it can be very complex. DNS is a hierarchical, distributed database, with records maintained on thousands of authoritative servers located all over the globe. A simple name resolution request might be handed off to many different DNS servers before an authoritative record for a given name is located.

DNS Naming

From the earliest days of TCP/IP networking, administrators gave their computers host-names as a user-friendly alternative to IP addresses. As the networks grew, maintaining individual lists of hostnames became unwieldy, so the DNS was designed to be a hierar-chical database for all of the hostnames everywhere. This database was distributed among many servers to provide fault tolerance and avoid network traffic bottlenecks.

The DNS namespace is based on a *global hierarchy*, a multilevel structure of domains. A *domain* is a container for hosts and for subdomains, which are the building blocks of the DNS hierarchy. To obtain IP addresses for a TCP/IP network, an administrator is assigned a network identifier by a service provider. Then, the administrator assigns a unique host iden-tifier to each network device. DNS works in much the same way. An administrator registers a domain and then assigns hostnames to individual devices in that domain. The result is a hierarchy that looks something like a filesystem, as shown in Figure 6.1.

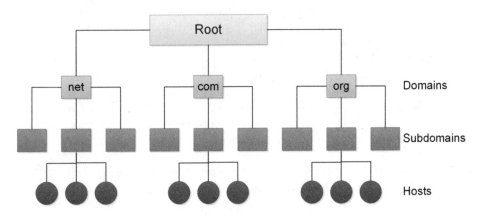

FIGURE 6.1 Domain Name System hierarchy

Starting at the root of the hierarchy, there are top-level domains, such as .com, .org, and .net, each of which has many subdomains. Each subdomain contains hostnames repre-senting individual devices. There can be additional layers of subdomains as well.

Therefore, to uniquely identify one host on the Internet, a DNS name must consist of a hostname plus all of its parent domain names up to the root. This is called a *fully qualified domain name (FQDN)*. An FQDN can be up to 255 characters long in total, with each name (between periods) no more than 63 characters. For example, the DNS name www.adatum .com consists of a hostname (www), a subdomain name (adatum), and a top-level domain name (com).

When a network administrator registers a domain name, control over the contents of the domain comes with it. The administrator can create any number of hosts in the domain, and any number of subdomains as well, in any number of layers. Thus, the administrator of the adatum.com domain could create subdomains for each of the company's branch offices and sub-subdomains for the various departments at each office, resulting in DNS names like the following: mail.sales.chicago.adatum.com.

The administrator of a domain is also responsible for maintaining two name servers for that domain, a primary and a secondary. These two servers become the *authoritative name servers*, the ultimate sources for information about that domain. If someone, anywhere on the Internet, tries to resolve a hostname in that domain, the IP address for that hostname will ultimately come from one of those two name servers.

DNS Name Resolution

The DNS client built into virtually every operating system is called a *resolver*. As noted earlier, the name resolution process begins when an application, such as a web browser, uses the resolver to generate a DNS name resolution request and send it to the DNS server specified in the system's TCP/IP settings. If that server happens to be the authoritative source for the domain containing the hostname to be resolved, then it can return a response containing the requested address to the resolver immediately. This rarely happens, however.

If the DNS server receiving the request has no information about the name to be resolved, then it must find that information by querying other DNS servers. To do this, the server traces the name to be resolved from the root down. Every DNS server is configured with the addresses of the root name servers, at the top of the DNS global hierarchy. These *root DNS servers* are the authoritative sources for the top-level domains.

If the client's DNS server is trying to resolve the name www.adatum.com, it begins by sending a query to one of the root name servers for information about the com domain. The root name server responds with the addresses of the authoritative name servers for the com domain.

This type of request is called an *iterative query*, because the root name server replies immediately with the best information it has available to it. The query that the resolver on the client system originally sent to its own DNS server is called a *recursive query*. When a DNS server receives a recursive query, it takes responsibility for the complete name resolution process, issuing queries to other servers as needed, until it arrives at the authoritative resolution of the name, which it returns to the resolver.

The client's DNS server, now with the addresses of the com servers, can send an iterative query to those servers to discover information about the adatum domain. The com servers return the addresses of the adatum name servers, and the client's server can now query the adatum servers for the IP address of the www host. Receiving this, the client's DNS server can now issue a reply to the original resolver containing the IP address of the www host on the adatum.com network. The resolver supplies the address to the web browser, and the browser can now connect to the web server using its IP address instead of its name.

DNS Servers

Name resolution is an essential part of Internet communications, and every client device that uses the Internet needs access to at least one DNS server. Depending on the size and complexity of the network, administrators might elect to use internal or external DNS servers.

Internal servers are located on the organization's private network. Most of the server operating systems in use today include a DNS server component, enabling administrators to create multiple DNS servers as needed. Smaller networks and residential customers are more likely to use *external servers* for DNS access, such as the ones on their Internet service provider's network.

DNS Caching

Despite its seeming complexity, the name resolution process is usually completed within a second or two. One of the reasons for this is that DNS servers maintain a cache of the information they have previously discovered. In *DNS caching*, each of the resource records that a DNS server receives from another server has a value called its *Time to Live (TTL)*. This value specifies how long the server receiving this record should hold it in its cache.

The duration of the TTL is typically based on how soon the authoritative resource record is likely to change. Longer TTL values allow the server to maintain a larger, more useful cache; shorter TTL values prevent the cache from storing outdated information.

DNS Records

The DNS database consists of resource records, the most basic of which contains a host-name and its IP address. However, there are several kinds of resource records that provide information about a domain and its resources, such as the following:

IPv4 Address (A)   Used for *forward name resolution*; maps a hostname to a 32-bit IPv4 address. This is the basic record used to resolve a hostname to an IPv4 address.

IPv6 Address (AAAA)   Used for forward name resolution; maps a hostname to a 128-bit IPv6 address. This is the basic record used to resolve a hostname to an IPv6 address.

Canonical Name (CNAME)   Creates an alias or alternative name for a hostname defined by an A or AAAA record. Both the original hostname and the alias resolve to the same IP address.

Mail Exchange (MX)   Identifies the server that will handle incoming email traffic addressed to the domain.

Name Server (NS)   Contains the name of a registered domain and the fully qualified domain name of a name server that is authoritative for that domain.

Pointer (PTR)   Used for *reverse name resolution*; maps an IP address in the `in-addr``.arpa` domain to a `host name`. The `in-addr.arpa` domain is a hierarchical name space based on IPv4 addresses that DNS servers use to look up IP addresses and resolve them to their hostnames. For example, the address 192.168.54.12 would appear in this domain as `12.54.168.192.in-addr.arpa`.

Service (SRV)   Specifies the server name and port number for a specific service available on the network. This general service location record was designed to prevent the need to create record types for specific applications, as with MX.

Start of Authority (SOA)   Identifies the server as the authoritative data source for the current zone and provides information needed to facilitate zone transfers.

Text (TXT)   Contains plain text added by administrators for their own purposes or to implement certain application-specific technologies.

Zones and Zone Transfers

For administrative purposes, it is possible to divide a DNS domain into zones, each of which has an authoritative server (identified by an SOA resource record). A simple two-level domain, such as adatum.com, consists of a single zone, but if adatum.com has multiple subdomains, creating zones makes it possible to delegate administrative responsibility for each one. A zone can be any contiguous part of the domain hierarchy, even spanning multiple levels, as shown in Figure 6.2.

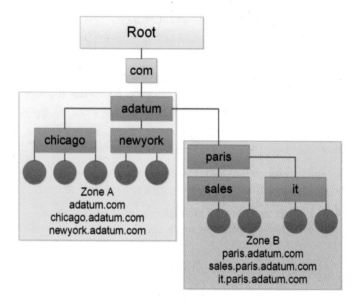

FIGURE 6.2 DNS zones

For fault tolerance and load balancing purposes, administrators typically designate two name servers as authorities for a given zone, called the *primary* and the *secondary*. Each server maintains a copy of the zone data on its local drive. To keep the DNS data on the two servers synchronized, administrators make changes to the primary master, which periodically updates the secondary with a process called a *zone transfer*.

Whenever the secondary restarts, it loads the zone data from its drive and checks with the primary to see if any updates have occurred. If so, the secondary initiates a zone transfer from the primary and updates the data on its local drive with the latest information. On a complex DNS implementation with many zones, a single DNS server can function as a primary or secondary for multiple zones at once, which can result in it performing multiple zone transfers to keep all of the DNS information for the domains updated.

NTP

Network Time Protocol (NTP) was designed to share time information among systems on a network. There are distributed applications that require servers at remote locations to synchronize their clocks periodically, such as email and directory services. This is to ensure that data modifications on various servers are applied in the correct order.

An *NTP client* sends periodic queries to a server to obtain a time signal with which it can synchronize its clock. A server functioning as a time provider uses NTP on UDP port 123 to transmit time signals to other devices so that they can synchronize their clocks accordingly.

An *NTP server* can be a computer on a private network, or administrators can use one of the many publicly available time servers on the Internet, such as those maintained by the National Institute of Standards and Technology (NIST) at various locations around the country.

NTP uses a *stratum* value to specify how close a time server is to its time source. A reference server with direct access to a calibrated time source, such as an atomic clock, is considered to have a stratum value of 0. A server that gets its time signal from a stratum 0 server is considered to be stratum 1, and a server synchronized with a stratum 1 server is stratum 2, and so forth. The higher the stratum value, the greater the possibility of a time discrepancy with the stratum 0 time source.

CERTMIKE EXAM ESSENTIALS

▶ Dynamic Host Configuration Protocol (DHCP) is an application layer protocol and service that provides TCP/IP clients with unique IP addresses and other configuration settings. DHCP servers lease addresses to clients and reclaim them when they are no longer in use.

▶ Domain Name System (DNS) is a distributed database of TCP/IP host names and their accompanying IP addresses. Because people work more easily with names but TCP/IP communications rely on addresses, DNS provides applications with the ability to resolve hostnames to addresses by sending queries to DNS servers located all over the world.

▶ Network Time Protocol (NTP) is a means by which computers can synchronize their clocks with reliable reference sources. Clients periodically send NTP queries to time servers and calibrate their clocks using the data in their replies.

Practice Question 1

Ralph is building a new network for a client and has just installed a DHCP server with a scope containing an entire /24 subnet: 254 addresses. There are to be 100 workstations in the office, and Ralph has figured that the 254 addresses will be enough to accommodate them plus the users' mobile phones and other Wi-Fi devices.

Some time later, Ralph begins receiving complaints from his client that users sometimes cannot connect to the network. Ralph examines the DHCP server and notices that the scope, at that moment, had only two available leases. He concludes that the scope has been exhausted at times, preventing any more users from connecting to the network. When some of the existing leases expire, more addresses become available. Ralph's client explains that their business gets a lot of visitors who use the company Wi-Fi on their phones, which helps to explain the address shortage.

Ralph wants to avoid having to add more addresses to the network. What can he do to relieve the occasional address shortages on his client's network?

A. Install a second DHCP server.
B. Create a second scope on the DHCP server.
C. Decrease the lease period for the scope.
D. Increase the lease period for the scope.

Practice Question 2

Ralph is working in his web browser and types the URL **www.contoso.com** in the Address text box. A DNS name resolution transaction occurs that consists of four query/reply message exchanges. Which of the following four message exchanges use iterative queries? (Choose all correct answers.)

A. The DNS client resolver sends a name resolution query to its designated DNS server, requesting information about the www.contoso.com address.
B. The client's designated DNS server sends a query to a root name server, requesting information about the com domain.
C. The client's designated DNS server sends a query to the com name server, requesting information about the contoso domain.
D. The client's designated DNS server sends a query to the contoso name server, requesting the IP address of the host www.

Practice Question 1 Explanation

A. is incorrect because installing another DHCP server without adding more IP addresses will not resolve the lease shortage problem.
B. is incorrect because creating a second scope without adding more IP addresses will not resolve the lease shortage problem.
C. is correct because decreasing the lease period for the scope will cause addresses to be returned to the pool for reassignment more quickly.
D. is incorrect because increasing the lease period for the scope will only worsen the problem by allocating addresses for a longer period of time.

Correct Answer: C, Decrease the lease period for the scope

Practice Question 2 Explanation

A. is incorrect because a DNS client resolver sending a name resolution request to its designated DNS server always uses a recursive query so that the server takes responsibility for resolving the name.
B. is correct because the client's designated DNS server, when messaging a root name server, always uses iterative queries. This is so that the root name server can respond immediately with information about the domain for which it is authoritative.
C. is correct because the client's designated DNS server, when messaging a top-level domain server, always uses iterative queries. This is so that the server can respond immediately with information about the domain for which it is authoritative.
D. is correct because the client's designated DNS server, when messaging a registered domain name server, always uses iterative queries. This is so that the server can respond immediately with information about the host for which it is authoritative.

Correct Answers: B, C, and D

CHAPTER 7

Network Architecture

Objective 1.7: Explain basic corporate and datacenter network architecture.

This chapter examines some of the elements of data center architecture and design, as well as the storage area networking technology available for use in data centers. The Network+ exam expects candidates to be familiar with these topics and their basic functions.

In this chapter, you'll learn everything you need to know about Network+ Objective 1.7, including the following topics:

▶ **Three-tiered**
▶ **Software-defined networking**
▶ **Spine and leaf**
▶ **Traffic flows**
▶ **Branch office vs. on-premises data center vs. colocation**
▶ **Storage area networks**

THREE-TIERED ARCHITECTURE

A *data center* is a facility that houses a collection of servers and the switches, routers, and other equipment needed to connect those servers to the resources they need, to each other, and to the users who must access them. Data centers can range in size from a dedicated room in a company office building to gigantic underground complexes with armed guards and vault doors. Whatever its size, however, a data center needs certain characteristics to function efficiently, including environmental controls, a stable power source, and most important, a carefully designed internal architecture that implements all of the necessary equipment connections in a manner that is organized, understandable, and easily serviceable.

The traditional data center architecture for a medium- to large-sized organization calls for the servers, switches, and routers to be deployed in three logical layers, as shown in Figure 7.1.

The three tiers or layers are as follows.

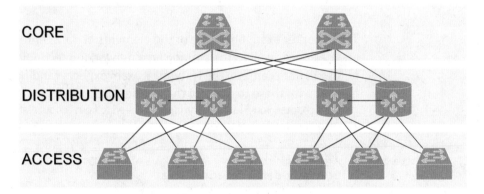

CORE

DISTRIBUTION

ACCESS

F I G U R E   7 . 1   Three-tiered data center architecture with two access layer pods

Core

The *core* tier is the figurative backbone of the enterprise; all of the network's data passes through the switches and routers at the core layer, so they must be the fastest ones the company can afford. Highest-speed routers and multilayer switches are common at the core tier. This is also where the wide area network (WAN) connections to branch offices and service providers enter the enterprise. Other technologies found at the core are typically those that can enhance the speed of the backbone processing or provide fault tolerance. Hardware redundancy is common at the core tier to ensure that electric power, processing power, and the necessary device interconnections are always maintained.

Distribution/Aggregation Layer

The *distribution or aggregation layer* functions as a buffer between the core and access layers, with switches that provide interconnections with all of the access layer switches. The distribution layer switches are all connected to each other so that if one fails, the others can take up the slack. These switches also have redundant connections to the access layer switches, with each access layer switch linked to at least two distribution switches. In some cases, the access layer switches are collected into groups called *pods*, along with their designated distribution switches.

The core layer sacrifices interconnectivity for pure packet forwarding speed. The distribution layer provides that interconnectivity by implementing the connections that the access layer needs. Some smaller networks combine the core and distribution layer functions into one, creating a two-tiered model called a *collapsed core* architecture. The distribution layer is also where services such as packet filtering, intrusion prevention, load balancing, and VLAN routing often occur. The switches at the distribution layer tend to be multilayer devices, with the connections to the access layer running on layer 2 and the high-speed core connections on layer 3.

Access/Edge

The *access or edge tier* is the location of the switches to which servers, workstations, printers, wireless access points, network-attached storage (NAS) arrays, and other end-user devices connect. These are typically layer 2 switches, less elaborate than those at the other tiers to keep the end-user cost-per-port relatively low, but often with higher-speed uplink ports for the connections to the distribution layer switches.

Physically, data centers typically consist of rack-mounted devices. One common design calls for each rack to have one or more switches in it, to which the devices in that rack are connected. This is called *top-of-rack switching*, and it tends to create a better organized data center layout while minimizing cable lengths.

EXAM TIP
The Network+ exam objectives provide alternative names for the distribution and access tiers, but all three tiers are often referenced using other names. The core tier might also be called a backbone, the distribution/aggregation tier the workgroup layer, and the access tier is sometimes referred to as the workstation or desktop layer, in addition to the edge tier. Candidates for the exam should be careful to acknowledge all of these terms when researching this topic.

SOFTWARE-DEFINED NETWORKING

The three-tiered architecture was created at a time when all of the devices in the data center were physical ones. Each physical server had one role, and each physical switch and router had to be managed individually. Today, virtualization and *software-defined networking (SDN)* have revolutionized the look, the organization, and the operation of the enterprise data center. A single physical server running a hypervisor can host many virtual servers, and SDN can centralize the management of the switches and routers.

Switches and routers traditionally had a management interface in the form of character-based terminal access. If there were any changes to be made to the overall switching and routing fabric of the network, it was necessary for administrators to reconfigure each device individually. Software-defined networking is an architecture for abstracting or decoupling the control and management functions of network devices from the physical hardware. This enables administrators to configure the network's switches and routers from a central management console at a remote location.

The SDN architecture consists of the following layers:

Application   The *application layer* is where devices such as firewalls, load balancers, and proxy servers are located, as well as many other network management, configuration, monitoring, and diagnostic functions. Whereas at one time, the network would use a separate physical device for each of these functions, in SDN they are realized as software, in the form of applications or APIs.

> **Northbound Interface**   The control layer communicates with the application layer through the *northbound interface (NBI)*, which is an API that allows application layer components to use the SDN controller to manage infrastructure layer devices.

Control   The *control layer*—sometimes called the *control plane* and/or the *management plane*—is the location of the SDN controller, the central console for all of the SDN elements, both logical and physical. As the intermediary between the application and infrastructure layers, the SDN controller accepts instructions from the application layer and converts them into commands recognized by the hardware devices at the infrastructure layer.

> **Southbound Interface**   The control layer communicates with the devices at the infrastructure layer through the *southbound interface (SBI)*, an API that provides the SDN controller with access to the infrastructure hardware.

Infrastructure   The *infrastructure layer*—sometimes called the *forwarding plane* or the *data plane*—is where all of the physical hardware is located. These are the devices being managed by the SDN controller. Also at this layer are the agents and other software components that monitor and report on the condition of the network to the SDN controller.

SPINE AND LEAF ARCHITECTURE

The use of virtualization and SDN in many data centers has led to a revision of the classic three-tiered architectural model. One of the most common architectures used in data centers today uses a two-tiered model with a mesh topology called *spine and leaf*, as shown in Figure 7.2. In this model, the top tier—or spine—is literally the *backbone* of the network, with high-speed switches, the only function of which is to forward data between leaf switches.

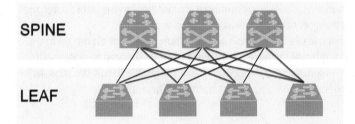

SPINE

LEAF

FIGURE 7.2 Two-tiered spine and leaf data center architecture

It is the leaf switches, in the bottom tier, to which the servers are connected, although they also have higher-speed layer 3 connections to the spine switches. In many implementations, the leaf switches use the same type of *top-of-rack switching* as the access layer switches in the three-tiered architecture, with a SDN providing the control plane for all of the spine and leaf switches.

The spine and leaf architecture calls for a type of mesh topology, in which each spine switch is connected to every leaf switch. However, the spine switches are not directly connected to each other, nor are the leaf switches connected to each other. This means that every leaf switch must go through the spine to connect to another leaf switch, which is always exactly two hops away from it.

Because of this topology, there are no switching loops, so the Spanning Tree Protocol (STP) is not needed. The switching fabric is also extremely fast, and the traffic patterns are entirely predictable, which makes the network's inherent latency predictable. The leaf switches are connected to all of the spine switches, so they can choose the link with the best conditions for transmission.

Finally, the spine and leaf model is easily scalable, even to the point of creating massively scalable data centers (MSDCs). In truly large implementations, servers can be grouped into pods, the only limitation for which is the number of ports in each leaf switch.

TRAFFIC FLOWS

One of the reasons for the evolution from the three-tiered architecture to the spine and leaf model is the alteration in the way traffic typically flows in a data center. Traffic that flows into or out of a data center is often referred to as *north-south* traffic. Southbound traffic is data entering the data center from outside, and northbound traffic is data leaving the data center. Traffic between devices within the data center is characterized as *east-west* traffic.

The terms *east-west* and *north-south*, in this context, do not reference specific compass directions. They refer rather to the directional lines typically used in network diagrams to indicate traffic flow, with horizontal lines representing traffic internal to the data center and vertical lines representing traffic entering and leaving the data center.

The increasingly prevalent use of virtualization and distributed application design in the data center has resulted in a general increase in east-west traffic compared to north-south traffic. The low latency of the spine and leaf model makes it preferable in this situation, as the three-tiered module does not handle east-west traffic as efficiently.

DATA CENTER LOCATIONS

Part of the process of designing and implementing a data center is deciding where it is going to be located. The traditional approach is to build a data center on company property, preferably near to the users who will be accessing it. An *on-premises data center* puts everything under the company's direct control, which is a benefit, but it also incurs a lot of additional costs, both in terms of initial outlay and ongoing expenses.

In addition to the network equipment itself, a data center requires a stable power source, special environmental systems, physical security measures, and a staff with the technical expertise to keep it all running. All of these things add to the cost. In addition, there is the question of fault tolerance. For many companies, at least one redundant data center—preferably at a remote location—is a necessity, to keep the network running and the company data available in the event of a disaster.

Another option is *colocation*, in which an organization leases data center space from a third-party company that is responsible for the entire data center environment, including power, cooling, security, and fault tolerance. In many cases, these providers maintain large purpose-built data centers that can outperform an average on-premises data center retrofitted into an existing office building in many ways. Colocation providers can typically provide several levels of service. A client might just want to lease rack space for their own equipment in the provider's data center, or they might want to lease an entire data center for their use. The provider might also be able to supply other services, such as onsite maintenance and technical support. Here again, the organization is dependent on WAN links for access to their data, but service provider contracts nearly always include a service-level agreement that guarantees a percentage of uptime.

Another issue is the question of whether an organization's *branch offices* should have their own data centers or just access the headquarters data center remotely. This question is largely dependent on the size and computing requirements of the branch offices. A small branch office might not be worth the expense of constructing its own data center. There is also the question of whether the company has—or even needs—full-time IT staff at each branch office. Remote access might be a more economical solution, but it leaves the branch offices fully dependent on the wide area network (WAN) links to the home office.

STORAGE AREA NETWORKING

Data storage is, of course, one of the primary functions of a business network, and as applications have constantly increasing demands for more storage space, new technologies for expanding the storage capacity of a network were developed. One of these technologies is the *storage area network (SAN)*, which is a means by which servers can access storage devices directly through the network.

Fibre Channel

In its original conception, a SAN is a completely separate local area network to which servers and storage devices are attached. The server can access the storage at the block level, just as though the drives were installed in the server itself. The SAN originally ran a protocol called *Fibre Channel (FC)* and typically used a dedicated Fibre Channel switch (or sometimes two, for fault tolerance), to which the storage devices and servers are connected. FC is a serial protocol, in comparison to the parallel signaling protocols commonly used for storage technologies, such as Small Computer Systems Interface (SCSI). In its current version, FC can support transmission rates of up to 128 gigabits per second (Gbps).

> **EXAM TIP**
>
> Fibre Channel is not a typographical error. The technology uses the British English spelling of "fibre" to distinguish the term from "fiber optic."

Fibre Channel originally required the use of multimode fiber-optic cable, but it now includes physical layer specifications supporting both copper and fiber-optic media. However, the FC technology is completely incompatible with standard LAN protocols, such as Ethernet and IP, and does not even conform to the layers of the OSI reference model; it has its own five-layer model instead. This is why the original SANs required a completely separate network, and servers required separate Fibre Channel host adapters to connect to it, in addition to their standard LAN adapters.

Fibre Channel over Ethernet

Fibre Channel is an efficient high-speed networking protocol, and the creation of a separate network for storage kept latency low and performance high, but the cost of building a separate SAN with nonstandard hardware was prohibitive to many potential users. Eventually, a variant of the protocol called *Fibre Channel over Ethernet (FCoE)* appeared, which encapsulates FC traffic within Ethernet frames and can coexist with Ethernet LAN traffic on the same cable. FCoE uses a host bus adapter with dual functionality; it is an FC adapter and a standard Ethernet LAN adapter in one device. The FC side of the adapter encapsulates the storage traffic (which is not routable) directly in Ethernet frames; no IP is needed.

iSCSI

For many years, Small Computer Systems Interface (SCSI) has been the protocol that storage devices use to communicate. SCSI commands implement the standard functions that storage devices use to read, write, and manipulate data. Fibre Channel is just a vehicle for carrying those SCSI commands to the storage devices on the network.

The next step in the evolution of SAN technology was an implementation that did not require any special hardware. *Internet Small Computer Systems Interface (iSCSI)* is just another means of transmitting SCSI commands over the network to the storage devices. However, in a major difference from FCoE, iSCSI encapsulates the storage traffic in IP datagrams and transmits them over the LAN to the attached devices. Also unlike FCoE, iSCSI traffic is routable. In an iSCSI implementation, all of the hardware is attached to one Ethernet network segment, and the iSCSI traffic is intermingled with all of the other IP traffic on the LAN.

These protocols that combine SAN and LAN traffic on the same network cannot hope to achieve the same level of performance as a dedicated storage area network, but with high-speed Ethernet hardware and Ethernet's support for jumbo frames up to 9,000 bytes, performance levels can be adequate.

CERTMIKE EXAM ESSENTIALS

▶ The classic data center architecture calls for switches and routers to be organized into three tiers: core, distribution/aggregation, and infrastructure.

▶ Software-defined networking (SDN) is a means of separating the management and control of the data center switches from the individual devices and centrally locating it in an SDN controller.

▶ Data center architecture has evolved into a two-tiered model called spine and leaf, which calls for switches connected using a mesh topology in which every spine switch is connected to every leaf switch. The servers, connected to the leaf switches, can access any other server with no more than two hops.

▶ A storage area network (SAN) provides servers with access to drive arrays and other storage devices. SAN technologies include Fibre Channel, which requires a separate network; FCoE, which encapsulates storage traffic in Ethernet frames using specialized host adapters on an existing LAN; and iSCSI, which encapsulates the storage traffic in IP datagrams and requires no specialized networking hardware.

Practice Question 1

Alice's company is planning to expand its network storage capacity by purchasing two new drive arrays and connecting them to a storage area network, which Alice is responsible for designing. Virtually the entire budget for the project will be spent on the drive arrays, so Alice wants to construct a SAN that does not require the purchase of any new networking hardware. Which of the following SAN technologies should Alice use to minimize additional hardware expenditures?

A. Fibre Channel
B. FCoE
C. iSCSI
D. None of the above

Practice Question 2

Ralph is helping to plan the switching fabric of the data center in his company's new headquarters complex. He is evaluating the three-tiered architectural model against the spine and leaf model. The plan so far is to create all of the servers as virtual machines and to use software-defined networking to remotely manage the switches and routers.

Which of the following is a valid statement that can help Ralph to recommend one architecture over the other?

A. The three-tiered architecture handles east-west traffic better than the spine and leaf architecture.
B. The traffic patterns of the spine and leaf architecture are predictable, with two hops between every two leaf switches.
C. A spine and leaf architecture is less expensive to implement because it has only two tiers instead of three.
D. The spine and leaf architecture is more prone to switching loops because it does not support the Spanning Tree Protocol (STP).
E. The three-tiered architecture is better suited to the use of virtualized servers because the hypervisor servers can be connected to the core layer.

Practice Question 1 Explanations

A. is incorrect because Fibre Channel requires the construction of a separate network for the storage devices, which calls for new cables, host bus adapters, and a Fibre Channel switch.

B. is incorrect because although Fibre Channel over Ethernet (FCoE) can use the existing network to connect the storage devices, the servers that will access the drive arrays require new dual-function host adapters that support both SAN and LAN communications.

C. is correct because Internet Small Computer Systems Interface (iSCSI) encapsulates storage traffic in standard IP datagrams and transmits them over the LAN, using the existing cables, host adapters, and switches.

D. is incorrect because iSCSI can support the new drive arrays without the need for any new networking hardware.

Correct Answer: C, iSCSI

Practice Question 2 Explanation

A. is incorrect because it is the spine and leaf architecture that handles east-west traffic better, not the three-tiered architecture.

B. is correct because the full-mesh topology does create a wholly predictable traffic pattern, with two hops between every pair of leaf switches.

C. is incorrect because the number of tiers in the architectural model does not dictate the number of switches required or their types.

D. is incorrect because the full-mesh topology used in the spine and leaf model eliminates switching loops and makes the Spanning Tree Protocol unnecessary.

E. is incorrect because no servers of any kind are ever directly connected to the core layer switches in the three-tiered architecture.

Correct Answer: B

CHAPTER 8

Cloud Computing
Objective 1.8: Summarize cloud concepts and connectivity options.

This chapter examines some of the fundamental concepts of cloud computing and how it is used in the enterprise. The Network+ exam does not dive too deeply into the cloud, which is a vast subject, but candidates should be familiar with these topics and their basic functions.

In this chapter, you'll learn everything you need to know about Network+ Objective 1.8, including the following topics:

▶ **Deployment models**
▶ **Service models**
▶ **Infrastructure as code**
▶ **Connectivity options**
▶ **Multitenancy**
▶ **Elasticity**
▶ **Scalability**
▶ **Security implications**

DEPLOYMENT MODELS

The use of the word *cloud* in the context of computing has become common at all levels of IT expertise, but not as many people can define the term. The *cloud* refers to any number of Internet-based services and solutions that are available on demand and typically purchased by lease or subscription. For end users, the cloud is typically a place where they can store their files and personal data. However, for IT professionals, the cloud can provide a huge variety of services in addition to storage, including virtualized implementations of the servers for which they would at one time have had to purchase a new computer. Organizations can now replace entire data centers and software libraries with cloud services.

One of the greatest advantages of the cloud in enterprise networking is its flexibility. Some companies start from nothing and build their entire network in the cloud. However, many organizations have already made large investments in data centers and physical computing hardware. Their expansion into the cloud is likely to be more modest, and they will be concerned about combining the new cloud services with their existing operations.

For this reason, there are several different cloud deployment models or architectures that enterprises can adopt, which are described in the following sections.

Public

A *public cloud* is a service or services provided by a third-party *cloud provider* that are available as a product to any qualified customer, called a *cloud consumer*. The facilities where the services are located are owned by the third-party provider, with access to the services provided to subscribers or lessors through the Internet.

As with renting a house instead of buying it, public cloud services require little or no initial outlay, but they also provide no equity. Public cloud services are highly flexible; consumers can expand their services to accommodate busy periods or company growth and then scale them back as needed. The consumers pay only for the resources they are actually using. Another benefit is that large cloud service providers often furnish additional fault tolerance and security features, such as redundant hardware, data backups, and colocated data centers.

Private

A *private cloud* is one in which the hardware and services are reserved for the consumer's exclusive use. The hardware and the facility where it is located can be owned and managed by the consumer or by a third party, and it can be located on the consumer's premises or elsewhere.

Technically, any private network that is purchased and operated by a private organization is, by definition, a private cloud. However, in most cases the term refers to the involvement of a third party in some capacity. For example, a company can purchase its own servers and other data center hardware and then engage a third-party provider to house them and provide power, environment, security, and other services. This is sometimes called a *hosted private cloud*.

Despite its requiring a substantial initial outlay for hardware, its ongoing depreciation in value, and the additional costs for personnel and upkeep, a private cloud can be beneficial for several reasons, including security and administrative control. A private cloud is also completely customizable to the consumer's needs and might provide features and services that are not available through public cloud offerings.

Community

A *community cloud* is one in which several organizations, usually engaged in the same business or concern and with common needs, share a cloud infrastructure that can be owned and operated by members of the community or by a third-party provider. Typical examples of community clouds are ones operated by educational or health-care communities.

Hybrid

A *hybrid cloud* is a combination of public, private, or community cloud resources that are connected by technology that enables them to interact and function together. For example, an organization with an internal data center functioning as a private cloud might use public cloud resources to temporarily add servers or expand the network's capabilities in other ways during busy times. The process of adding cloud resources to enhance an existing network infrastructure is called *cloudbursting*.

SERVICE MODELS

Cloud providers can typically provide products using a variety of service models, which specify how the administration tasks are split between the consumer and the provider. The cloud infrastructure can be split into eleven layers, as shown in Table 8.1.

T A B L E 8 . 1 Cloud infrastructure layers

Layer	Function
People	The end users running applications
Data	The information created or utilized by applications
Application	A software program running on a virtual machine
Runtime	An intermediate software layer, such as .NET or Java
Middleware	Software that provides intermediate services between an operating system and applications
Operating System	Software providing the basic functions of a virtual machine
Virtual Network	The logical connections between virtual machines

Layer	Function
Hypervisor	Software running on physical servers that creates virtual machines and enables them to share the server's physical resources
Servers	The physical computers hosting the virtual machines that provide cloud services
Storage	The hardware subsystem that provides data storage for the physical servers
Physical Network	The cables, switches, routers, and other equipment that physically connect the servers to the Internet

The service models defined by the National Institute of Standards and Technology (NIST) specify which party—the cloud consumer or the cloud provider—is responsible for the administration of each of the layers (see Figure 8.1).

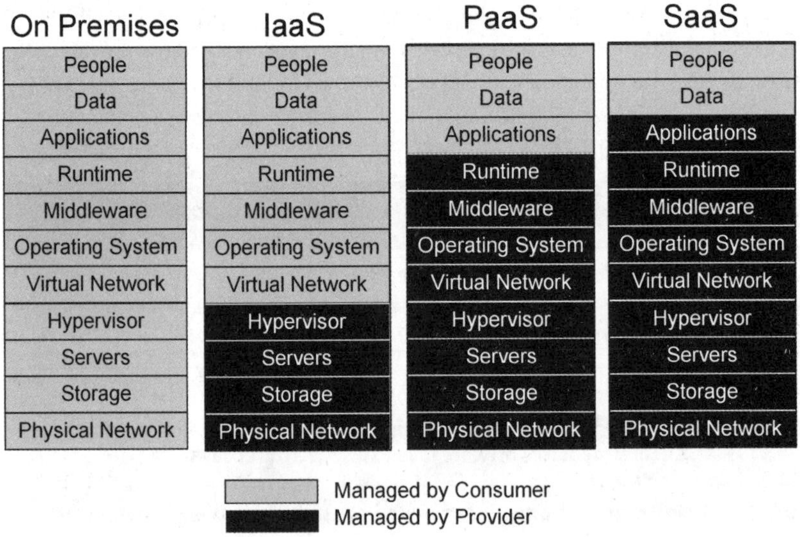

FIGURE 8.1 Infrastructure layers for the cloud services models

Infrastructure as a Service (IaaS)   A third-party cloud provider supplies the consumer with access to a physical server running a hypervisor. The consumer can then create *virtual machines (VMs)* on the server, install operating systems and applications on them, and manage them as needed. In this service, the bulk of the system administration tasks—everything above the Hypervisor layer—is left to the consumer. The cloud provider is responsible for the physical server, the operating system running the hypervisor, and the physical network that connects it to the world, but the VMs and the software running on them are the sole responsibility of the consumer.

Platform as a Service (PaaS)   A third-party cloud provider supplies the consumer with access to a physical server running a hypervisor and with the virtual machines running on that hypervisor. In PaaS, the responsibility of the provider is extended up through the Runtime layer, meaning that provider must update and maintain the operating systems on the VMs. The consumer is only responsible for the applications they install on the VMs, for their own data, and for the users that run the applications. PaaS was originally designed as a tool for Internet-based application development that allowed people to run their code on a consistent platform without having to create new VMs and reinstall the OSs for each test.

Software as a Service (SaaS)   A third-party cloud provider supplies the consumer with Internet-based access to an application or service running on their servers. In an SaaS environment, the provider's responsibility extends up through the application layer. The consumer supplies only the data the application will use and the people who will run the application. The consumer sees only the application and a limited set of configuration settings; they have no way of knowing anything about the server running the application, the VM hosting the server, or the hypervisor providing the VM.

Desktop as a Service (DaaS)   Not a NIST designation but included in the Network+ exam objectives, DaaS is a new designation for a technology that has been known at times as desktop virtualization, remote desktop, and terminal services. A third-party cloud provider supplies the consumer with a fully configured desktop workstation running on a VM, which users can access from any location using a thin client, such as a web browser. The client and the VM only exchange interface information, such as keystrokes, mouse movements, and display video; all operating system and application processing occurs in the cloud.

> **EXAM TIP**
> In today's IT world, appending the phrase "as a Service" to almost any word increases its marketing value. As a result, Network+ exam candidates might run across many other -aaS abbreviations, but they should be aware that the only official NIST designations are IaaS, PaaS, and SaaS.

Infrastructure as Code

Infrastructure as Code (IaC) is a technique for automating the process of building a platform for the development and testing of code. In a large software development environment, there might be many people working on the code for one application, all of whom have their own work habits. Testing code typically requires a standardized test platform, but with many different people performing tests, the process of repeatedly building the test platform can be time-consuming and error-prone.

IaC defines the infrastructure of the test platform as code in the form of scripts and configuration files. This allows the process of building the environment for a test deployment to be automated by the developers themselves, resulting in faster deployments and a consistent platform for every test. IaC also prevents the developers from having to request a new platform from the IT department for each test.

The scripts that define the platform infrastructure can be of two types: imperative and declarative. In the *imperative* approach, the scripts consist of all the commands needed to create the environment in the order of their execution. The *declarative* approach specifies the desired final state for the environment, and the system does what must be done to achieve that state.

Scripting the infrastructure deployment process can provide *automation* of frequently performed tasks, but the term automation usually refers to a single task. The automation process can go even further by working with multiple tasks, toward what is known as orchestration. *Orchestration* is a more comprehensive approach to the automation of workflows, consisting of configuration and management tasks for multiple operating systems, services, and applications.

Connectivity Options

Most end users, when they connect to the cloud, do so using the public Internet. However, for some cloud consumers and for some applications, an open Internet connection does not provide sufficient security. For example, a company running a hybrid cloud might have sensitive data stored in their private data center that their cloud services need to access. If the threat of the data being compromised precludes the use of an open Internet connection between the data center and the cloud, there are alternative connection types, such as the following:

Virtual Private Network (VPN)   A VPN connection is a virtualized private link between two points, such as a database server in a private data center and a cloud provider on the Internet. The VPN link, often referred to as a tunnel, can protect the data passing through it using digital signatures, data encryption, or both. Although the tunnel is protected by security protocols such as IPsec, the traffic still passes over the public Internet. Attackers could conceivably intercept the VPN packets while they are in transit, but the encrypted tunnel prevents the data from being compromised.

Private-Direct Connection to Cloud Provider   Some cloud providers offer a means to connect to their network without using the public Internet at all. A *private-direct connection* is a dedicated link between the cloud consumer's data center and the cloud provider's network. The link could be a physical cable—usually fiber optic—installed expressly for the purpose of making this connection, or it could be a leased line contracted through a telecommunications provider. This is the most expensive alternative to an open Internet connection, but when the data in question is highly classified, the cost might be warranted.

Multitenancy

Multitenancy refers to the sharing of cloud resources among multiple consumers. When a consumer enters into a contract with a provider for access to certain cloud resources, there is usually no mention of what servers will be used, where they are located, or what other consumers might be sharing the same hardware. For most consumers, this is not a major problem because virtual machines are generally well isolated from each other. That isolation is not perfect, however, and if a consumer's application or data is extremely sensitive, providers can usually provide a consumer with dedicated hardware that is not shared with other tenants (at an additional cost).

In a private cloud environment, multitenancy and isolation between networks in the same enterprise can be an issue. For example, a development network in which people are testing their code must be kept separate from the production network.

Elasticity

One of the major advantages of cloud-based networking is the ability of the services to expand and contract based on the needs of the consumer. Because the servers and other network components are virtualized, it is a simple matter to enhance or expand them based on the consumer's business needs and regress or contract them again, if necessary. With many cloud providers, the process by which this *elasticity* is applied can even be automated so that when a website's incoming traffic during their busy season reaches a certain threshold, for example, additional virtual machines are automatically added to the server farm. At the end of the busy season, when traffic dies down, the additional servers are removed, and the consumer only pays for the time they were actually running.

Scalability

Elasticity refers to the ability of cloud resources to expand and contract based on the needs of the consumer. Typically, this means adding more servers, a process known as *scaling out*. With cloud services, however, it is also possible to *scale up* by enhancing the capabilities of the existing servers.

This *scalability* in two directions enables consumers to provision their networks with additional servers and their servers with additional memory, storage, bandwidth, or virtually any other resource in minutes, instead of hours or days. The cloud consumers pay only for the resources they use. To the consumer, the pool of available resources they can access seems virtually limitless.

Security Implications

Security is a vital concern for all networks, and cloud-based networks add some special security implications that administrators should address. Risk management is a part of every network operation, but when dealing with a third party, such as a cloud provider, all security issues of concern should be documented in the contract between the parties involved. The contract should clearly delineate the responsibilities of both the provider and the consumer with regard to security.

Cloud service contracts nearly always include a service-level agreement (SLA) specifying that the cloud services furnished by the provider be available a certain percentage of the time. However, the contract should also specify other aspects of the provider's security posture, such as what steps the provider should take to protect the consumer's data. Questions such as whether the data is backed up, where the backups are stored, whether the data is encrypted when at rest, and whether the cloud facility has adequate physical security should all be documented. Depending on the services provided and the nature of the contract, some of these tasks might be left to the consumer, but the contract should make that clear.

By definition, using public cloud services takes some of the most vital network security issues out of the hands of the consumer. User identities are typically maintained in the cloud, so there might be authentication and authorization traffic passing between the consumer's site and the cloud provider's network. This traffic is vulnerable and should be encrypted, as should any sensitive data transmitted to or from the cloud.

Hybrid cloud implementations are particularly vulnerable, due to the exchange of data that frequently occurs between local, private cloud storage and the public cloud services. Administrators must be conscious of where their data is located at all times and how it is used. For example, if a company that maintains a private data center because they work with highly sensitive data decides to add some cloud services, they must consider whether the data will have to leave the private network and be transmitted to the cloud. Cloud consumers often take the step of creating a VPN tunnel to the cloud facility so that the data can be encrypted and digitally signed for transit. In some cases, consumers restrict their use of the cloud to applications and services that are not particularly sensitive and leave their most classified data on the private network.

CERTMIKE EXAM ESSENTIALS

▶ NIST defines cloud deployment models that specify the basic architecture of a cloud network implementation, including *public*, in which a third-party cloud provider makes services available to any consumer; *private*, a cloud implementation reserved for a consumer's exclusive use; community, in which a group of consumers in the same business share a cloud infrastructure; and *hybrid*, which is an implementation that combines public and private cloud resources.

▶ NIST's cloud service models define how responsibility for the cloud network is divided between the provider and the consumer. IaaS provides access to a hypervisor on which the consumer can create VMs. PaaS provides consumers with installed VMs on which they can deploy applications for development and testing. SaaS is a fully installed application or service, access to which is furnished to consumers.

▶ Infrastructure as Code (IaC) is a technique for scripting the process of infrastructure deployment to automate the creation of development platforms.

▶ Multitenancy, in which many consumers share the same hardware infrastructure; elasticity, which enables cloud services to scale out by adding servers when the consumer's needs change; and scalability, which allows consumers to scale up their servers by adding memory, storage, or other resources, are all aspects of cloud networking that administrators must consider when evaluating cloud services.

Practice Question 1

Alice's company is planning to open a new branch office and she is considering using cloud resources for it instead of constructing a new data center. There are no plans to hire IT personnel for the new office, so Alice and her staff must be able to manage the branch office network remotely. After assessing the capabilities of the cloud, Alice decides that the best course of action is to virtualize the branch office workstations. This way, the users can access them in the cloud using older computers that the company has in storage as thin clients. Which of the following service models should Alice use to implement her plan with the least administrative overhead?

A. IaaS

B. PaaS

C. SaaS

D. DaaS

Practice Question 2

The company Ralph works for as IT director is growing rapidly, and their busy season is fast approaching. Ralph is concerned that the company's on-premises server farm hosting their e-commerce website might not be able to handle the additional traffic. With time short and his budget for the year nearly depleted, Ralph is pondering different strategies to keep the company website running with a minimal cash expenditure. Reading about the cloud services available, Ralph is surprised to learn that their in-house data center is actually a private cloud. He wonders if he could make use of public cloud servers somehow. After more research, Ralph devises three possible plans of action:

A. Enlarge the company's private cloud by purchasing new physical servers to augment the existing server farm.

B. Create a separate public cloud implementation by migrating the entire website server farm to virtual servers in the cloud.

C. Create a hybrid cloud by leasing new virtual servers with a public cloud provider to augment the existing on-premises server farm.

Which plan would enable Ralph to ensure the continued operation of the company's website for the lowest cost?

Practice Question 1 Explanation

A. is incorrect because while the Infrastructure as a Service (IaaS) model can support virtual desktops, Alice would be responsible for creating virtual machines on the cloud network, installing the servers, and implementing a virtual desktop solution.

B. is incorrect because while the Platform as a Service (PaaS) model can support the virtual desktops and provides virtual machines with the operating systems already installed, Alice would still have to install and configure the users' applications on the VMs.

C. is incorrect because while Alice could use the Software as a Service (SaaS) model to provide the branch office users with the applications they need, she would still have to install and configure the individual user desktops on site.

D. is correct because the Desktop as a Service (DaaS) model makes virtualized desktops available to the users with only a minimal amount of application configuration from Alice and her team, all of which can be accomplished remotely.

Correct Answer: D, DaaS

Practice Question 2 Explanation

A. is incorrect because purchasing new physical servers would be the most expensive solution and would also be wasteful, as the new servers won't be needed after the busy season is over.

B. is incorrect because planning and implementing a migration of the entire server farm to the cloud would be a large and complex undertaking that could take too long and require a substantial investment in cloud technology. In addition, the company's substantial investment in the existing data center and server farm would be largely wasted.

C. is correct because the hybrid deployment model leaves the existing server farm in place and requires only sufficient cloud servers to support the additional busy season traffic. Once the busy season is over, Ralph can decommission the cloud servers. The only expenditure would be leasing the cloud servers for the duration of the busy season, which would cost far less than either of the other two strategies.

Correct Answer: C

Domain 2.0: Network Implementations

Network Implementations is the second domain of CompTIA's Network+ exam. It covers the core knowledge that networking professionals must understand about routing, switching, and wireless standards. This domain has four objectives:

2.1 **Compare and contrast various devices, their features, and their appropriate placement on the network.**

2.2 **Compare and contrast routing technologies and bandwidth management concepts.**

2.3 **Given a scenario, configure and deploy common Ethernet switching features.**

2.4 **Given a scenario, install and configure the appropriate wireless standards and technologies.**

Questions from this domain make up 19% of the questions on the Network+ exam, so you should expect to see approximately 17 questions on your test covering the material in this part.

CHAPTER 9

Network Devices

Objective 2.1: Compare and contrast various devices, their features, and their appropriate placement on the network.

This chapter examines some of the fundamental components of a typical enterprise network and their functions. The Network+ exam expects candidates to be familiar with these devices and their basic functions.

In this chapter, you'll learn everything you need to know about Network+ objective 2.1, including the following topics:

▶ Networking devices
▶ Networked devices

NETWORKING DEVICES

The Network+ exam requires candidates to be familiar with a large collection of networking devices. The following sections describe these devices, some of which are currently in wide use, while others are all but obsolete.

Hubs

A *hub*—also known as a *multiport repeater*—is a cabling nexus—that is, a network connectivity device that takes the form of a box with a row of ports, typically for unshielded twisted pair (UTP) cables. Plugging computers and other devices into the ports connects them together, forming a local area network (LAN) with a shared network medium.

A hub is a physical layer device that forwards all signals entering through any one of its ports out through all of the other ports. Hubs do not recognize or process data in any way; they simply relay electrical signals.

The first Ethernet specification to use UTP cable—called 10BaseT—required the use of a hub to create a shared network medium. As the Ethernet specifications evolved, so did the capabilities of hubs. However, once switches began to appear on the market at comparable prices, hubs quickly obsolesced and are rarely used today.

Repeaters

A *repeater* is a device that extends the range of a network medium by amplifying signals as they pass through it. By adding a repeater, the network can mitigate the effects of signal attenuation, the gradual reduction of a signal's amplitude as it passes through a network medium.

In computer networking, the term *repeater* was originally used to refer to devices that extend the range of cable connections. The hubs used in early UTP data networks were multiport repeaters. Long-distance fiber-optic connections also use repeaters to boost their signals. Today, the term is more often used to refer to wireless repeaters, which extend the range of Wi-Fi signals.

Media Converters

A *media converter* is essentially a repeater that connects two different network media. The device appears as a simple box with two different types of cable connector in it. Internally, the media converter receives signals through one connector, translates the signals from one media type to the other, and then retransmits them out through the other connector.

For example, on an Ethernet network, a media converter can connect a UTP cable segment to a fiber-optic segment. This can extend the range of a network connection because fiber-optic cables can exceed the 100 meter limit of nearly all UTP Ethernet segments. The conversion to fiber-optic cable can also provide immunity to electromagnetic and other types of interference. There have been a variety of media converters used in data networking, for connections between UTP and fiber optic, between single-mode and multimode fiber optic, and between coaxial and UTP or fiber optic.

Switches

A *switch* is a network connectivity device that operates at the physical and data link layers (layers 1 and 2) of the OSI reference model. A switch is essentially an intelligent hub that reads the data link layer header of incoming packets and keeps track of the MAC addresses assigned to each connected device. Data entering through any one of the switch's ports gets forwarded, as in a hub, but only through the port providing access to the intended recipient. This means that, unlike a hub, a switch does not create a shared network medium; each connected device has its own *collision domain*, essentially a dedicated full-duplex connection to every other device. This reduces the amount of extraneous traffic on the network, eliminates the packet collisions that are a normal occurrence on a hub-based Ethernet network, and enables the connected devices to transmit and receive data simultaneously.

Switches are the essential building blocks of today's local area networks. At the low end, a switch looks very much like a hub—that is, a box with a row of ports in it. Small, unmanaged switches with four to eight ports are typically used for residential and small business networks. Many of the multifunction routers used for residential Internet installations have some switched ports for cabled device connections.

At the high end, enterprise datacenters typically have large rack-mounted switches with dozens of ports. These switches often have additional features built into them, including support for virtual LANs (VLANs) and management capabilities that allow administrators to configure and monitor them remotely.

The basic functions of a switch are performed at *layer 2* of the OSI model. Data link layer protocols always include a header containing the MAC addresses of each packet's source and its destination. By reading this information, the switch compiles a table containing the MAC address of each device and the number of the switch port to which the device is connected. This allows the switch to know which port to use to forward packets to a specific device. By connecting multiple switches together, each network device can communicate with every other device.

In addition to their layer 2 functionality, some switches have routing capabilities. These are called *layer 3 switches* or *multilayer switches* because, in addition to their normal switching function, they can operate at the network layer by routing data packets to other subnets. Multilayer switches typically have the same capabilities as a stand-alone router; they maintain routing tables based on IP addresses and support the same routing protocols.

Bridges

A *bridge* is a data link layer connectivity device that predates switches but that performs essentially the same function, on two ports instead of many. A bridge connects two similar network segments together, and by reading the MAC addresses from incoming packets—just like a switch—it keeps the traffic on the two segments separated as much as possible. For example, when a device on one side of the bridge transmits to a device on the other side, the bridge forwards the packets to the other segment. However, if a device transmits to a recipient on the same segment, the bridge does not forward the packets, thus reducing unnecessary traffic.

Switching has made physical bridges unnecessary on most cabled networks, but the bridging concept is frequently used to control traffic between wireless and wired networks. For example, in the case of a multifunction home router that has both Wi-Fi capability and ports for Ethernet cables, one of the device's multiple functions is to function as a wireless bridge between the two types of connections.

Routers

A *router* is a network layer (layer 3) device that connects two network segments together, forming an internetwork. The public Internet is the ultimate example of an internetwork, with thousands of segments connected by routers. Unlike switches, which work with MAC addresses at the data link layer, routers identify systems by their network layer IP addresses.

Every router maintains a routing table, which contains information about other networks. As incoming data packets arrive, the router reads each packet's destination address in its IP header and uses the information in the routing table to forward the packet toward its destination.

As with switches, routers can range from small, inexpensive devices used in homes and small businesses to hugely elaborate devices found in data centers. High-end routers can incorporate a variety of additional functions, including management capabilities, network address translation, and firewalls.

> **EXAM TIP**
>
> Routers are known by many different names, depending on the context in which they are used. In TCP/IP parlance, a router is called a *gateway*. When routing is incorporated into a switch, it is called a *layer 3 switch* or a *multilayer switch*.

Access Points

An *access point (AP)*—sometimes referred to as a wireless access point (WAP)—is a layer 2 connectivity device that enables wireless clients to join a wireless LAN (WLAN) in infrastructure mode. In its most basic form, that is an access point's only function; it is a switch that connects the wireless devices and enables them to communicate with each other. In an enterprise environment, there might be access points scattered around the facility to provide widely dispersed users with access to the wireless network.

However, in many cases, access points have other capabilities as well. Access points intended for residential or small business use are typically multifunction devices that can function as a DHCP server, a firewall, and a router to an Internet service provider's (ISP's) network, as well as a bridge to wired network devices.

Wireless LAN Controllers

Large enterprise networks with many wireless clients might have dozens of access points, and configuring and managing them individually can become a time-consuming chore for IT personnel. A *wireless LAN controller* is a device that functions as a central connection point for all of the access points. Instead of configuring the APs individually, administrators can create the network configuration once, on the wireless LAN controller, and the controller then pushes it out to all of the individual access points using a specialized protocol, such as Control and Provisioning of Wireless Access Points (CAPWAP).

Load Balancers

Load balancers are devices that enterprise networks use when they have multiple servers running the same application or service. Balancing the load means that the incoming traffic destined for those servers is distributed among them so that no one server is being over- or underworked. For example, highly trafficked websites typically have multiple web servers functioning as a cluster. Load balancing ensures that each of the servers in the cluster handles approximately the same amount of incoming traffic.

Proxy Servers

A *proxy server* is a networking device that functions as an intermediary between client computers and the Internet. The browser on the clients is configured with the address of the proxy server so that any attempts they make to access the Internet are redirected to the proxy. The proxy server then accesses the Internet server, receives its responses, and relays them back to the clients. This way, only the proxy server accesses the Internet; the clients remain hidden on a private network.

Firewall

A *firewall* is a hardware or software device that functions as a barrier between a private network and the Internet outside. Its primary objective is to protect the resources on the internal network from unauthorized access—whether accidental or deliberate—by external systems. A firewall is essentially a filter that examines the incoming traffic and allows or denies packets access to the private network based on their contents. The most basic packet filtering technique that most firewalls use is to examine the IP addresses and port numbers in packet headers to determine where the traffic is going. Administrators can configure firewall with rules that include or exclude specific types of traffic based on these criteria. More advanced firewall techniques examine packets—including their data—in much greater detail.

Intrusion Prevention and Detection

An *intrusion detection system (IDS)* is a hardware or software device that examines network traffic, looking for anomalous patterns that might indicate the presence of an intruder or an actual attack. Some IDS products base their detection routines on signatures provided by the product manufacturer, usually on a subscription basis, much like an antivirus product. Others take a more behavioral approach by watching for deviations from baseline traffic patterns and other anomalies.

Unlike a firewall, which is located at the border between the private and public networks, an IDS is located inside the private network, enabling it to monitor for both internal and external threats. When an IDS product detects a potential intrusion, it gathers information about it in the form of logs and reports; captures pertinent traffic samples, if necessary; and notifies the administrators responsible.

IDS products detect, document, and notify, but they can do nothing to mitigate any trouble that they find. An *intrusion prevention system (IPS)* can intervene, however, using measures such as discarding packets and locking out specific IP addresses. Apart from this additional capability, the primary difference between IDS and IPS products is where they are located on the network.

An IDS product typically operates in promiscuous mode, meaning that it receives a copy of every packet transmitted on the network. The actual traffic proceeds normally, so there is no additional network latency. An IPS product is situated such that it monitors the live traffic as it is transmitted over the network. This enables the device to remove objectionable traffic from the network, but it also introduces an additional measure of latency as it processes the traffic.

Modems

A modem is a device that enables a computer or network to access another network, typically that of an ISP. The term *modem* is derived from the terms *modulation* and *demodulation*. A modem takes the digital signals generated by a computer, modulates them into analog signals suitable for transmission over a telephone connection, and then demodulates the incoming analog signals back into digital form.

In the early days of the Internet, computers used dial-up modems and standard telephone lines to communicate with other networks. Today, dial-up modem connections are virtually obsolete, but the term modem is still used for devices that provide broadband connections, including the following:

DSL Modem   A digital subscriber line (DSL) connection still uses a standard telephone line to access an ISP's network, but instead of monopolizing the entire telephone connection, it uses only the frequencies over 3.4 MHz for data. This allows voice communication to continue over the lower frequencies.

Cable Modem   A cable modem uses the same modulation/demodulation technique to enable the connection that supplies television signals to carry data and voice traffic as well so that the cable network can provide Internet and voice over IP (VoIP) services.

Voice Gateway

As many large organizations migrate from traditional telephone services to Voice over IP (VoIP), they must endure a period of overlap between the systems. A *voice gateway*—also called a VoIP gateway or a PBX gateway—is a device that bridges between a traditional Public Switched Telephone Network (PSTN) installation, such as a private branch exchange (PBX), and a Voice over IP (VoIP) provider, enabling the two to interact. The voice gateway can enable the PBX and other traditional telephone devices, such as fax machines, to invisibly use VoIP connections to make outside calls instead of the PSTN.

VPN Headend

A *virtual private network (VPN) headend*—also called a *VPN concentrator*—is a hardware device that functions as an endpoint for multiple VPN connections from remote users.

Many servers and routers include this capability in software, but there are advantages to using a dedicated headend device for this purpose.

The VPN headend is responsible for maintaining one end of the multiple encrypted VPN tunnels through the Internet to the remote users' locations. As encryption and decryption are highly processor-intensive applications, it can be advantageous to offload that processing to a separate hardware device.

NETWORKED DEVICES

In addition to the devices that make up the network, the Network+ exam also expects candidates to be familiar with some of the devices that are now being networked, some for the first time.

VoIP Phones

With the increasing use of VoIP in the business world, the average user's desktop phone has had to evolve along with the rest of the telecommunications system. *VoIP telephones* can be standard physical devices similar in appearance to any other desk phone, except that they connect to an Ethernet network, rather than a separate telecommunications network. Some phones can use Power over Ethernet (PoE) rather than a standard power cord. In some cases, the phone is not a physical device at all, but rather a software application running on the user's workstation, requiring only a headset to make it a fully functional VoIP telephone.

Printers

Printer calls are often the bane of an IT worker's existence, frequently because printers are left to the control of their end users. While printers have been networked for decades, this is often accomplished by sharing printers attached to workstations. Many printers are equipped with network interfaces, either wired or wireless, which allow users to connect them directly to the network. However, the best way to centralize control of printers is to create one print server that feeds jobs to the appropriate print devices. This approach allows administrators to control access to the printer with permissions and monitor its activities.

Physical Access Control Devices

Physical access control devices, such as doors with swipe card readers, have made it possible for businesses to monitor and track the locations of their employees, visitors, and sometimes their intruders.

An access control device typically has a combination of authentication mechanisms, such as a swipe card reader and a keypad for input of a PIN. There must also be a solenoid or other mechanism that controls the door lock and a central console where administrators can manage permissions and monitor activities. Connections to a standard Ethernet network allow the various components to communicate, and there might be separate low-voltage connections to supply devices with power.

Cameras

Apart from live sentries, there is no better security mechanism than *cameras* scattered about a facility. At one time, installing cameras for security required a proprietary closed-circuit network. However, today there are relatively inexpensive cameras that can connect to a standard network, either cabled or wireless, allowing them to be monitored from a central location and video saved to a network server. Some cameras are fixed, whereas others are capable of panning, tilting, and zooming. Cameras with cabled network connections can sometimes use Power over Ethernet (PoE) to supply the cameras with electricity.

HVAC Sensors

Heating, ventilation, and air conditioning are major expenses in any facility, and controlling them efficiently can help to manage that expense. Networking the various components of an HVAC installation can allow administrators to both monitor and control them from remote locations.

Some HVAC control products can also enable administrators to create rules that cause the equipment to self-adjust in certain conditions, such as turning down the heat or air conditioning when the equipment detects that no one is in the building.

Networked HVAC systems have a central console that is the control station, as well as sensors and actuators scattered about the facility. The sensors monitor the environmental conditions throughout the building and the condition of the HVAC equipment. The actuators can turn devices on or off or adjust them as needed, all from the central console. As with access control devices, a low-voltage connection linking the controls supplies them with power.

Internet of Things (IoT)

The *Internet of Things (IoT)* is the designation that has been applied to the growing class of devices that have been made "smart" with the integration of a TCP/IP network client. The client allows the device to obtain an IP address from a DHCP server, just like any computer, and communicate with the network using Wi-Fi, Bluetooth, or other wireless protocols. End users can typically monitor and control IoT devices from any location with a cellphone app.

Many IoT products are household devices, including the following:

Refrigerators   Because of their size and central location, IoT refrigerators typically have touchscreens on them and can download and run apps, just like a smartphone or tablet. Some refrigerators even include internal cameras that users can access with a smartphone to see what groceries they need as they are shopping in the market.

Smart Speakers   A smart speaker is a wireless device that is essentially a voice-activated interface to a search engine. The device allows users to ask questions, play music, and control lights and other home automation products.

Smart Thermostats   A smart thermostat can not only respond to remote commands from a smartphone, but can also execute rules that automatically adjust the temperature setting based on the time of day, the temperature outside, or the presence of people in the home.

Smart Doorbells   Smart doorbells typically have cameras integrated into them so that the homeowner can see who is at the door using a smartphone, speak to the callers, and capture video of any motion seen by the camera.

ICS and SCADA

An *industrial control system (ICS)* does for factories and other manufacturing facilities what HVAC systems do for a building environment. An ICS includes sensors and actuators on the equipment and a central controller that administrators can use to monitor and control the factory's various processes. The sensors monitor the conditions of manufacture, such as the temperature, pressure, and speed of a particular process, and the actuators allow an operator to modify those conditions by adjusting controls from a remote location.

Supervisory Control and Data Acquisition (SCADA) is a standardized architecture for this type of industrial control, but it is designed for use by utility companies and other large-scale industries that are typically distributed across multiple facilities, such as electrical production, oil and gas pipelining, and railroads.

CERTMIKE EXAM ESSENTIALS

▶ The devices that make up a modern network include switches, repeaters, bridges, media converters, and access points at layer 2 of the OSI model, routers and multilayer switches at layer 3, and firewalls, proxy servers, and intrusion detection/ prevention systems at the upper layers.

▶ Networked communication devices include cable and DSL modems, voice gateways, and VPN headends.

▶ Devices now being connected to networks include VoIP telephones, printers, access control devices such as door locks, cameras, HVAC sensors, and industrial control systems.

Practice Question 1

Ralph is an IT consultant working for a new video production client, who has a Fast Ethernet LAN with 50 workstations and three servers, all of which are connected to three hubs that are uplinked together. The users routinely share large video files among themselves, and they all require access to the servers. The owner of the firm has called Ralph because the network's users are complaining that file transfers across the network are too slow, and video streaming on the internal network is jittery and inconsistent. The owner knows that his network is outdated, but he wants to know if he can improve its performance without spending a lot, as his budget is limited.

Which of the following upgrades should Ralph recommend in this situation?

A. Replace the three hubs with switches.
B. Add a router to split the network into two 25-node LANs.
C. Replace the hubs with a layer 3 switch and create two 25-node VLANs.
D. Replace the Fast Ethernet hubs with Gigabit Ethernet hubs.

Practice Question 2

Alice is consulting for a client who has a network configured like the one in Figure 9.1. After capturing a traffic sample and analyzing it, she is troubled by the number of collisions that are occurring on the network. How many collision domains and how many broadcast domains are there on this network? (Choose two answers.)

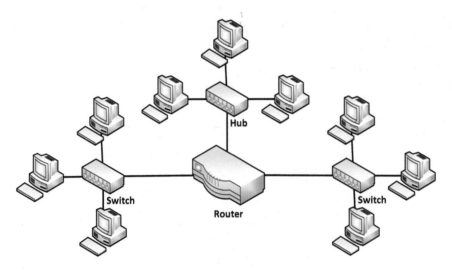

FIGURE 9.1 **A network with nine workstations**

A. There is one collision domain.
B. There are 3 collision domains.
C. There are 7 collision domains.
D. There are 9 collision domains.
E. There is one broadcast domain.
F. There are 3 broadcast domains.
G. There are 7 broadcast domains.
H. There are 9 broadcast domains.

Practice Question 1 Explanation

A. is correct because workgroup switches are relatively inexpensive and can replace the hubs without additional modifications to the network. Fast Ethernet hubs create a single 100 Mbps network medium that is shared by all of the computers. Replacing the hubs with switches creates a separate collision domain for each computer, each with a full 100 Mbps of bandwidth.

B. is incorrect because while adding a router and dividing the network into two LANs could yield some modest performance improvement, due to the non-propagation of broadcasts, the users frequently share data among themselves. This would result in a lot of traffic forwarded to the other LAN by the router.

C. is incorrect because adding a layer 3 switch and creating two VLANs would result in roughly the same traffic conditions as option B. Layer 3 switches are also extremely expensive, making the solution impractical in this case.

D. is incorrect because replacing just the hubs would not result in a performance improvement. For the network to run at Gigabit Ethernet speeds, both the computers and the hubs must use Gigabit Ethernet networking equipment.

Correct Answer: A

Practice Question 2 Explanation

A. is incorrect because routers only forward traffic that is destined for another network. Therefore, there must be at least three collision domains.

B. is incorrect because switches create a separate collision domain for each of the devices connected to them, so there must be at least six collision domains.

C. is correct because switches create a separate collision domain for each of the devices connected to them and hubs create a single collision domain for all of their connected devices.

D. is incorrect because hubs only create a single collision domain for all of their connected devices. Therefore, there cannot be nine collision domains.

E. is incorrect because routers do not propagate broadcasts, so there must be more than one broadcast domain.

F. is correct because each hub or switch forms its own broadcast domain.

G. is incorrect because all of the broadcast messages reaching a hub or switch are propagated to all of the devices connected to that hub or switch, so there cannot be more than three broadcast domains.

H. is incorrect because all of the broadcast messages reaching a hub or switch are propagated to all of the devices connected to that hub or switch, so there cannot be more than three broadcast domains.

Correct Answers: C and F

CHAPTER 10

Routing and Bandwidth Management

Objective 2.2: Compare and contrast routing technologies and bandwidth management concepts.

This chapter examines fundamental routing concepts in a typical enterprise network and techniques for manipulating network traffic to optimize bandwidth. The Network+ exam expects candidates to be familiar with these basic networking functions.

In this chapter, you'll learn everything you need to know about Network+ Objective 2.2, including the following topics:

▶ Routing
▶ Bandwidth management

ROUTING

As noted in earlier chapters, a *router* is a device that connects networks together and selectively forwards traffic toward its destination. A router, by definition, has interfaces to two or more networks. A group of networks, connected by routers, is called an *internetwork*. The Internet is a gigantic internetwork consisting of thousands of individual networks, all connected by thousands of routers.

To get network traffic to a specific location on the Internet, or on any internetwork, the routers forward packets based on the destination IP addresses in the packets' IP headers and on the information stored in each router's routing table. A registered IP address is a unique identifier for one specific host somewhere on the Internet, but transmitting packets to that particular host might require them to pass through dozens of routers on the way. Each of those routers is responsible for forwarding each packet to the next router on the path to the network where the destination address is located.

A routing table consists of network destinations and specifies the interface the router should use to send traffic to each network. Table 10.1 contains a sample of a routing table from a router that is connected to two networks (192.168.2.0 and 192.168.14.0), as shown in Figure 10.1. Routers and server operating systems can use different routing table formats, but they all contain the same information and function in roughly the same way.

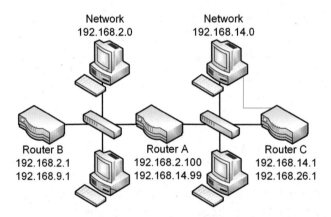

FIGURE 10.1 Router A connected to two networks

TABLE 10.1 Sample routing table from Router A

Network destination	Netmask	Gateway	Interface	Metric
0.0.0.0	0.0.0.0	192.168.2.1	192.168.2.100	10
127.0.0.0	255.0.0.0	127.0.0.1	127.0.0.1	1
192.168.2.0	255.255.255.0	On-link	192.168.2.100	10

Network destination	Netmask	Gateway	Interface	Metric
192.168.14.0	255.255.255.0	On-link	192.168.14.99	10
192.168.9.0	255.255.255.0	192.168.2.1	192.168.2.100	20
192.168.26.0	255.255.255.0	192.168.14.1	192.168.14.99	20
127.0.0.1	255.255.255.255	127.0.0.1	127.0.0.1	1
192.168.14.99	255.255.255.255	127.0.0.1	127.0.0.1	10
192.168.2.100	255.255.255.255	127.0.0.1	127.0.0.1	10
192.168.2.1	255.255.255.255	192.168.2.1	192.168.2.100	10
192.168.14.1	255.255.255.255	192.168.14.1	192.168.14.99	10

The columns in this routing table contain the following information:

Network Destination   Identifies a host or network address of a destination reachable by the router.

Netmask   Contains the subnet mask value for the network destination address that indicates the division between the network bits and the host bits.

Gateway   Identifies the router that will be the next hop for packets going to the network destination address.

Interface   Specifies which of its network interfaces the router should use to reach the intended gateway.

Metric   Specifies the relative value of the route. When a routing table contains multiple routes to a specific destination, the router uses the gateway with the lowest metric value.
   The functions of the entries in the sample routing table are as follows:

▶ The first entry in the routing table (0.0.0.0) is the *default route* (also known as the *default gateway*), which specifies the router that the system should use when it fails to find a packet's destination address in its routing table.

▶ The second entry (127.0.0.0) is the standard IP loopback network address, which sends traffic directly to the system's input buffer without transmitting it over the network.

▶ The third and fourth entries specify the networks to which Router A is directly connected: 192.168.2.0 and 192.168.14.0.

▶ The fifth entry indicates that to send traffic to the 192.168.9.0 network, Router A must use its 192.168.2.100 interface to forward the traffic to Router B's

192.168.2.1 interface. Router B is also connected to the 192.168.9.0 network, so it can forward the traffic from Router A directly to its destination.

▶ The sixth entry indicates that to send traffic to the 192.168.26.0 network, Router A must use its 192.168.14.99 interface to forward traffic to Router C at 192.168.14.1. Router C can then forward the traffic to its destination on 192.168.26.0.

▶ The 7th through 11th entries are all host destinations that Router A can access directly through its connected networks.

There are two types of routing, depending on how the routing table is formed: static routing and dynamic routing, as defined in the following sections.

Static Routing

In *static routing*, administrators create the entries in the routing table manually, using a tool such as *route*, a command-line utility that can display, modify, and create routing table entries. In static routing, those manual entries remain in force until someone changes them. For smaller networks that do not change frequently, this is an acceptable solution. However, some routers have extremely large routing tables, and some large enterprise networks have traffic conditions that change frequently, requiring updates to the routing tables. For cases such as these, static routing is impractical.

Dynamic Routing

For installations where static routing is impractical, usually because the routing tables are too large or too volatile to maintain manually, dynamic routing is the preferred solution. *Dynamic routing* is a technique for automatically building and updating routing tables. Routers do this by running specialized routing protocols that allow them to exchange routing information with other routers in the area.

By publishing their routing table information using these protocols, routers learn about what lies beyond the network segments to which they are directly connected. This allows the routers to make more intelligent decisions about how to forward packets to a particular destination most efficiently.

Dynamic routing is where the metric value included for each entry in a routing table becomes important. Routing protocols modify this value for specific destinations to indicate the relative efficiency of a route to that destination. If a router providing access to a particular destination is many hops away, it will have a higher metric value. Large networks can have multiple routes to a destination, which take the form of multiple routing table entries. When there are multiple entries to choose from in the routing table, routers always choose the one with the lowest metric value.

There are many routing protocols designed to service particular types of routers. Some of the most commonly used routing protocols are described next.

Routing Information Protocol (RIP)

The *Routing Information Protocol (RIP)* is one of the oldest and simplest of the routing protocols. RIP works by transmitting the entire routing table over all available interfaces every

30 seconds. Routers receiving the transmissions incorporate the information into their own routing tables, modifying the metric values to reflect the distance from the transmitting router.

The first RIP standard was published in 1988, but it has since been enhanced several times, as follows:

RIP Version 1 (RIPv1)   Transmits the entire routing table using broadcast messages; supports classful addresses only; does not transmit subnet masks

RIP Version 2 (RIPv2)   Transmits the entire routing table using multicast messages, to conserve bandwidth; supports classless addressing; includes a subnet mask for each entry

RIP Next Generation (RIPng)   Transmits the entire routing table using IPv6 multicast messages

RIP is a *distance vector routing protocol*, meaning that it measures the distance between routers in terms of the number of hops between them. Each *hop* represents one router that packets must pass through on the way to the destination. Therefore, traffic destined for a network that is 10 hops away must be forwarded by 10 routers to get there.

Open Shortest Path First (OSPF)

Distance vectoring is not a terribly precise way to measure the proximity of a router. A single hop could be a local area network (LAN) connection running at 1,000 Mbps, or it could be a much slower wide area network (WAN) connection. This is why many of the other routing protocols use alternative measurements to calculate their metric values.

Open Shortest Path First (OSPF) is an open standard *link state routing protocol*. Unlike distance vector protocols, link state protocols gather information about the network by transmitting messages called link state advertisements (LSAs) to other routers in multicast messages. Using the information in the LSAs, the routers create a neighbor table and a topology table, essentially a map of the entire network. The routers then use that information to build their routing tables.

Unlike distance vector protocols, link state protocols use various criteria to calculate the efficiency of routes through the network. In addition to hop counts, OSPF factors in the transmission speeds of the various network links, the current levels of traffic congestion on the various routes, and a route cost specified by an administrator. The routers then use the Dijkstra algorithm to calculate the relative efficiency of routes to a given destination. OSPF routing tables support multiple routes to the same destination with the same metric and administrative distance values. When this occurs, the router balances the outgoing traffic among the duplicate routes.

Unlike RIP, OSPF does not transmit its entire routing table at regular intervals. Instead, it generates updates containing only the data that has changed, which conserves bandwidth and speeds up convergence. OSPF also does not have a hop count limit, as RIP does. OSPF has many advantages over RIP, including route efficiency and convergence speed, but it also requires more processing power, memory, and storage from the router.

Enhanced Interior Gateway Routing Protocol (EIGRP)

The Enhanced Interior Gateway Routing Protocol (EIGRP) is an updated version of the earlier Interior Gateway Routing Protocol (IGRP). Although ostensibly a distance vector protocol, EIGRP is sometimes referred to as a *hybrid routing protocol* because it includes both distance vector and link state routing characteristics.

EIGRP uses neighbor discovery messages to gather information about other routers. The protocol encapsulates its messages directly within IP datagrams; there is no TCP or UDP port number. Using the neighbor discovery information, the router creates a neighbor table and a topology table, much as in OSPF. The topology table contains all of the routes gathered from other routers. After calculating the best route to each network destination, the router places the selected entries in the routing table.

EIGRP does not rely solely on hop counts to calculate metrics; it also considers several characteristics of the link to the destination network, including its bandwidth, traffic congestion levels, transmission delay, reliability, and its maximum transfer unit (MTU) size. To calculate the relative efficiency of a route, EIGRP uses the Diffusing Update Algorithm (DUAL).

Like RIP, EIGRP transmits distance vector updates to other routers. However, it does not send the entire routing table as RIP does; it generates incremental updates containing only the information that has changed, much like OSPF.

Compared to RIP, EIGRP is much more scalable, due to its support for numbered autonomous systems. An *autonomous system (AS)* is a group of adjacent routers that share their routing tables and run the same routing protocol. This capability enables EIGRP to support larger networks by splitting them up into multiple ASs.

Border Gateway Protocol (BGP)

RIP, OSPF, and EIGRP are all *interior gateway protocols*, meaning that they are intended for use inside an enterprise internetwork. *Border Gateway Protocol (BGP)* is an *exterior gateway protocol*. In fact, BGP is *the* exterior gateway protocol, responsible for the IPv4 and IPv6 routing between autonomous systems all over the Internet. The routers in an AS that communicate with other AS routers using BGP are sometimes called *border routers* or *edge routers*.

BGP is classified as a *path vector routing protocol*. This is similar to a distance vector protocol, except that it shares AS path information with other routers, such as the numbers of the autonomous systems on the way to a destination and the addresses of the networks inside an AS, rather than just router hop counts.

While it is possible to use BGP within an AS as an interior gateway protocol, in which case it is called the *Interior Border Gateway Protocol (iBGP),* RIP and OSPF are better suited to that role. In the case of a large enterprise network consisting of multiple autonomous systems, an interior protocol such as RIP or OSPF might be suitable for the routing within each AS, but not for the routing between ASs, which might require a more scalable protocol such as BGP.

RIP and OSPF could never handle the volume of routing needed for a multihomed Internet router. A BGP router on the Internet, sometimes known as an *Exterior Border Gateway Protocol (eBGP)* router, must discover all of the routes between ASs, which number in the hundreds of thousands. The complete IPv4 routing table for the Internet is nearly a gigabyte in size, and a BGP router needs substantial processing, memory, and storage resources to manage it.

EXAM TIP

There are many other routing protocols, but RIP, OSPF, EIGRP, and BGP are the only ones named in the Network+ exam objectives. Candidates for the exam should be aware of these four protocols, their types, and in what situations they are used.

Administrative Distance

Administrative distances (ADs) are set values that routers use to evaluate the trustworthiness of paths through the network to a given destination, based on the source of each path. AD values range from 0 to 255. When selecting a route to a destination, a router always chooses the path with the lowest AD value. Directly connected networks have an AD value of 0, and static routes have a value of 1, so these are always the routes chosen first. Table 10.2 lists the AD values for the most commonly used routing protocols.

The primary function of administrative distance values is to allow routers to compare routes generated by different routing protocols. Routers use AD values to evaluate routes first. It is only when the AD values for two routes are the same that the router uses their metrics to evaluate them.

TABLE 10.2 Administrative distance values for route sources

Route source	Default AD
Connected network interface	0
Static route	1
External BGP	20
Internal EIGRP	90
OSPF	110
RIP	120
External EIGRP	170
Internal BGP	200
Route never used	255

BANDWIDTH MANAGEMENT

Routers are network layer (layer 3) devices. As the layer primarily responsible for the end-to-end communication between source and destination systems, the network layer is the perfect place to implement other networking technologies. One of these is *bandwidth management*, which refers to mechanisms for controlling the allocation of bandwidth to specific types of traffic.

Networks frequently carry different types of traffic with different transmission requirements. For example, file transfers must be bit-perfect, but they can tolerate a transmission delay and some retransmitted packets. Web traffic can also tolerate delays and even some lost bits. Streaming audio and video can buffer their traffic and tolerate a few dropped frames caused by lost or corrupted packets. However, applications such as Voice over IP (VoIP) and iSCSI work in real time. Transmission delays and lost bits can result in calls being dropped or data being corrupted. By managing the network's bandwidth, administrators can see to it that the traffic is prioritized so that applications requiring it receive the bandwidth they need.

Traffic Shaping

Traffic shaping is a technique for delaying network traffic—usually in a buffer—to achieve an agreed-on transmission rate. The technique can be applied to all traffic or to that generated by specific applications. For example, Internet service providers can use traffic shaping to limit the bandwidth used by peer-to-peer file sharing applications, while allowing other types of traffic to proceed without limits. In other cases, service providers can use traffic shaping to ensure that their clients receive the bandwidth specified in their service level agreements. Enterprise administrators can also limit the bandwidth they receive from their own providers, to avoid exceeding data rates that incur additional charges.

Traffic shaping tools—sometimes called *traffic conditioners*—allow administrators to monitor the traffic on their networks, to determine who is using bandwidth, at what time, and for what purpose. With that information, administrators can decide what limits need to be imposed and create rules to implement them. Traffic shaping can work by regulating either the bandwidth used to transmit data or the time during which the transmission occurs. For example, to prevent a 1 Gbps interface from exceeding a transmission speed of 500 Mbps, a router can transmit at its normal speed for half the time and buffer the outgoing data for the other half.

Quality of Service (QoS)

When a network becomes overly congested with traffic, there are two possible solutions: increase the bandwidth or use the existing bandwidth more effectively. *Quality of Service (QoS)* is a means of doing the latter, by prioritizing network traffic so that applications can always have the bandwidth they require available to them. To use QoS, network administrators must evaluate the different types of traffic carried by the network, create categories for them, and establish priorities among the categories.

QoS works by embedding codes in packets' IP headers. Routers that support QoS read the codes on incoming packets and act on each packet according to the priorities assigned to its code. For example, high-priority traffic, such as VoIP calls, would always be transmitted immediately, whereas packets with lesser priorities might be buffered for a period of time before transmission or even discarded entirely, depending on the network's traffic congestion level.

The most commonly-used mechanism for coding traffic at layer 3 is called *Differentiated Services, or DiffServ*. Most of the traffic shaping and conditioning tools mentioned earlier can also function as traffic classifiers by applying DiffServ codes to packets as they enter the network. The Differentiated Services field in a standard Internet Protocol (IP) header contains a 6-bit differentiated services code point (DSCP) that identifies the traffic category of the data in the packet. The DiffServ standards leave the creation of categories to the administrators of the network.

EXAM TIP

Quality of Service (QoS) can be implemented by routers at the network layer (layer 3) or by switches at the data link layer (layer 2). At layer 2, QoS works by reading a 3-bit Class of Service (CoS) code in the 802.1Q frame. Exam candidates should be aware that they might encounter QoS in discussions of switches as well as routers.

CERTMIKE EXAM ESSENTIALS

► A router is a network layer device that connects two or more networks together and forwards traffic between them. Each router maintains its own routing table, which consists of destinations on other networks and the addresses of the gateways used to send traffic there.

► The two basic types of routing are static routing, in which administrators manually create the routing table entries, and dynamic routing, in which specialized routing protocols share information with other routers and compile their own routing table entries.

► Bandwidth management is a collective term for various technologies that allow administrators to regulate their network traffic, including traffic shaping, which is a technique for buffering traffic to regulate its transmission rate, and Quality of Service (QoS), which is a means of prioritizing traffic by applying codes to IP packet headers.

Practice Question 1

Ralph is an IT consultant working on a network that consists of a headquarters facility and several branch offices. The branches are connected to the headquarters network using a variety of WAN technologies running at different speeds. Ralph wants to implement a single routing protocol at all of the offices but is not sure which one to use. Which one of the following routing protocols is the least suitable for Ralph's network?

A. RIP
B. OSPF
C. EIGRP
D. BGP

Practice Question 2

Alice is working as a consultant for a client who has a network running RIPv1 as a routing protocol. The client wants Alice to divide their existing Class C network into three subnets with 32 hosts in each. Alice explains that while she can create the requested subnets, the network will no longer be able to use RIPv1 as its routing protocol.

Which of the following is a valid reason why Alice must change routing protocols on the network?

A. RIPv1 only uses broadcast messages to share its routing table.
B. RIPv1 only shares routing table entries that have recently changed.
C. RIPv1 only supports classful addressing.
D. RIPv1 only uses hop counts to evaluate routes.

Practice Question 1 Explanation

A. is correct because the Routing Information Protocol is a distance vector protocol that evaluates routes based on the number of hops between the source and the destination. Because the branch offices are connected using WAN links running at different speeds, hop counts are not a reliable means of evaluating the efficiency of the branch office routes.

B. is incorrect because Open Shortest Path First (OSPF) is a link state routing protocol that does not rely on hop counts to evaluate routes.

C. is incorrect because the Enhanced Interior Gateway Routing Protocol (EIGRP) is a hybrid routing protocol that relies on other factors in addition to hop counts to evaluate routes.

D. is incorrect because Border Gateway Protocol (BGP) is a path vector routing protocol that does not rely solely on hop counts to evaluate routes.

Correct Answer: A, RIP

Practice Question 2 Explanation

A. is incorrect because although RIPv1 does use broadcast transmissions, this is not a reason why the routing protocol must be changed.

B. is incorrect because the statement is untrue. RIPv1 always transmits the entire routing table every 30 seconds.

C. is correct because RIPv1 does not include the netmask (or subnet mask) value in its routing table transmissions. Therefore, the routes included in the messages must conform to the standard IP address classes. Once Alice creates the requested subnets, the routing table will no longer contain the Class C address, and the entries in the RIPv1 messages will be incorrect.

D. is incorrect because although RIPv1 does use only hop counts to evaluate routes, this is not a reason why the routing protocol must be changed.

Correct Answer: C

CHAPTER 11

Switching
Objective 2.3: Given a scenario, configure and deploy common Ethernet switching features.

This chapter examines some of the fundamental switching concepts in a typical enterprise network. The Network+ exam expects candidates to be familiar with these basic networking functions.

In this chapter, you'll learn everything you need to know about Network+ Objective 2.3, including the following topics:

▶ **Switching**
▶ **Address Resolution Protocol (ARP)**
▶ **Neighbor Discovery Protocol**

ETHERNET BASICS

Ethernet is one of the first local area networking (LAN) protocols to be released commercially in 1980, and it still persists today as the primary data link layer (layer 2) protocol for cabled networks. The term *Ethernet* is actually a misnomer; the original standard for the network was called Ethernet, but the current standards are published by the IEEE as part of the 802.3 working group. Therefore, the Ethernet networks being built today are actually IEEE 802.3 networks.

The original Ethernet standards specified three basic components for an Ethernet network: the Ethernet frame, the CSMA/CD media access control mechanism, and a series of physical layer specifications. These components are discussed in this section.

The Ethernet Frame

The Ethernet frame is the outermost envelope in a packet transmitted over a local area network. The frame consists of a header and a footer that encapsulate the payload that the Ethernet protocol receives from the network layer protocol above it, usually Internet Protocol (IP).

In the same way that IP uses IP addresses to identify hosts on the network, Ethernet uses media access control (MAC) addresses to identify systems on a LAN. A MAC address is a 6-byte value, expressed in hexadecimal notation, as in the following example:

```
52-E7-AD-C5-96-18
```

Ethernet network interface adapters have a MAC address hard-coded into them. The first 3 bytes identify the manufacturer of the device, and the last 3 bytes are a unique identifier for that adapter. Ethernet headers have Destination Address and Source Address fields that contain the MAC addresses of the sending and receiving systems on the LAN.

Carrier-Sense Multiple Access with Collision Detection (CSMA/CD)

In its early iterations, the Ethernet standards called for a shared network medium, such as that on a coaxial bus or a hub-based star network. In a shared network medium, when two hosts transmit at the same time, a packet collision occurs, usually requiring the retransmission of both packets.

Collisions were a normal occurrence on these networks, but to minimize them, Ethernet includes a MAC mechanism called *Carrier Sense Multiple Access with Collision Detection (CSMA/CD)*.

CSMA/CD defines a method by which hosts can access a shared network medium with a reduced chance of collisions occurring and detect collisions when they do occur. The phases of the process are as follows:

Carrier Sense   Before a host transmits, it listens to the network to see if it is in use. If it is in use, the host pauses before listening again.

Multiple Access   When the network is clear, the host begins transmitting. The transmitted packet fills the entire shared network medium before the host finishes transmitting it. It is during this time that a collision can occur.

Collision Detection   When the transmitting host detects signals on both its transmit and receive wires simultaneously, it declares a signal quality error (or collision), stops transmitting data, and starts transmitting a jam signal instead. The jam signal alerts any other transmitting systems of the collision, causing them to discard any incoming data they have received.

Wireless devices cannot use CSMA/CD because they turn off their receivers when transmitting, so they use an alternative mechanism called *Carrier Sense Multiple Access with Collision Avoidance (CSMA/CA)*.

When switches replaced hubs in the IT marketplace—and in data centers around the world—Ethernet networks no longer needed a shared network medium or CSMA/CD, and packet collisions as a normal occurrence became largely a thing of the past.

Physical Layer Specifications

The Ethernet standards include a large collection of physical layer specifications, which have been updated over the years to reflect advancements in networking technologies. There are dozens of specifications supporting different network media, but only a few have remained in general use.

An Ethernet specification defines the characteristics of the network medium, such as what category of UTP cable to use, and also provides installation guidance, such as the maximum length of a cable segment. The limitations on cable length exist primarily to support the collision detection mechanism in CSMA/CD.

> **EXAM TIP**
>
> An Ethernet network, by today's standards, typically consists of UTP cable segments connecting hosts to switches. Switches have replaced hubs in all but the most outdated network installations. Candidates for the Network+ exam should be conscious of the effect that switching has on an Ethernet network.

SWITCHING

A *switch*, as noted elsewhere in this book, is a network connectivity device that operates at the data link layer (layer 2) of the OSI reference model. Unlike hubs, which are purely electrical devices operating at the physical layer, switches have the ability to learn about the devices on the network and maintain a record of the information they discover.

A switch is essentially a multiport bridge that forwards traffic selectively to its destination on the local network, rather than flooding each packet to every connected host, as a hub does. This provides each device connected to the switch with a dedicated, full-speed link to every other connected device.

So, although the devices connected to the switch are all included in a single broadcast domain, every pair of devices has its own separate collision domain. This eliminates the routine Ethernet packet collisions and the need for CSMA/CD.

> **EXAM TIP**
>
> All of the information on Ethernet and switching in this chapter is concerned with layer 2 local area networking only. An Ethernet packet can only be addressed to a destination on the local network, either a host or a router. Network+ exam candidates should be aware that while a single packet must have a data link layer (MAC address) destination on the local network, it can also have a network layer destination IP address located on a distant network.

Switches are available at price points ranging from the cost of a meal to that of a substantial house. Usually, as prices go up, so does the list of features the switch provides. Many switches include capabilities that exceed the strictly defined role of a switch, even to the point of including functions from other OSI model layers. For example, multilayer switches—sometimes called layer 3 switches—include routing as well as switching capabilities.

MAC Address Tables

The heart of the switching process is the creation and maintenance of *MAC address tables*; this is how the switch learns about the devices on the network. As traffic arrives at a switch, the device reads the Ethernet header of each packet, specifically the MAC address fields. The switch then compiles a table containing those MAC addresses, associating each packet's Source Address with the number of the switch port over which the packet arrived. Switches frequently store MAC address tables in *content addressable memory*, a high-performance memory type that speeds up the switch's table searching process.

In the future, when packets arrive that are destined for that same source address, the switch will know to forward the packets out through that same port. When packets arrive that are addressed to destinations not yet in the switch's table, the switch forwards them through all of its ports. Eventually, all of the devices connected to the switch will be added to the MAC address table.

To discover the MAC addresses of specific hosts on the network, systems use the *Address Resolution Protocol (ARP)*. ARP is a data link layer protocol that generates request messages containing an IPv4 address and broadcasts them on the local network. The host using that IP address is then responsible for generating a reply message containing its MAC address, which it transmits as a unicast. The original requestor therefore receives the MAC address it needs, but at the same time, the switches processing the ARP messages are adding those MAC addresses to their own forwarding tables.

In addition to the protocol itself, ARP maintains a cache of IP addresses and their MAC address equivalents. Systems search the ARP cache for IP addresses before they generate new ARP request messages. There is also an ARP utility with which users can add static entries to or remove them from the ARP table, or just display the contents of the cache, as follows:

```
Interface: 192.168.5.22 --- 0xe
  Internet Address      Physical Address      Type
  192.168.5.1           28-80-88-1e-87-e5     dynamic
  192.168.5.12          84-b8-b8-2d-18-69     dynamic
  192.168.5.255         ff-ff-ff-ff-ff-ff     static
  224.0.0.2             01-00-5e-00-00-02     static
  239.255.255.250       01-00-5e-7f-ff-fa     static
  255.255.255.255       ff-ff-ff-ff-ff-ff     static
```

On networks using IPv6, the equivalent to ARP is called the *Neighbor Discovery Protocol (NDP)*. NDP performs the same address resolution function as ARP, but it does so without using broadcasts (because there are no broadcasts in IPv6). Instead, it generates multicasts using Internet Control Message Protocol version 6 (ICMPv6) messages. As with ARP, the system generating the reply messages transmits them as unicasts.

Connecting Switches

Switches are typically marketed by the number of ports they provide. Simple switches might have four or eight ports, while high-end devices often have 24 or 48. For large enterprise networks, switches are rack-mountable, and administrators can link them together to create larger networks.

On an Unshielded Twisted Pair (UTP) network, a host transmits a packet by sending signals out over the Transmit wire inside the cable. At the destination, those signals must arrive over the Receive wire. Therefore, at some point in the cable connection between the two hosts, there must be a crossover between the Transmit and Receive wires. Cables for a UTP LAN are always wired "straight through," meaning that each pin in the connector at one end is wired to the corresponding pin at the other end. Therefore, that necessary crossover between the Transmit and Receive wires must occur inside the switch.

When connecting two switches together, administrators must be careful to avoid a double crossover situation, in which one switch is transposing the wires and the other switch is transposing them back again. For example, this would occur if the switches were connected by a patch cable plugged into a standard port on each one. To avoid the double crossover, switches can use any of the following techniques:

Crossover Cable   For a low-end switch with no other capabilities, a special UTP cable with the Transmit and Receive wires transposed—called a *crossover cable*—can connect two switches together.

Uplink Port   Some switches are equipped with a designated uplink port, which is a port that either does not have a crossover circuit or has a toggle to enable and disable it.

To connect two switches, plug a standard patch cable into the uplink port on one switch and a standard port on the other. Connecting an uplink to an uplink would negate the crossover.

Auto-Medium-Dependent Interface Crossover (MDI-X) Some newer switches can automatically sense the Transmit and Receive wires in the connected cables and enable or disable the crossover for the port as needed.

Switching Loops

Large enterprise networks might have dozens or even hundreds of switches, and it is common practice to create redundant links between them, for fault tolerance purposes. When a host transmits a packet, it travels over the cable to its connected switch. If that switch has redundant connections to two other switches, then each of the other switches will receive an identical copy of the packet. The other switches then forward the packets over their own redundant connections, so more copies of the packet start circulating around the network. This is called a *switching loop*, and it can monopolize large amounts of bandwidth and cause corruption of the switches' MAC address tables.

There is no Time-to-Live field in data link layer switching, as there is in network layer routing, so packets don't expire; they just circulate endlessly. The situation only worsens when a host generates broadcast transmissions, which the switches forward out through all of their ports, flooding the network with hundreds or thousands of copies. This is called a *broadcast storm*.

To avoid switching loops and broadcast storms, switches typically use a specialized protocol called the *Spanning Tree Protocol (STP)*. STP is a protocol that allows switches to communicate and organize the switching fabric of the network.

Using messages called *bridge protocol data units (BPDUs)*, one switch is elected to the role of *root bridge,* and every nonroot bridge has a designated *root port*. These selected elements work together to elect one port on each network segment as its *designated port*. The designated port is the one that forwards traffic to other switches.

All of the other ports—the *nondesignated ports*—are blocked to data traffic by their switches to prevent looping but continue to receive STP communications from other switches. This communication allows the switches to self-adjust when a link goes down and a designated port becomes unavailable. In that case, one of the nondesignated ports is elected to take over and transitions through several operational phases on its way to becoming the designated port for the segment.

The convergence period of the original STP version—published by the IEEE 802.1 working group in 1990—is 50 seconds. *Convergence* is the time needed to configure all of the ports in a switch with their STP roles. Each time there is a change in the switching fabric of the network, such as when a link to a designated port goes down, there is a 50-second convergence delay as the switches readjust.

In 2001, the working group published a revised version of the STP technology called *Rapid Spanning Tree Protocol (RSTP)*, which modifies some of the port designations and transition phases, as well as the process by which switches calculate their port roles. The result is a greatly reduced convergence period, down to 5 seconds from 50.

VLANs

As noted earlier, switches create a separate collision domain for each pair of connected devices, eliminating the collisions and the media access control problems that occur on hub-based networks. However, a network interconnected by switches is still one big broadcast domain. On a large network with many switches, the propagation of broadcast messages to all of the switches and hosts can generate a huge amount of traffic throughout the network.

It is possible, however, to segment a switched network into multiple broadcast domains by creating *virtual local area networks (VLANs)*. This also makes it possible to secure a group of hosts by adding them to a VLAN that isolates them from the other VLANs on the network.

By default, switches that support VLANs have a default VLAN, typically called VLAN1. All of the switch's ports are in VLAN1 by default, resulting in a single broadcast domain. Administrators can then create additional VLANs on the switches, calling them by the name VLAN plus a numeral, and add ports to the new VLANs as needed. Each new VLAN becomes a separate broadcast domain.

VLANs are virtual, but they are functionally the same as if they were separate physical networks. As with physical LANs, the only way for VLANs to communicate with each other is through routers. The routing can be virtualized as well, however, which is why multilayer switches with routing capabilities built into them are common.

Trunking

A VLAN can have ports from any switch on the network in it, as long as the switches are connected in such a way that the ports in a VLAN can communicate with each other. To make this possible, each switch must have a port dedicated to inter-switch communication called a *trunk port*. The trunk ports in the switches exchange all traffic, regardless of the VLAN to which it belongs. The other ports—called *access ports*—carry only the traffic for the VLANs to which they are assigned.

Trunk ports work with traffic from all of the network's VLANs at once, so switches must have a means of identifying the VLAN for each packet. This is called *802.1Q port tagging*. IEEE 802.1Q is a standard that defines the format of a 4-byte field that switches add to the Ethernet header of each frame they transmit using the trunk port. This field contains a 12-bit VLAN identifier value, which means that the network can support up to 4,094 (2^{12}–2) VLANs.

Only trunk port traffic includes an 802.1Q field in each packet. When a switch receives incoming traffic that is destined for a host in the same VLAN and connected to the same switch, it forwards the packets directly to the host using its access port. However, if the destination is in the same VLAN but physically connected to another switch, the sending switch adds an 802.1Q field to the packets and transmits them out to the other switches through its trunk port. The switch to which the destination host is connected receives the packets over its trunk port, removes the 802.1Q fields, and then forwards the packets to the destination host using its access port.

Voice VLANs

As a general rule, an access port on a switch can only be associated with one VLAN. However, as with most networking rules, there is an exception. On some switches, it is possible to create a *voice VLAN* that allows administrators to prioritize VoIP traffic over standard data traffic, while leaving the default VLAN in place to accommodate the data traffic. This makes it possible to support a VoIP phone and a computer with a single switch port.

Plugging the phone into the switch port and the computer into the phone's auxiliary jack connects both to the network. The packets carrying VoIP traffic are tagged with a 4-byte field in the Ethernet header, similar to 802.1Q tagging. Ordinary data packets are left untagged. VoIP phones can scan packets for the tags. They process the tagged packets as voice traffic and forward the untagged packets to the computer.

> **EXAM TIP**
>
> The Network+ objectives use the term *data virtual local area network* to refer to regular VLANs and distinguish them from voice VLANs. The term is nonstandard, however, and exam candidates should know that it refers to a normal VLAN.

Port Configuration Settings

The simplest unmanaged switches, intended for home and small office use, have a row of UTP ports and a power cable. There is nothing to configure. Higher-end managed switches have a variety of settings that administrators can configure, many of which they can set for each port individually.

The administrative interface of a managed switch varies by product and manufacturer. Some switches have a console port, into which it is possible to plug a laptop running a terminal emulation program with a command-line interface. This is called *in-band management*. Other switches require administrators to access the switch over a network connection, again using a terminal emulator. Still other switches include a built-in website that provides the switch with a graphical configuration interface. These are examples of *out-of-band management*.

Some of the configurable features often found on managed switches are as follows:

Duplex   Most switches autodetect the traffic on the network and use *full duplex* communication by default, which allows hosts to transmit and receive data simultaneously. Older (usually hub-based) networks might use *half duplex* communication, meaning that hosts can transmit or receive data at any one time, but not both. Although it is rarely necessary, switches typically allow administrators to manually specify full duplex or half duplex communication for a particular port.

Speed   The speeds of Ethernet networks have increased over the years, but the standards are backward compatible. Connecting a Fast Ethernet host to a Gigabit Ethernet switch causes the switch port to adjust its speed down from 1,000 to 100 Mbps. It is also possible to manually configure a switch port to run at a specific speed, but this is not usually necessary.

Port Aggregation   A mechanism for combining the bandwidth of two or more ports to create a single aggregated port with increased bandwidth. Many switches use the *Link Aggregation Control Protocol (LACP)* to manage port aggregations.

Flow Control   An Ethernet standard for the regulation of transmission speed based on network congestion levels. A host can generate an Ethernet Pause frame with a specific delay value, which causes the switch to stop forwarding traffic to that host until the delay expires or the host sends another Pause frame with a delay value of 0.

Port Mirroring   Switches forward packets only to their destinations, which makes it difficult for administrators to monitor network traffic for a specific port. Port mirroring, when enabled, creates a mirror relationship between the selected port and another unused port. This allows administrators to connect a protocol analyzer to the mirror port and capture network traffic.

Port Security   To help prevent potential intruders from connecting unauthorized devices to the network, administrators can secure individual switch ports by specifying the MAC addresses of the only devices permitted to use them.

Jumbo Frames   In the IEEE 802.3 standards, the default maximum payload size for an Ethernet frame is 1500 bytes. However, Ethernet equipment manufacturers have for many years been supporting larger frame sizes, collectively called *jumbo frames*. Jumbo frame sizes can vary, but a 9,000-byte maximum payload is common. Jumbo frame capability is not defined in any of the 802.3 standards, and administrators can configure switch ports to support it or not. To use jumbo frames on a network, all of the switches and adapters processing the packets must support the feature and have it enabled.

Power over Ethernet (PoE)   is a standard published by the IEEE 802.3 working group that defines a method for Ethernet networks to supply power to remote devices over UTP cables. This enables devices such as Voice over IP (VoIP) phones, wireless access points, and remote video cameras to function on the network without the need for a separate power source. The first PoE standard called for the transmission of 12.95 watts of power. In later standards, *Power over Ethernet Plus (PoE+)* increased the power to 25.5 watts, and PoE++ increased it further, with power levels of 51 and 71.3 watts.

CERTMIKE EXAM ESSENTIALS

▶ Ethernet consists of three elements: a frame format, a media access control mechanism called CSMA/CD, and a series of physical layer specifications.

▶ Switches have replaced hubs on local area networks, creating a separate collision domain for each pair of connected hosts and eliminating routine Ethernet collisions. Switches learn about the network and compile MAC address tables that associate addresses with specific switch ports.

▶ Large networks frequently have redundant switches, which can result in switching loops and broadcast storms. To avoid this, networks use the Spanning Tree Protocol (STP).

▶ Virtual LANs allow administrators to segment a switched network into multiple broadcast domains. VLANs can include systems connected to different switches. The switches use a technique called trunking to share traffic among themselves.

Practice Question 1

Ralph has an 8-node LAN in his business office, with a single unmanaged switch and eight workstations. He wants to add more workstations, but his switch only has eight ports, and they are all occupied. Ralph purchases a second, identical 8-port switch and plans to cable the two switches together.

On both switches, there is a toggle next to port number 8 that is labeled Uplink. Ralph enables the toggle on both switches and connects the two number 8 ports using a standard patch cable. Ralph then tests the network and finds that all of his attempts to make hosts on different switches communicate with each other fail.

Which of the following are possible solutions to Ralph's problem that will enable all of the hosts on the network to communicate with each other? (Choose all correct answers.)

A. Disable the Uplink toggle on one of the switches.
B. Replace the patch cable connecting the number 8 ports with a crossover cable.
C. Disable the Uplink toggle on both switches.
D. Move the patch cable on one of the switches from port number 8 to one of the other ports.
E. Move the patch cable on both switches from port number 8 to one of the other ports.

Practice Question 2

Alice is working as a consultant for a client with an outdated hub-based Ethernet network. She has recently replaced all of the network's hubs with switches and is generally pleased with the results. Monitoring the network traffic, she has noticed a marked reduction in the number of collisions, which was extremely high using hubs. However, although the number of collisions has gone down, the broadcast traffic on the network has increased alarmingly.

Alice realizes that the switches have created one huge broadcast domain, so she decides to create departmental VLANs to segment the network into several smaller broadcast domains. At first, Alice thought that she could dedicate a whole switch to each department, but that has turned out to be impossible. The VLANs will have to include members on different switches.

Which of the following will Alice need to implement the VLANs? (Choose all correct answers.)

A. Crossover cables
B. Trunking ports
C. Access ports
D. 802.1Q

Practice Question 1 Explanation

A. is correct because disabling the Uplink toggle on one switch will leave the connection with a single crossover circuit, which is the proper configuration.

B. is correct because the Uplink crossovers on the two switches are canceling each other out, and using a crossover cable will add the required crossover circuit to the connection.

C. is incorrect because disabling the Uplink toggle on both switches will remove all crossovers from the connection, preventing communication.

D. is correct because moving the patch cable on one switch will remove one of the two crossover circuits currently in the connection, leaving a single crossover, which is the proper configuration.

E. is incorrect because moving the patch cable on both switches will remove all of the crossover circuits currently in the connection, preventing communication.

Correct Answers: A, B, and D

Practice Question 2 Explanation

A. is incorrect because switches that support VLANs have uplink ports that eliminate the need for crossover cables.

B. is correct because the switches must exchange tagged traffic with each other through dedicated trunking ports.

C. is incorrect because all switch ports that are not trunking ports are access ports, and these provide no special function for VLANs.

D. is correct because the switches use IEEE 802.1Q tags to identify packets exchanged through the trunking ports.

Correct Answer: B and D

CHAPTER 12

Wireless Standards

Objective 2.4: Given a scenario, install and configure the appropriate wireless standards and technologies.

This chapter examines some of the fundamental wireless networking concepts in a typical enterprise network. The Network+ exam expects candidates to be familiar with these basic networking functions.

In this chapter, you'll learn everything you need to know about Network+ Objective 2.4, including the following topics:

▶ **802.11 standards**
▶ **Frequencies and range**
▶ **Channels**
▶ **Channel bonding**
▶ **Service set identifier (SSID)**
▶ **Antenna types**
▶ **Encryption standards**
▶ **Cellular technologies**
▶ **Multiple input, multiple output (MIMO) and multi-user MIMO (MU-MIMO)**

WIRELESS NETWORKING

Wireless networking has existed for decades, but the wireless local area networks (WLANs) that we now know as Wi-Fi were first standardized in 1997. Since then, wireless networking has become a critical part of business and residential computing. With the ever increasing use of smartphones and other mobile computing devices, WLANs provide network access to users without tethering them to the desktop.

A simple WLAN consists of one or more wireless access points (WAPs) and a group of client devices that connect to it. In a residential or small office setting, the WAP is usually incorporated into a multifunction device that also includes routing and other capabilities. In an enterprise environment, which often has multiple WAPs to service larger areas, the WAPs are typically connected to a wired Ethernet network. In that case, the WAPs function as bridges (not routers) between the wired and wireless segments.

802.11 Standards

The Institute of Electrical and Electronics Engineers (IEEE) *802.11* working group has released a series of wireless networking standards that represent the evolution of the underlying wireless technologies. Wireless networks have become faster and more reliable over the years, and the standards reflect the changes they have undergone.

The various 802.11 standards are identified by the letters following the working group number. There are also equivalent designations created by the Wi-Fi Alliance. The various standards released over the years have increasing transmission speeds, but they also vary in the frequencies they use and the number of MIMO streams they support. Table 12.1 lists the various standards and their specifications. The earlier standards, such as 802.11, 802.11a, and 802.11b, are rarely seen today.

T A B L E 1 2 . 1 Wireless LAN standards

IEEE standard	Wi-Fi Alliance designation	Supported frequencies (GHz)	MIMO streams	Maximum speed (Mbits/s)	Year ratified
802.11	Wi-Fi 0 (unofficial)	2.4	N/A	2	1997
802.11a	Wi-Fi 2 (unofficial)	5	N/A	54	1999
802.11b	Wi-Fi 1 (unofficial)	2.4	N/A	11	1999
802.11g	Wi-Fi 3 (unofficial)	2.4	N/A	54	2003

IEEE standard	Wi-Fi Alliance designation	Supported frequencies (GHz)	MIMO streams	Maximum speed (Mbits/s)	Year ratified
802.11n	Wi-Fi 4	2.4/5	4	600 (150 x 4)	2008
802.11ac	Wi-Fi 5	5	8	6933 (867 x 8)	2014
802.11ax	Wi-Fi 6	2.4/5	8	9608 (1201 x 8)	2019
802.11ax	Wi-Fi 6E	6	8	9608 (1201 x 8)	2020

Frequencies and Range

The earliest Wi-Fi networks all used the *2.4 GHz* frequency band, and many of them still do. The 2.4 GHz band actually consists of the 83 MHz between 2.4000 and 2.4835 GHz. The main problem with the 2.4 GHz band is the number of devices that use it. Apart from WLANs, there are also many Bluetooth devices, microwave ovens, and other appliances that use the same frequencies, which has led the band to become crowded with signals in some locations.

The *5 GHz* band is far less crowded that the 2.4 GHz band and has a wider range of available frequencies, so there is generally less interference to be found. However, lower frequencies like 2.4 GHz generally have better ranges than higher ones, such as 5 GHz. This is because the 2.4 GHz signals are less likely to be absorbed by walls and other surroundings than the 5 GHz signals. The more signal that is absorbed, the less that reaches the destination, so the effective range of the network connection is reduced. The speed of the connection is also affected by the distance between the devices. Longer distances mean lower transmission speeds.

The latest standard, a variation on 802.11ax called Wi-Fi 6E, uses the 6 GHz frequency band for the first time in wireless LANs.

Channels

Wi-Fi divides the frequency bands into *channels*, which are discrete frequency ranges that wireless devices use to communicate with the network. The 2.4 GHz band, for example, consists of 14 channels, each 22 MHz wide. The channels are offset by 5 MHz each, resulting in an overlapping array like that shown in Figure 12.1.

Countries make their own laws regarding the frequencies that private networks are permitted to use. For example, the 2.4 GHz band has 14 channels, but networks in North America only use the first 11, due to these *regulatory impacts*. Channel 14 is restricted, and while channels 12 and 13 are technically legal, Wi-Fi products in North America do not use them, to avoid getting too close to the forbidden frequencies. Networks in Japan are permitted use channel 14, but only for 802.11b networking.

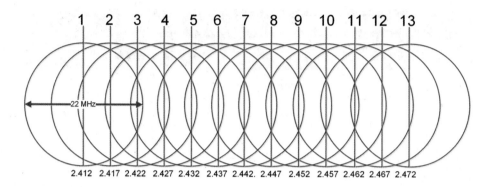

FIGURE 12.1 **22 MHz channels in the 2.4 GHz band**

Channel Overlap

Because the 2.4 GHz band is relatively narrow, there is a lot of overlap between channel frequencies. This can result in interference if there are two devices near each other using adjacent channels. In fact, to avoid interference from adjacent channels altogether on a 2.4 GHz network, only three channels are safe: 1, 6, and 11, as shown in Figure 12.2.

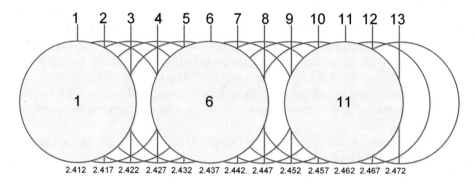

FIGURE 12.2 **Nonoverlapping 22 MHz channels in the 2.4 GHz band**

Many network administrators have made it a standard rule to use only these three channels on their networks, even though not every Wi-Fi technology uses the same channel spacing. For example, 802.11g networks use a type of radiofrequency modulation that creates 20 MHz channels instead of 22 MHz ones. Adjusting the overlap to account for the narrower bandwidths, the non-conflicting channels on an 802.11g network are 1, 5, 9, and 13, as shown in Figure 12.3.

In the 5 GHz band, there are many more channels, and overlap is not as much of a problem as in the 2.4 GHz band. The 802.11a standard was the first to use the 5 GHz band, and at the time, it was a high-priced alternative for networks that could not use 2.4 GHz.

Prices eventually came down, however, and beginning with the 802.11n standard, dual-frequency devices became common.

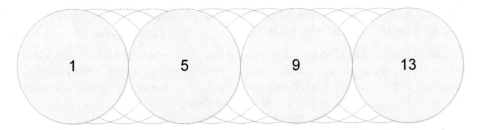

FIGURE 12.3   **Nonoverlapping 20 MHz channels on an 802.11g network**

Channel Bonding

Another new feature included in the 802.11n standard is *channel bonding*, which is the ability to combine the bandwidth of adjacent channels together to increase throughput. Two bonded channels provide 40 MHz of bandwidth, which is practical on a 5 GHz network, but not on a 2.4 GHz network, which would be monopolized by just one bonded channel.

In the subsequent 802.11ac and 802.11ax standards, the ability to bond channels is expanded, allowing multiple 20 MHz channels to be combined up to a 160 MHz maximum channel throughput. As the bonded channels get larger, however, they consume more of the available bandwidth, so the network supports fewer of them. For example, bonding eight channels creates a 160 MHz connection, but a 5 GHz network can only support two of these connections. The same network could support up to six 80 MHz or 12 40 MHz channels.

Service Set Identifiers

A *service set identifier (SSID)* is the name by which a WLAN is identified on the network. Wireless access points advertise their SSIDs by transmitting beacon announcements. When connecting to a wireless network, a device receives the beacon announcements and displays a list of SSIDs identifying all of the WLANs in the area. In addition to the SSID, access points have a 48-bit *basic service set identifier (BSSID)*. A network can have multiple access points servicing the same set of devices with a single SSID, but each WAP has a unique BSSID, which is how they tell each other apart.

SSIDs can be up to 32 bytes long and can also be configured with a null value to create what the 802.11 standards call a wildcard SSID. A *wildcard SSID*—sometimes called a no-broadcast SSID—is still operational but does not appear in the list of advertised WLANs. Some administrators use wildcard SSIDs as a security mechanism, figuring that intruders cannot attack a network if its SSID is not visible, but this is a technique that is only modestly effective.

Three operational modes for wireless networks are defined in the 802.11 standards:

Basic Service Set (BSS)   Also known as *infrastructure mode*, a group of wireless devices using the same type of modulation, frequency band, and security protocol, connected to a single access point. All wireless communication goes through the WAP, whether to connect to other wireless devices or to a bridged Ethernet network.

Extended Service Set (ESS)   A collection of two or more BSSs that function together as a single network servicing a common pool of wireless devices. All of the WAPs use the same SSID, and devices can *roam* from one WAP to another as needed without having to reconnect. While not required, many ESSs use a *wireless LAN controller (WLC)* to authenticate clients, coordinate roaming among WAPs, and prevent channel duplication.

Independent Basic Service Set (IBSS)   Also known as *ad hoc mode*, a point-to-point link between two wireless devices connected directly to each other without an intervening access point.

Encryption Standards

To prevent unauthorized users from accessing a wireless LAN, the devices use a security protocol that encrypts the traffic between the clients and the WAP. As is typical with security protocols, they evolve over time as attackers develop exploits for the existing security measures.

WPA

The first protocol developed for Wi-Fi, called *Wired Equivalent Privacy (WEP)*, was found to be vulnerable and was deprecated. To replace WEP, the Wi-Fi Alliance developed *Wi-Fi Protected Access (WPA)* in 2003. WPA uses 256-bit encryption keys, rather than the smaller keys that contributed to the vulnerability of WEP. WPA also introduced the *Temporal Key Integrity Protocol (TKIP)*, which uses the same underlying cipher as WEP (called RC4) but adds a message integrity check (MIC) and other security features, in addition to the larger keys.

WPA2

The similarities in design between WEP and WPA were deliberate so that existing hardware devices with WEP could be upgraded to WPA with just a firmware update. However, the initial version of WPA was also found to be exploitable and was deprecated in 2006 in favor of *Wi-Fi Protected Access 2 (WPA2)*, also known as *802.11i*, which is the wireless encryption protocol still in common use today.

WPA2 continues to support TKIP, for backward compatibility purposes, but the WPA2 standards require that implementations include more advanced algorithms, including *Counter Mode with Cipher Block Chaining Message Authentication Code Protocol (CCMP)* for integrity checking, which is part of the *Advanced Encryption Standard (AES)* that WPA2 uses for data encryption. This combination is sometimes notated as *CCMP-AES*.

WPA and WPA2 both have two operational modes:

▶ *WPA2 Personal*—Also known as WPA2-PSK or Pre-Shared Key, this mode requires client devices to supply a 32-byte alphanumeric key previously specified on the access point. All devices use the same pre-shared key for both encryption and decryption of data, which makes the protocol vulnerable to brute-force attacks.

▶ *WPA2 Enterprise*—Also known as WPA2-802.1X, this mode requires a *Remote Authentication Dial-In User Service (RADIUS)* server on the network to authenticate users with the *802.1X* protocol prior to granting them access to the wireless network. Although a more complicated deployment, this option provides much greater security than a pre-shared key.

As the names imply, WPA2 Personal is best suited for residential sites or small offices in which the users can be trusted not to share the pre-shared key with unauthorized personnel. On a larger network with many users, the chances of a pre-shared key being compromised are much greater. When it does happen, changing the key requires that all of the access points and client devices be reconfigured with the new key value, which can be a highly time- and labor-intensive task.

WPA2 Enterprise not only eliminates the need for a single pre-shared key; it also provides centralized authentication, authorization, and accounting (AAA) for individual network users. Clients connecting to the network must supply their individual credentials before they can access wireless resources on the network. Because it requires an external RADIUS server, WPA2 Enterprise is considerably more complicated and expensive to deploy than WPA2 Personal, but on larger networks, it is much more secure. Although they didn't exist when the WPA2 standard was designed, cloud-based RADIUS servers are now available that can make the WPA2 Enterprise deployment process simpler and less expensive.

EXAM TIP

There is no standardized set of security options for access points and wireless client devices, since their configuration interfaces vary. Some products just use the term WPA2 Personal, for example, but others use PSK and might also specify the encryption cipher, as in *WPA2-PSK (AES)*. Candidates for the Network+ exam should be aware of the various components used in the Wi-Fi security protocols and the names used to refer to them.

Antennas

WLAN devices all have transceivers to transmit and receive radio signals, but for those processes to function efficiently, the devices must have antennas. The *antenna* on (or inside) a wireless device transmits electromagnetic signals that it receives from the internal transceiver as electrical signals. To receive data, the antenna works in reverse by capturing the EM signals and converting them back into electrical signals. In most cases, access points have swiveling antennas built into the unit, as do some network interface adapter cards. These antennas can typically be detached from the device and replaced with a different model.

Many devices, especially mobile ones, have internal antennas that are not accessible from the outside of the case. It might be possible to replace the internal antenna on these devices, but it will not be a simple matter and will almost certainly void the warranty.

Most wireless users never think about the antenna; they just use the one supplied with the device. However, in large network environments, administrators might replace an access point's antenna, either to provide the WAP with additional range or to regulate the operational area of the access point.

Antenna Types

There are several types of external antennas available, including the following.

▶ *Omni*—An omni (or omnidirectional) antenna radiates in a spherical pattern with roughly the same signal strength in every direction. Many omni antennas are designed to be used on one floor of a building, so their vertical radiation is not as strong or precisely spherical as the horizontal,

▶ *Directional*—A directional (or unidirectional) antenna radiates in one general direction, providing better range than an omni antenna of the same power and making the antenna suitable for point-to-point links between two devices. There are various types of directional antennas, such as *panel*, *patch*, and *Yagi*, which differ in the width of the operational area. Some highly focused directional antennas are designed for point-to-point links, such as those connecting two buildings. Others have a wider radiation pattern, such as those designed to be placed indoors near an outer wall and pointing inward. This provides network access to the internal users while helping to prevent unauthorized users outside the building from accessing the network.

MIMO

Beginning with the 802.11n standard, Wi-Fi has supported the use of multiple antennas on a single device with a technology called *multiple input, multiple output (MIMO)*. The MIMO support in a particular hardware product is notated by specifying the number of antennas at the access point and the client, in the form 2×2, 3×3, and so on up to 8×8. Devices supporting four or eight antennas are relatively rare; devices with two or three antennas are more common.

MIMO is a technique in which both the access point and the client have multiple antennas transmitting the same signal. The devices use a technique called *multipath signal propagation* that takes advantage of reflective surfaces in the environment to bounce signals—called *spatial streams*—to the destination using multiple paths. The receiving device compares the arriving signals and uses them to enhance the strength and reliability of the transmission.

The MIMO technology has advanced in subsequent wireless standards, as follows:

- ▶ 802.11n—MIMO
- ▶ 802.11ac—*Multi-user MIMO (MU-MIMO)* (downstream only)
- ▶ 802.11ax—Multi-user MIMO (MU-MIMO) (bidirectional)

Multi-user MIMO in 802.11ac builds on the technology by enabling access points to transmit spatial streams to multiple users simultaneously. The 802.11ax standard enhances the technology further by making it bidirectional, enabling both client devices and WAPs to transmit spatial streams to multiple users. With the introduction of MU-MIMO, the original MIMO implementation is sometimes referred to as single-user MIMO (SU-MIMO).

CELLULAR TECHNOLOGIES

The other main type of wireless network in use today is the *cellular* networks that provide voice, text, and data services to millions of users. Unlike WANs, the infrastructure of a cellular network is owned by third-party service providers, so there are no access points for consumers or IT personnel to locate and configure. This saves on time and expense, but it also means that the back end of the cellular network is out of the consumer's control.

As with WLAN technology, cellular networking is based on standards that have evolved over the years to increase the speed and reliability of wireless devices. The most common terms used to reference cellular technologies are the generational indicators, such as 2G, *3G*, *4G*, and now *5G*. However, while there are certain standards that networks branded with these designations have to meet, they are more marketing names than official standards. Providers use different underlying technologies to implement the generations of their products. Some of those underlying technologies are as follows:

Global System for Mobile Communications (GSM)　Developed by the European Telecommunication Standards Institute (ETSI), GSM was developed for use on the 2G networks that replaced the original analog 1G networks. Used at first strictly for voice telephony, the standard was later enhanced to include data, using protocols such as *Enhanced Data Rates for GSM Evolution (EDGE)*.

Code-Division Multiple Access (CDMA)　Developed as a competitor to GSM, CDMA became the dominant 3G technology in the US, while Europe and Japan used the *Universal Mobile Telecommunications System (UMTS)* for their 3G networks. CDMA is not compatible with GSM hardware.

Long-Term Evolution (LTE)　Developed by the 3rd Generation Partnership Project (3GPP) and based on earlier GSM and EDGE technologies, LTE is one of the dominant 4G technologies on wireless networks around the globe. LTE is a viable upgrade path for both GSM and CDMA.

5G NR (New Radio)　Developed by the 3GPP to be the standard for 5G networks, NR can operate in a non-stand-alone mode that uses an existing 4G LTE network for its control plane, simplifying its initial deployment. Stand-alone mode uses NR for both the control and user planes.

All of these technologies have themselves undergone multiple revisions to increase their transmission speeds and make other improvements. Individual implementations vary widely in the speeds they profess to achieve, but their actual realized performance often fails to meet expectations.

CERTMIKE EXAM ESSENTIALS

▶ Wi-Fi networking is based on a series of standards developed by the IEEE 802.11 working group. The standards call for the use of the 2.4 GHz, 5 GHz, and now the 6 GHz frequency band.

▶ Wi-Fi infrastructure mode requires a wireless access point, which can bridge the wireless devices to a wired Ethernet network. Ad hoc mode is a direct connection between two wireless devices without an access point.

▶ The Wi-Fi frequency bands are split into channels, which prevent interference between devices. The standards beginning with 802.11n support channel bonding, which combines channels to increase available bandwidth.

▶ Cellular-based wireless networking is based on the technologies chosen by individual service providers, such as GSW, CDMA, LTE, and NR. The development of cellular technologies is represented by the generational designations 2G, 3G, 4G, and 5G.

Practice Question 1

Alice is configuring security for a new wireless LAN she has installed for a client that already has a large, cabled network. The cabled network has a RADIUS server installed, which already has accounts for the users of the wireless network. Which of the following security options should Alice select for the access point and the wireless client devices that will provide the best possible security for the WLAN?

A. WEP
B. WPA-PSK
C. WPA-802.1X
D. WPA2-Personal
E. WPA2-Enterprise

Practice Question 2

Ralph is consulting for a new client that is running an 802.11b/g wireless LAN in a busy office complex. The client is having problems with wireless device users losing their connections or connecting only at slow speeds. Ralph scans the 2.4 GHz frequency band and sees dozens of other networks spread across all of the available channels. Choose two tasks from the following options that will enable Ralph to resolve the client's problem and improve the performance of the wireless network.

A. Configure the access point to suppress SSID broadcasts.
B. Configure the wireless devices to use the 5 GHz band.
C. Configure all of the network devices to use WPA2 encryption with AES.
D. Upgrade all of the network devices to the latest firmware.

Practice Question 1 Explanation

A. is incorrect because Wired Equivalency Protocol (WEP) was an early wireless encryption protocol that was found to be vulnerable and deprecated.

B. is incorrect because the first version of the Wi-Fi Protected Access (WPA) protocol has been deprecated in favor of WPA2 and because the pre-shared key version of the protocol is intended for smaller networks and is less secure than the Enterprise version.

C. is incorrect because although the 802.1X option calls for a RADIUS server, the first version of the Wi-Fi Protected Access (WPA) protocol has been deprecated in favor of WPA2.

D. is incorrect because the Personal version of the WPA2 protocol uses a pre-shared key, which is less secure than the Enterprise version.

E. is correct because WPA2 is the most secure of the protocols listed, and the Enterprise variant calls for the use of a RADIUS server for user authentication, authorization, and accounting.

Correct Answer: E

Practice Question 2 Explanation

A. is incorrect because suppressing the SSID broadcasts will do nothing to improve the network's connectivity.

B. is correct because the 5 GHz band is less populated than the 2.4 GHz band and provides many more channels to choose from.

C. is incorrect because changing the encryption protocol the network uses will not improve the network's connectivity.

D. is incorrect because the network problems are being caused by interference from other networks, and upgrading the firmware on the wireless devices will not affect that interference.

Correct Answer: B

PART III

Domain 3.0: Network Operations

Chapter 13 Network Availability
Chapter 14 Organizational Documents and Policies
Chapter 15 High Availability and Disaster Recovery

Network Operations is the third domain of CompTIA's Network+ exam. In this domain, you'll learn about the ways that networking professionals maintain high availability networks, create organizational documents and policies, and undertake disaster recovery efforts. This domain has three objectives:

3.1 Given a scenario, use the appropriate statistics and sensors to ensure network availability.

3.2 Explain the purpose of organizational documents and policies.

3.3 Explain high availability and disaster recovery concepts and summarize which is the best solution.

Questions from this domain make up 16% of the questions on the Network+ exam, so you should expect to see approximately 14 questions on your test covering the material in this part.

CHAPTER 13

Network Availability

Objective 3.1: Given a scenario, use the appropriate statistics and sensors to ensure network availability.

This chapter examines some of the fundamental network statistics and sensors found in a typical enterprise network. The Network+ exam expects candidates to be familiar with these basic networking functions.

In this chapter, you'll learn everything you need to know about Network+ Objective 3.1, including the following topics:

- ▶ Performance metrics/sensors
- ▶ SNMP
- ▶ Network device logs
- ▶ Interface statistics/status
- ▶ Interface errors or alerts
- ▶ Environmental factors and sensors
- ▶ Baselines
- ▶ NetFlow data
- ▶ Uptime/downtime

PERFORMANCE METRICS

Users can frequently detect variations in the performance of a device or a network, but these are just subjective impressions, not objective studies. To track the performance of a device, you must quantify its activity by observing the changing values of certain hardware components and system processes. These values are called *performance metrics*.

There are many different tools for measuring performance metrics, some of which are software built into the device's operating system, whereas others are third-party software or hardware products. This section describes some of the most important performance metrics for network devices and for the network itself.

Device Metrics

Individual network devices all have performance metrics, but they differ both in what metrics they can measure and in the importance of each metric to the overall performance of the device. For example, servers, like all computers, have many components that administrators should monitor on a regular basis. Servers are among the most important devices to monitor because many users depend on them. However, workstations need monitoring as well, as do other network devices, such as switches and routers.

Some of the most critical performance metrics are described next.

Temperature

Most electronic devices generate heat and also have some means of dissipating it. Excessive heat can shorten the life of a device, cause it to shut down, or in extreme cases physically damage the components.

Chief among the computer components that generate heat is the central processing unit (CPU). Fans and vents keep air circulating to dissipate heat, and there are typically sensors in the computer that monitor the temperature and can take action by shutting down the system if it gets too hot. In addition, tools such as the Simple Network Management Protocol (SNMP) can access the data generated by the temperature sensors, enabling administrators to monitor the system and detect a potential problem before it occurs.

Computers are not the only devices that can overheat. Switches and routers have CPUs and other heat-generating components as well. Monitoring temperatures throughout the data center is an important part of keeping the network running smoothly.

CPU Usage

The *central processing unit (CPU)* utilization metric for a computer or other network device indicates how hard the device is working. The more applications and services running on a server, for example, the higher its CPU utilization figures will be. CPU utilization is typically expressed as a percentage of the processor's maximum capacity. The higher the metric value, the more heat the processor is generating.

On a large network with many servers, it is a good idea for administrators to monitor the CPU utilization metric on all of them and try to keep them balanced. If the CPU utilization on one specific server frequently runs high, though, administrators might consider taking action in one of two ways:

▶ Add more processing power to the server with more or better CPUs.
▶ Migrate some applications or services to other servers.

Switches and routers have CPUs also, and high utilization values can be one indicator of high traffic levels, along with network metrics such as latency.

Memory

Memory utilization can be another indicator that a device is working too hard and might be suffering a reduction in performance. Computers and other network devices might have several types of memory in them, but *random access memory (RAM)* is the one that is dependent on the applications the device is running. Some operating systems, when they start to run low on RAM, begin swapping some of the memory contents out to disk. Since disk storage access times are far slower than RAM access times (milliseconds versus nanoseconds), swapping memory to disk can cause high RAM utilization values that are typically accompanied by increased values of CPU and storage metrics. When this problem occurs, administrators can address it in one of two ways:

▶ Reduce the system's application load
▶ Add more RAM to the system

Network Metrics

In addition to monitoring the metrics for the components of individual devices, it is important to monitor the performance of the network itself.

Bandwidth

The most essential network performance metric to monitor is its *bandwidth*. There are two bandwidth metrics to consider:

Available Bandwidth   The amount of bandwidth that the network is capable of providing

Bandwidth Utilization   The amount of bandwidth that is actually being utilized at a given time, also known as the network's *throughput*.

The available bandwidth, essentially the speed of a network connection, is usually measured in megabits or gigabits per second (Mbps or Gbps). This is the transmission speed that the network hardware—cables, switches, routers, and network adapters—is designed to provide.

Depending on the tool being used, the bandwidth utilization metric can be notated as a percentage of the available bandwidth or as a raw Mbps or Gbps figure. Bandwidth utilization values can differ depending on where the measurement is taken, the time of day it is taken, and how the network is being used at the time.

When bandwidth utilization values are high, it can indicate a temporary traffic condition, but when they are consistently high, the connection might be overloaded with traffic. When this occurs, administrators can take any of the following actions:

- ▶ Increase the available bandwidth by upgrading the network hardware.
- ▶ Move servers or other devices to a less-trafficked network segment.
- ▶ Move applications or services that generate large amounts of traffic to servers on another network segment.

EXAM TIP

The abbreviations Mb and Gb, with a lowercase b, stand for megabits and giga-bits, which are typically used to measure network speeds. MB and GB, with a capital B, stand for megabytes and gigabytes, which are used to measure storage transfer rates. Network+ exam candidates should be aware of the differences in the abbreviations and how they are used.

Latency

Latency is the delay that is incurred between the transmission of a packet and its receipt at the destination. Typically measured in milliseconds, latency and its value as a metric vary depending on the location of the destination being measured. There are many reasons why packets can be delayed, including excessive traffic on the network, an overloaded switch, a malfunctioning network adapter, or any number of other causes.

The effect of latency is different depending on the type of traffic on the network. A brief delay in accessing a file from a server is not a big problem, but for real-time protocols such as VoIP or iSCSI, even a slight amount of additional latency can affect the quality of a voice call or data transfer.

Jitter

The latency of a network is usually a relatively stable condition. Metric values can vary over time, but they tend to remain consistent from second to second. If they don't, and there are different latency measurements for successive packets transmitted to the same destination, this is called *jitter*.

The value of the jitter metric is a calculation of the difference between latency values for successive packets, usually expressed in milliseconds.

Networks can tolerate latency far better than they can tolerate jitter. In particular, jitter can interfere with real-time data transmissions such as those for VoIP.

SNMP

There are many tools that can monitor performance metrics. Operating systems typically have some means of gathering metric values, such as the Windows Performance Monitor, for example, but one of the oldest and most comprehensive network-based tools of this kind is the *Simple Network Monitoring Protocol (SNMP)*. SNMP is a centralized monitoring tool that can gather information from devices all over the network—including servers, workstations, switches, routers, and printers—and display it to administrators on a central management console.

SNMP consists of three basic components, as follows:

SNMP Agents   Software components that run on a managed network device and gather data they will send to the NMS (see next item). Some agents are built into devices such as switches and routers, whereas others have to be installed by users.

Network Management System (NMS)   The NMS is the central console that receives all the information from the SNMP agents.

Management Information Base (MIB)   An MIB is a database of components on a managed device called *object identifiers (OIDs)*, which are capable of supplying performance metrics and other information to the NMS. The OIDs store information about the components as variables. The NMS can modify variables in the OIDs to remotely reconfigure the managed device.

SNMP agents communicate with the NMS using various message types, including Get-Request messages that an NMS sends to an agent, requesting the values of specific OID variables; SetRequest messages that supply revised values for specific OID variables; and *traps*, unsolicited messages sent by an agent to the NMS containing information about an important event.

NETWORK DEVICE LOGS

Most network devices generate logs of their activity, and in some cases many different types of logs. Monitoring logs is an important part of maintaining a network. Some of the log types are described in this section.

Traffic Logs

Many devices can maintain *traffic logs* of their experiences, and in some cases, administrators can specify exactly what traffic should be logged. For example, a firewall can handle a great deal of traffic, and the vast majority of log entries will probably be for traffic that is successfully admitted through the firewall. However, it is also possible, in the case of some firewalls, to adjust the *logging levels* to retain only the exceptions—that is, the packets that are blocked by the firewall because they do not conform to its rules.

Audit Logs

Auditing is a feature provided in many operating systems and network devices that allows administrators to specify what information should be captured to the device's *audit logs*. Auditing generally provides administrators with more granularity in what components to monitor and what activities to log. For example, an administrator can opt to audit user logins to a server. Selecting all of the logins will produce a lot of log entries, including many successful logins. Administrators might have reason to monitor all of the logins, but it is also possible to select just the failed logins to let administrators know when someone attempts a brute-force password attack.

Auditing can also be centralized on the network. One way to do this is to use an authentication, authorization, and accounting (AAA) server such as Remote Authentication Dial-In User Service (RADIUS).

Syslog

One of the problems with monitoring logs is that devices typically store their logs locally, and the prospect of examining the logs on every network device individually can be daunting to administrators. *Syslog* is a mechanism for sending log entries from a network device to a central syslog server, where they are added to a single log covering all of the devices in one place.

Syslog consists of the following elements:

> ▶ A central syslog server
> ▶ Client applications on the individual network devices
> ▶ A syslog message format

Syslog messages, in addition to the actual log information generated by the device, include a timestamp to indicate when the event occurred. Though not required by the standard, many network devices include a Facility code that identifies the type of message and a Severity code that indicates the nature of the event stimulating the log entry. The *Severity level* codes used in syslog messages are shown in Table 13.1.

T A B L E 1 3 . 1 Syslog severity values

Code	Severity	Keyword	Description
0	Emergency	emer	System is unusable
1	Alert	alert	Action must be taken immediately
2	Critical	crit	Critical conditions
3	Error	err	Error conditions
4	Warning	warning	Warning conditions
5	Notice	notice	Normal but significant condition
6	Informational	info	Informational messages
7	Debug	debug	Debug-level messages

Log Reviews

Log reviews are an important part of monitoring network and device performance. How-ever, the biggest problem with reviewing logs is the sheer amount of data they often contain. For example, the logs maintained by a web server typically have entries for every user that connects to it. A busy website might handle thousands or even millions of hits each day, resulting in massive logs that administrators cannot easily read and interpret manually. Instead, most use tools that read and interpret the log files for them, so they can concentrate on the most important data.

INTERFACE ERRORS OR ALERTS

Operating systems maintain statistics for every network interface adapter, speci-fying elements such as how many bytes and packets it has transmitted and received. The means of accessing this information differs depending on the device, but in many cases, there are command-line utilities that display interface information, such as the Get-NetAdapterStatistics cmdlet in Windows PowerShell or the ifstat command in Linux.

NetFlow is a proprietary tool that administrators can use to gather statistical data about the IP traffic that routers and switches send and receive through each of their ports. Routers and switches periodically send the *NetFlow data* they gather to a central server. That server, called a *NetFlow collector*, collates the data from all the devices into a single timestamped log so that administrators can visualize the network as a whole and locate bottlenecks and other problems.

Some of the most important statistics are as follows:

Link State (Up/Down)   Specifies whether the interface is physically connected to the network. A down state could be the result of an issue with the interface itself, a configu-ration setting on the device, a hardware problem with the network medium, or a problem with the device at the other end of the connection.

Speed/Duplex   Specifies the connection's available bandwidth and whether it is func-tioning in full-duplex or half-duplex mode. Mismatched duplex settings at either end of a connection prevents the device from accessing the network.

Send/Receive Traffic   Specifies the number of packets and/or bytes that the interface has transmitted and received, as shown in the following excerpt from the Windows Get-NetAdapterStatistics output:

```
SentBroadcastBytes        : 2183533
SentBroadcastPackets      : 43528
SentBytes                 : 9726451193
SentMulticastBytes        : 21784625
SentMulticastPackets      : 91080
SentUnicastBytes          : 9702483035
SentUnicastPackets        : 37057942
```

Cyclic Redundancy Checks (CRCs)   Specifies the number of packets that have failed the interface's data link layer checksum test.

Protocol Packet and Byte Counts   Break down by protocols the number of bytes and/or packets that the interface has transmitted and received.

Interfaces can also track the number of packet errors that occur, generating statistics like the following:

CRC Errors   Indicate that packets are arriving through the interface in a damaged state. Regularly incrementing values could indicate a problem with the device's interface, the network medium, or the device at the other end of the connection.

Giants   Frames received by the interface that are larger than the network's maximum transmission unit (MTU) size, which on Ethernet networks is 1500.

Runts   Frames received by the interface that are smaller than 64 bytes. Giants and runts can be the result of collisions on a half-duplex network or a malfunctioning network adapter.

Encapsulation Errors   Indicate that the data link layer encapsulation process is not occurring properly. One common cause is plugging a host into a switch port that has been configured as a trunk port. The switch is expecting 802.1X frame headers but is receiving standard 802.3 headers.

ENVIRONMENTAL SENSORS

As noted earlier, high temperatures are bad for computers and other electronics. Network devices can overheat because of internal problems, certainly, but one of the other possible causes of overheating is external: the temperature and other environmental factors in the room where the devices are located.

Large networks typically have their sensitive equipment located in a data center, and most data centers have environmental systems that maintain appropriate *temperature* and *humidity* levels. Data centers are also often equipped with sensory equipment that not only monitors the climatic conditions, but also detects smoke, fire, *flood*, and other environmental disasters. Other sensors can monitor the data center's *electrical* power supply, checking for surges, sags, and other fluctuations. Any of these conditions, when their levels fall outside of a safe range, can negatively affect the performance of the network and even damage the hardware.

BASELINES

All of the metrics that indicate the performance level of a network fluctuate over time. Most of the actual metric values are meaningful only in relation to their previous values.

A specified number of collisions or CRC errors, for example, are only cause for alarm if the values increase over time.

To maintain records of a network's performance, administrators typically take baseline readings of important metrics. A *baseline* is a reading of metric levels under normal operational conditions, taken with the same tools that administrators will use to monitor the levels in the future. One common practice is to take readings both during a normal business day and during off hours, when the business is not operating. This provides a comparison indicating how certain metrics increase when the network is actively in use. With the baselines in place, administrators can continue to monitor the network's metrics and, comparing them with the baselines, determine if the network's performance levels are changing over time.

UPTIME/DOWNTIME

A network's *uptime/downtime* figure indicates the total amount of time that a particular network service is online and accepting requests from clients. The statistic is usually expressed as a percentage of a particular time period. Uptime/downtime figures are frequently specified in the contracts that clients sign with service providers. For example, the provider and the client might agree that the service must be available to the client 99.99 percent of the time, colloquially called a "four nines" contract, or a penalty applies. Both parties to an agreement like this should monitor the uptime/downtime of the service independently. SNMP is capable of doing this, as are many other tools.

CERTMIKE EXAM ESSENTIALS

▶ Performance metrics are statistics that enable administrators to objectively monitor the ongoing operations of networked devices and of the network itself. Metrics for computers include CPU usage and memory consumption, whereas network metrics include the available bandwidth and bandwidth utilization.

▶ Logs are an excellent resource that administrators should monitor regularly. Auditing enables administrators to select the precise information to gather about a particular resource. Many tools are available for filtering and interpreting voluminous log files.

▶ Network interfaces maintain statistics about their configuration settings and the amounts and types of traffic they send and receive. Operating systems typically have some means of displaying this information, often a command-line utility.

Question 1

It's Ralph's first day in the IT department, and his supervisor asks him to check the memory and CPU utilization on all the servers in the data center and compare the values with the baselines stored on the department server. Ralph knows how to check the statistics on the servers but isn't quite sure what a baseline is supposed to be, so he does some research. Which of the following is the best description of a baseline?

A. A record of performance metric values captured under a simulated workload

B. A record of performance metric values captured before the system is deployed in a production environment

C. An estimation of expected performance metric values, based on manufacturers' specifications

D. A record of performance metric values captured under an actual workload

Practice Question 2

As the newest employee in the IT department, Ralph is pulling the night call duty. At 2:45 a.m., Ralph receives the first of several texts from automated systems on his company network. One said it was a trap, which Ralph assumed was some kind of spam, and another was an error message with a syslog severity of 0, so Ralph went back to sleep. The next day, Ralph was in big trouble. The company's e-commerce servers had been offline from 2:45 a.m. until the day shift arrived at 8:00. The logs said that Ralph had been notified. Why hadn't he done something about it?

Ralph was forced to admit that he wasn't familiar with syslog severity codes and didn't know what a trap was. Which of the following describe what Ralph should have known? (Choose all correct answers.)

A. Syslog severity levels range from 0 to 7, with 0 the most severe, indicating that a serious situation had occurred.

B. Syslog severity levels range from 0 to 7, with 0 the least severe, but still indicating that an error has occurred.

C. A trap is a type of error message generated by syslog when a severe error occurs.

D. A trap is a type of SNMP notification generated by an agent when an important event occurs.

Practice Question 1 Explanation

A. is incorrect because a comparison of the servers' current levels with those saved under a simulated work-load would provide no definitive proof of a problem.

B. is incorrect because a comparison of the servers' current levels with those saved in a different operational environment would provide no definitive proof of a problem.

C. is incorrect because a comparison of the servers' current levels with those specified by the manufacturer would provide no definitive proof of a problem.

D. is correct because a baseline performance level must be taken when the system is operating under real-world conditions.

Correct Answer: D

Practice Question 2 Explanation

A. is correct because syslog severity level 0 indicates an emergency situation in which a system was unusable.

B. is incorrect because syslog security level 0 is not the least severe, but rather the most.

C. is incorrect because a trap is an SNMP message, not a syslog message.

D. is correct because a trap is an unsolicited notification message sent by an SNMP agent to its NMS.

Correct Answers: A and D

CHAPTER 14

Organizational Documents and Policies

Objective 3.2: Explain the purpose of organizational documents and policies.

This chapter examines some of the documentation procedures for a typical enterprise network. The Network+ exam expects candidates to be familiar with these basic networking concepts.

In this chapter, you'll learn everything you need to know about Network+ Objective 3.2, including the following topics:

▶ Plans and procedures
▶ Hardening and security policies
▶ Common documentation
▶ Common agreements

PLANS AND PROCEDURES

While small businesses often go without IT plans and procedures and documentation, preferring to deal with issues as they arise, larger businesses need them for the network and its services to run smoothly. *Plans* are an early part of the process, one step beyond brainstorming. After appropriate discussion and consideration, plans become *policies*, documented rules that everyone must observe. Once policies are in place, it is common for organizations to develop *procedures* for implementing and enforcing them.

This section describes some of the most commonly used plans and procedures for enterprise networks.

Change Management

Change is inevitable in the IT business. Hardware and software need to be upgraded, network devices need configuration changes, departments might expand or contract, and personnel might enter or leave the company. Before IT personnel make any of the changes associated with these events, it is a good idea to assess their potential ramifications and present a proposal for the changes to a designated *change management* committee. This committee, typically composed of people from various departments and disciplines, evaluates change proposals from different perspectives and rules on whether they should be implemented.

The proposal for a change might include the following elements:

Proposed Change   Describes in detail the changes that are to be made if the proposal is approved

Reasons for Change   Specifies why the proposed changes are necessary and how they will benefit the company

Change Procedures   Specifies how the changes will be implemented, including step-by-step procedures

Rollback Procedures   Specifies a plan for returning the network to its previous state if the proposed changes yield negative results

Personnel Required   Specifies who will be needed to implement the proposed changes and when

Maintenance Schedule   Specifies the time frame for the proposed changes and how long the implementation will take

Proposed Downtime   Specifies whether the proposed changes require an interruption of network services, and if so, how long an interruption and at what time of day

Required Notifications   Specifies who should be notified of events regarding the proposed changes, including the steps of the approval process and those of the actual change procedure

Approval Process   Specifies the steps of the approval process and lists the personnel who must approve the proposed changes

Documentation   Specifies in detail everything about the change proposal process, and after the proposal is approved, documents the tasks involved in implementing the changes

EXAM TIP

While this discussion emphasizes change management in the IT department, in many organizations the change management infrastructure spans the entire firm, evaluating changes in personnel, finance, and the organizational structure of the company, as well as computer and network hardware and software. Candidates for the Network+ exam should be aware that change management is not limited to the IT department.

Incident Response Plan

The Network+ objectives cover three types of *contingency plans*: incident response, disaster recovery, and business continuity. The three plans differ primarily in the severity of the incident that triggers them. An *incident* is any event that interferes with the smooth operation of the company's business. Incidents can be anything from an Internet-based attack on the computer network to a catastrophic weather event that endangers not only the network but the company's employees as well.

An *incident response plan* includes the policies and procedures that IT personnel should follow when an incident of a specific type occurs. When an attack occurs from outside the network, for example, the incident response plan should include the procedures for protecting the network and its data, including diagnosing and remediating the attack, while preserving any evidence that might be needed to identify the attackers, prosecute them, and prevent the same type of attack from happening again.

Disaster Recovery Plan

Most of the incidents accounted for in the incident response plan are relatively minor, internal matters, but incidents that are extreme enough to be considered a disaster are handled differently. A disaster is an event that causes significant damage to the network infrastructure that prevents the business from functioning. Disasters typically fall into three categories: catastrophic equipment failures, natural disasters, and user error.

A *disaster recovery plan* has the goal of getting the network back to a functional state so that business can continue. One aspect of the plan deals with replacing any hardware that was damaged in the disaster. An organization can maintain a store of redundant equipment for this purpose or have standing orders with vendors that they can fill quickly. The other, most crucial, aspect of a disaster recovery plan is protecting and restoring the company data to operational status.

Protecting the company data from disaster requires planning and procedures before any disaster occurs, in the form of offsite network backups that are available to the disaster recovery team immediately after the incident. In addition to the application data that the network's users will need, backups suitable for disaster recovery should include the configuration data and system state for all of the network devices affected. This additional data enables the disaster recovery team to restore the network infrastructure more quickly because they do not have to re-create the device configurations manually. Finally, the document should include detailed procedures specifying the duties of each member of the disaster recovery team when an incident occurs.

Business Continuity Plan

While a disaster recovery plan is designed to get the network back up and running at the site of the event, there are some disasters for which this is not possible. If the network infrastructure is largely or completely destroyed by a major catastrophe, such as a hurricane or other natural disaster, a *business continuity plan* describes the contingencies for restoring the network to functionality at a remote site.

Like disaster recovery, business continuity requires considerable planning and preparation before any damage occurs. Depending on the size of the organization, its budget, and how vital it is to get the business back into operation as soon as possible, a business continuity plan might range from procedures for rebuilding the network elsewhere to fully operational redundant data centers located in other cities. The plan should also include instructions for the succession of personnel, specifying who is going to do what job in the remote location and who should take over if someone should be unavailable.

For more information on disaster recovery and high availability concepts, see Chapter 15, "High Availability and Disaster Recovery."

System Life Cycle

As years pass, computer and network equipment ages, depreciates, and obsolesces and must eventually be replaced. Each type of device has its own *system life cycle*, and in a well-run enterprise network, those life cycles are carefully planned and documented.

A typical system life cycle consists of the following phases:

Evaluation and Purchasing   Before purchase, IT personnel typically evaluate devices by comparing specifications, physical examination, and in some cases, a period of in-house testing. The purchasing process might include negotiation with vendors that involves executive or financial personnel from other departments.

Acquisition and Deployment   After purchase, all new devices must be inspected and registered as an asset of the company, both on paper and by the use of serialized asset identification devices. Devices are prepared for deployment by the installation and configuration of operating systems, applications, and other software, either manually or by an automated process.

Maintenance and Upgrading   Once deployed, all devices need monitoring to some degree, and many also require regular software or firmware updates. Maintenance processes can be the responsibility of the end users or the IT department.

Decommissioning and Retirement   As a device nears the end of its life, its replacement should already be somewhere in the first phase of its life cycle. Decommissioning must include the permanent erasure of all licensed software and data. Retirement can consist of reassignment to another less critical task, resale outside the company, or responsible disposal of the device.

Standard Operating Procedures

In a well-organized IT operation, personnel perform tasks according to *standard operating procedures (SOPs)* that should be carefully documented and maintained. This makes it possible for anyone in the department to complete a particular task using consistent and approved company procedures.

While SOPs might be conceived and created at various times by people in various departments and locations, the resulting documents should be gathered into a single manual that can function as a centralized resource for the entire department.

HARDENING AND SECURITY POLICIES

Network administrators must consider a great many security issues when designing, implementing, and maintaining an enterprise network. The Network+ exam objectives devote an entire objective domain to security issues, but this section concerns the policies that many organizations use to document their security procedures.

Some of these policies are as follows:

Password Policy   Specifies the administrative requirements for user passwords, such as minimum length, complexity, reuse limitations, and frequency of change. Other, less tangible policies might include restrictions on choosing appropriate passwords, sharing passwords, and writing passwords down in obvious places. In addition to documentation of such policies, many operating systems and applications can enforce them by requiring users to comply with established policies.

Acceptable Use Policy (AUP)   Specifies the approved and disapproved uses for the company's network equipment and services, including hours of use, personal use restrictions, and forbidden practices. For example, the AUP for email might specify how the firm has the right to read and retain all email content created using the company's domain name and how users are not permitted to use the company email for illegal purposes. The creation of this policy will likely require input from the organization's Legal and Human Resources departments.

Bring Your Own Device (BYOD) Policy   The increasing mobility of network users and the use of employees' personal smartphones and other devices for business purposes has led to the establishment of policies regarding the types of devices that employees are permitted to use on the company network, how they are permitted to use them, and the security settings they must configure on them. In some cases, users ae required to register their devices with a mobile device management (MDM) product that enforces a secure configuration on their devices and provides a means for the company to recover or erase company data from a lost or stolen phone.

Remote Access Policy   Specifies who is permitted to access company network resources from remote locations, using virtual private network (VPN) connections or other means, and what they are permitted to do with those resources. The policy can also describe the security infrastructure for remote network access, such as required authentication and authorization mechanisms.

Onboarding and Offboarding Policy   Specifies the procedures for adding new users to and removing them from the company network, including discussion of the other required policies and revocation of access to all network services and company data immediately on separation from the firm.

Security Policy   Functions as an umbrella document that includes all of the other policies applicable to company employees, including the password, BYOD, and AUP policies.

Data Loss Prevention (DLP)   A mechanism, such as an email filter, that prevents confidential company data from being sent outside the company, either accidentally or deliberately.

COMMON DOCUMENTATION

Documentation is a critical part of any IT department's operations. Keeping track of who has done what and when they did it prevents unnecessary repetition of tasks, and documenting the layout of the network enables technicians to locate equipment easily.

Documentation maintained by a typical enterprise IT department includes the following:

Physical Network Diagram   Indicates how network devices are physically connected to each other, but not necessarily their physical proximity, nor is the diagram drawn to scale.

Floor Plan   Depicts the physical layout and dimensions of the network site and the locations of the cables, wireless access points, and other network devices within each room. The diagram is typically drawn to scale and is often based on an overlay of the architectural blueprint for the facility. A floor plan should also include the locations of equipment and architectural barriers that might interfere with cable installations or wireless network transmissions.

Rack Diagram   Most data centers use vertical equipment racks to house servers, switches, routers, and other devices, as shown in Figure 14.1. Racks are typically 73.5 inches high and divided vertically into 42 units, each 1.75 inches high and numbered from bottom to top. Many rack-mounted devices are similar in appearance, and a rack diagram identifies the precise locations of the devices housed in each of a data center's racks.

Intermediate Distribution Frame (IDF)/Main Distribution Frame (MDF) Documentation   The MDF is the location in the facility where the internal network and the demarcation points for any external network services, such as WAN and telephone connections, meet. The MDF is often located in the company's data center itself or in a separate room near the place where cables for outside services enter the building. In addition to equipment such as patch panels and punchdown blocks, the MDF houses the backbone network switch, which provides connections to multiple IDFs scattered

F I G U R E   1 4 . 1   **A set of data center racks housing switches, routers, servers, and storage resources**

around the site, as shown in Figure 14.2. The backbone network connecting the MDF to the IDFs is often fiber optic, with as much speed and bandwidth as the budget will allow. IDFs are often server closets located on each floor, containing patch panels and work-group switches that connect to the workstations and other end-user devices on that floor. The MDF and the IDFs must be documented to specify what equipment and connections can be found in each one, as well as what building services they use, such as power conditioning and HVAC.

Logical Network Diagram   Depicts the flow of data between network devices. A logical network diagram is typically not drawn to scale because it is less about the physical locations of the network equipment and more about how the various devices interact with each other, regardless of their physical proximity. Administrators typically create logical network diagrams using a specialized software product intended for that purpose.

Wiring Diagram   Specifies the locations of all network cables and the devices to which they are connected, including the numbers assigned to all wall plates, patch panels, and switch ports. Wiring diagrams are particularly important because much of the cable infrastructure is typically hidden from view, and cables are often installed by outside contractors rather than employees of the firm. An efficient wiring contractor should provide a detailed diagram of every cable run they install that specifies the cables

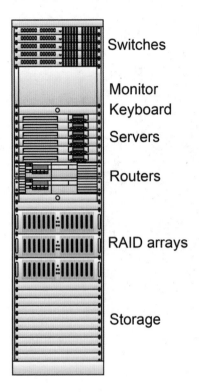

Switches

Monitor
Keyboard

Servers

Routers

RAID arrays

Storage

FIGURE 14.2 **The MDF and IDFs of a network installed in an office building**

and connectors used, the route the cable takes from one end to the other, the exact locations of the cable ends, and the numbers of the ports to which both ends of the cable are connected. This provides IT personnel with valuable troubleshooting information, should there be a problem with a particular patch panel or wall plate port, for example.

Site Survey Report   Details the layout of a wireless network in a particular facility, taking into account all of the walls, barriers, and other architectural elements that can cause interference that affects the range and speed of wireless transmissions, as well as any existing access points in the area and the frequencies they are using. Site surveys are typically performed before the wireless LAN installation, as part of the network design process, and might be repeated periodically as conditions or requirements change.

Audit and Assessment Report   A periodic examination of the network's overall security posture, which might include an examination of the existing network policies and penetration testing by a third party.

Baseline Configurations   Specifies the normal operating configurations of network devices, in the form of either documentation or backups of configuration files. If a device needs to be replaced for any reason, the settings needed to configure it are readily available. These baseline configurations are distinct from the performance baselines discussed in Chapter 13, "Network Availability."

COMMON AGREEMENTS

IT personnel often have to sign a variety of agreements as a condition of employment and might also be party to the negotiation of agreements with clients, vendors, or partners. Some of these agreements are as follows:

Nondisclosure Agreement (NDA)   Employees are sometimes party to proprietary internal information that could be damaging if disclosed outside the company. For that reason, part of the employee on-boarding process for many companies is signing an NDA that limits the employee's rights to share company information. The NDA typically specifies the duration of the agreement, which might stretch well beyond the worker's separation from the company, as well as the penalties for violating the terms of the agreement.

Service-Level Agreement (SLA)   In a contract between a service provider and a client, the SLA specifies the amount of service uptime guaranteed by the provider. Typically expressed as a percentage of the annual uptime, the SLA is often referred to as "the nines" because the agreement is nearly always 99 percent or over. For example, a "four nines" SLA guarantees that the service will be up 99.99 percent of the time, which allows the provider just under an hour of downtime per year before they are in violation of the agreed-on terms. A "six nines" SLA guarantees 99.9999 percent uptime, which allows the provider only 31 seconds of downtime per year. The SLA also specifies the penalties to which the provider is subject on breach of contract.

Memorandum of Understanding (MOU)   Sometimes called a *letter of intent*, an MOU specifies the terms of an agreement between two parties in a situation in which a formal contract is not appropriate. However, the terms of an MOU can be legally binding, particularly when the two parties already have a formal contract between them.

CERTMIKE EXAM ESSENTIALS

▶ Well-organized IT departments begin with planning. The plans are eventually developed into policies, and the policies are implemented using documented procedures. The plans and procedures document and regulate the changes the network undergoes, specify what to do in the event of a serious incident or disaster, and define the operational life cycle of network devices.

▶ There are IT policies used in many organizations to enhance the security of the network. Employees typically must observe password policies that define how and when users must change passwords, acceptable use policies that specify how employees can utilize the company's network and its services, BYOD policies that define how employees can use their own smartphones, and remote access policies that specify restrictions for mobile users.

▶ IT personnel should document all aspects of the company network by maintaining a library of diagrams and reports, including logical and physical network diagrams, floor plans, wiring diagrams, rack diagrams, and MDF/IDF documentation.

Practice Question 1

Ralph is working as an IT contractor for a new client with a large Ethernet network. The cables for the network were installed several years ago by an outside contractor, and some of the paper labels on the wall plates and patch panels have begun to fall off. Ralph's troubleshooting is being severely hampered by his not knowing, in some cases, which wall plate is connected to which patch panel port.

Which of the following is the best way for Ralph to determine which wall plates and patch panel ports are cabled together?

A. Call the cable installation contractor and ask them if they can remember which ports go with which wall plates.

B. Plug a tone generator into an unidentified wall plate and then test each patch panel port with a locator until you hear a tone indicating the correct one. Repeat for each port that needs labeling.

C. Consult the wiring diagram provided by the cabling contractor at the time of the installation.

D. Use a cable certifier to locate the patch panel port associated with each wall plate port.

Practice Question 2

Alice has been asked to create a proposal for a companywide password policy that would prevent the abuses that have been reported recently, including password sharing, reuse, and overly simple passwords. She has been considering a variety of password strategies and has narrowed down her list of policy requirements. Which of the following would not be necessary to prevent the abuses that have been reported?

A. Unique passwords

B. Minimum password length

C. Frequent password changes

D. Company-assigned passwords

Practice Question 1 Explanation

A. is incorrect because a busy cable installer is not likely to remember specific details about a job completed years before.
B. is incorrect because while testing each port individually with a tone generator and locator would be an effective solution, it would also be an incredibly slow and time-consuming process.
C. is correct because a reputable cable installer should supply a wiring diagram that indicates the locations of all the cable runs on a plan or blueprint of the site. Ralph should be able to use this diagram to determine which ports go with which wall plates.
D. is incorrect because although a cable certifier can test a cable run and discover its length, it cannot tell the user which wall plate is associated with a specific patch panel port.

Correct Answer: C

Practice Question 2 Explanation

A. is incorrect because a unique password policy is necessary to prevent users from reusing the same passwords.
B. is incorrect because a minimum password length policy is necessary to prevent users from creating overly simple passwords.
C. is incorrect because frequent password changes are necessary to make password sharing ineffective.
D. is correct because assigning passwords to users would cause more noncompliance problems than it would prevent.

Correct Answer: D

CHAPTER 15

High Availability and Disaster Recovery

Objective 3.3: Explain high availability and disaster recovery concepts and summarize which is the best solution.

This chapter examines some of the high availability and disaster recovery concepts implemented on a typical enterprise network. The Network+ exam expects candidates to be familiar with these basic networking concepts.

In this chapter, you'll learn everything you need to know about Network+ Objective 3.3, including the following topics:

▶ **Load balancing**
▶ **Multipathing**
▶ **Network interface card (NIC) teaming**
▶ **Redundant hardware/clusters**
▶ **Facilities and infrastructure support**
▶ **Redundancy and high availability (HA) concepts**
▶ **Network device backup/restore**

LOAD BALANCING

Load balancing is a high availability technique in which there are multiple servers performing the same task and a mechanism that divides the incoming traffic among those servers. This prevents any one server from being overwhelmed with requests.

One of the most common load balancing scenarios is that of a server farm hosting a busy website. There are multiple web servers clustered together, each of which hosts a fully functional copy of the website. A load balancer functions as a gateway to the server farm. Incoming requests from clients on the Internet arrive at the load balancer, which distributes them evenly among the servers.

This arrangement enables administrators to add servers to the cluster when the traffic load increases or remove them for maintenance. Even if a server should fail, the load balancer can redistribute the traffic among the remaining servers, ensuring the continued availability of the website.

The load balancing mechanism can be a software or hardware product, and it can distribute the traffic in various ways. For example, some load balancers use a round-robin algorithm, in which the device distributes the incoming requests by sending one to each server in turn. Others monitor the servers in the farm and send incoming requests to the server with the fewest active client connections.

MULTIPATHING

Multipathing—also known as *multipath IO* or *MPIO*—is a fault tolerance mechanism usually associated with storage area networks (SANs). SANs can provide a flexible and scalable storage infrastructure, but they also add points of failure. When a server is connected to its storage through a SAN, there are intervening cables, switches, and disk housings that could one day fail.

To provide fault tolerance and high availability, administrators often design the network to have redundant paths between the server and the storage devices so that if one path should fail, the other continues operating. To implement a multipath infrastructure for a SAN, the server needs at least two network interface adapters, each of which is connected by a cable to a different switch. The switches are then connected to the drive array, which should also have redundant network interfaces.

With this arrangement, the server can tolerate the failure of a network adapter, a cable, or a switch. The more redundant components there are on the path from the server to its storage, the more tolerant of faults the SAN will be.

NIC TEAMING

Network interface card (NIC) teaming—also called *NIC bonding*—is a technique for joining two network interface adapters together, either to combine their bandwidth or to provide fault tolerance. When creating a NIC team, the administrator typically has a choice of operating in either of the following modes:

▶ **Active-active:** When both NICs are active, each has its own MAC address and its own connection to a switch. The NICs can both be connected to the same switch, but connecting them to different switches enables the system to tolerate a switch failure as well as a NIC or cable failure. When both NICs are active, the bandwidth of the adapters is aggregated to provide greater performance.

▶ **Active-passive:** One NIC is aways operational, while the other remains in passive standby mode so that it can function as a failover option should the active NIC malfunction. In some cases, the teamed NICs exchange heartbeat messages so that the passive NIC can detect when the active NIC fails and activate itself to take over its role.

EXAM TIP

The Network+ objectives and many other sources frequently use the term *network interface card* and the abbreviation NIC, even though many computers and other devices have integrated network interface adapters instead of separate expansion cards. Candidates for the Network+ exam should be aware that the term NIC is used here generically and applies to all network interface adapters, not just those on expansion cards.

REDUNDANT HARDWARE/CLUSTERS

The key to network fault tolerance is *redundancy*. Providing duplicate devices for as much of the network infrastructure as possible will make the network more resilient.

For servers, redundancy can mean duplicate components inside the computer, such as redundant processors, power supplies, hard disks, and network interface adapters, or it can mean duplicating entire servers, creating what is known as a failover cluster or server farm. As mentioned earlier with regard to NIC teaming, redundant servers can operate in active-active or active-passive mode. In either case, the server cluster has a single IP address that represents the cluster itself, including all of the servers in it.

Another typical use of redundancy is in the storage infrastructure. Servers and disk arrays can use the various levels defined in the *Redundant Array of Independent Disks (RAID)* standards to maintain duplicate copies of important data on different disks, either standard hard drives or *solid-state drives (SSDs)*, which use memory chips to store data, rather than spinning platters.

For both servers and storage, a key part of component redundancy is having an automatic failover mechanism that detects when a component malfunctions and brings its fallback online without administrative intervention.

In addition to servers and storage, other network devices can have built-in redundancies, including the following:

Switches   As noted in Chapter 11, "Switching," designing a network with redundant switching paths is relatively common in enterprise networking. However, when the switches run in active-active mode, there is a tendency for packets to circulate endlessly around the network in switching loops. Switches use the Spanning Tree Protocol (STP) to put individual switching paths into passive mode to prevent switches from repeatedly processing the same packets.

Routers   Unlike switches, which are invisible to the average network user, workstations must have a default gateway address configured, which specifies the router that the device will use to access outside networks. This makes it difficult to create redundant routers because each has its own IP address, and there is no mechanism to dynamically change a workstation's default gateway address as network conditions change. Instead, administrators use specialized protocols called first hop redundancy protocols (FHRPs), which create a virtualized router with its own IP and MAC addresses that stands in for the redundant physical routers. By using the virtual router's IP address for a workstation's default gateway, the physical routers can change their active and passive roles without affecting the workstation.

Firewalls   For load balancing or fault tolerance reasons, an enterprise network can use redundant firewalls that operate as a cluster, much as servers do, with a single IP address representing the cluster itself. This splits the packet processing load among the cluster nodes, ensures high availability, and enables administrators to add nodes to and remove them from the cluster as needed. Duplicate firewalls might also be required for a network with connections to multiple Internet service providers.

FACILITIES AND INFRASTRUCTURE SUPPORT

High availability applies not just to the devices that make up the network, but also to the environment in which those devices run. To run efficiently, the network equipment in a data center or server closet requires a stable power source and an atmosphere with controlled temperature, humidity, and other factors. The data center should also have some means of protection against disasters, such as fire suppression equipment and sensors to detect flood conditions and toxic gasses, such as carbon monoxide and radon.

This section describes some of the devices needed to maintain an environmental infrastructure.

Uninterruptible Power Supply (UPS)

An *uninterruptible power supply (UPS)* is a battery-based backup power source and power conditioner. The UPS protects the devices connected to it from damage due to power sags or spikes and also provides a short-term source of power when there is an AC outage. UPSs are designed for two purposes: to provide power long enough to execute a controlled shutdown of the equipment and to keep the equipment running until a generator can start up and supply a stable, long-term power source.

UPS products range from small, inexpensive units intended for protecting a single computer to large, costly devices used in data centers. A UPS accepts power from an AC source and also contains a battery; it uses both of these to supply AC power to the devices connected to it. However, the way in which the UPS handles the changeover between AC and battery power is what differentiates the three types of UPSs, which are as follows, from most to least expensive:

▶ **Online:** The UPS supplies power to the connected devices from its battery at all times and uses the incoming AC source to supply power to the battery circuit and also charge the battery. There is no need for switching between power sources and no transition delays.

▶ **Line-interactive:** The UPS uses the incoming AC source to supply power to the inverter that provides the outgoing AC power. When the incoming AC fails, the inverter begins supplying outgoing AC from the battery. There is no circuit switch from AC to the battery-based inverter, so the transition time is minimal.

▶ **Standby:** The UPS normally supplies the connected device with AC power direct from the source. When the AC power fails, the UPS switches its output over from AC to the battery-based inverter in a relatively long transition that can take 25 milliseconds or more.

Power Distribution Units

A *power distribution unit (PDU)* is a device that provides multiple electrical outlets from a single AC source. The power strip that is probably sitting under your desk is technically a PDU, but the one used in data centers are larger, rack-mounted devices and often include specialized features.

When a data center has equipment, such as servers or switches, with redundant power supplies for fault tolerance purposes, the recommended practice is to connect each of the power supplies to a separate AC source. Some organizations do just that by installing a rack with two separate PDUs connected to different AC sources, thus providing separate circuits for each of a device's two power supplies. If one power supply should fail, the other is always available to keep the equipment running. Depending on the degree of fault tolerance required and the organization's budget, each PDU might also be connected to its own UPS and even its own separate generator.

Generator

Battery-based power sources, such as UPSs, are designed only for short-term use. A UPS can provide power to last through a brief AC outage, but for an extended power failure, a UPS is only a stopgap measure. Batteries eventually run down, and when they do, the situation is no different from running without a UPS.

Battery power can enable administrators to execute a controlled shutdown of the equipment, but for an extended backup power source, a generator is needed. A *generator* is a device that burns some type of petroleum product to create electricity. Large enterprise data centers often have inline generators connected to their power circuits, with a sensor that detects an AC failure and brings the generator online automatically. UPSs are still needed, however, even with a generator, because it can take a few minutes for a generator to spin up and start supplying a stable current. The UPS can fill in for those few minutes until the generator is online. Once the power source is active and stable, the equipment can keep running as long as the generator's fuel supply holds out.

HVAC

Heating, ventilation, and air conditioning (HVAC) are critical services in any location where network equipment is running. Data centers can have dozens or hundreds of electrical devices in them, all generating large amounts of heat and all highly sensitive to variations in temperature and humidity. Most people know that overheating can shorten the life of electrical equipment, but excessive cold can lead to moisture condensation that is also damaging. In the same way, humidity can cause problems if too high (condensation) or too low (static). In a well-planned data center, HVAC is an integral part of the overall design, with sensor locations and airflow paths carefully selected to provide an ideal operational environment.

One common design calls for rows of equipment racks arranged face-to-face and back-to-back. Rack-mounted equipment takes in cool air from the front and exhausts it out the back, much hotter. In this design, the face-to-face rows are the cool rows, and the back-to-back rows are the hot rows. The ventilation system is then designed with intake vents for hot air in the ceiling of the hot rows and output vents for cool air in the floors of the cold rows.

HVAC can be more of a problem with server closets and other intermediate distribution frames, which are sometimes located in smaller spaces that are not specifically designed for that purpose and might be difficult to heat and cool.

Fire Suppression

In addition to conditioned power sources and the HVAC system, a data center should also have some means of fire suppression, both to limit the data center's vulnerability to fire outside and to prevent fire originating within the data center from spreading. There are various types of fire suppression systems, the most effective and most expensive of which floods the data center with inert gas that displaces the oxygen, choking out the fire (and any people in the area without breathing equipment).

The main advantage of an inert gas fire suppression system is that the gas has no permanent effect on electrical equipment. These systems are far more expensive than those that use water or foam, but the potential cost of replacing water-damaged equipment likely far outweighs the cost of the fire suppression system.

> **EXAM TIP**
>
> Inert gas fire suppression systems are often incorrectly identified as Halon systems. These products no longer use Halon gas, which was found to be toxic, but rather another inert gas that has the same fire-dampening effect. Candidates for the Network+ exam should be aware that many Internet sources still use the outdated terminology.

REDUNDANCY AND HIGH AVAILABILITY CONCEPTS

Redundancy is a key concept in the design of network components, as well as in the design of the network itself. As with many things, redundancy is a trade-off between expense and efficiency. Administrators typically choose to install redundant components for two reasons: fault tolerance and *high availability (HA)*. Some of the concepts involved in designing and building redundant systems are discussed next.

Active-Active vs. Active-Passive

As noted earlier in this chapter, redundant systems can typically operate in one of two ways, as follows:

Active-Active   Both devices are fully operational at all times, providing fault tolerance as well as the opportunity for load balancing.

Active-Passive   One device is operational at all times, with the other left in a standby mode, ready to take over if the active device should fail.

The active-active and active-passive techniques are common to redundant systems at all levels. However, when dealing with redundancy at the enterprise level, there are other HA concepts to consider, such as whether the enterprise is prepared for a major disaster that renders an entire facility unusable.

Redundant Data Centers

The ultimate in data center redundancy is simply to have another data center at a different location. For organizations with service requirements that cannot tolerate any major downtime, a duplicate data center that can replace the one at the company headquarters, should it be damaged or destroyed, is a critical requirement.

Obviously, building an entire redundant data center is a major expense, as is keeping it updated and ready for use. To that end, there are three basic configurations for redundant data centers. These three types of sites balance the expense of construction and maintenance with the time needed to restore the full functionality of the network using the alternative site. The site types are as follows:

Cold Site   Not yet a data center at all, a cold site is a leased property with all of the building services required for a data center in place, such as power, HVAC, and plumbing, but no network equipment at all. A cold site is the least expensive to construct and maintain but requires the longest time to obtain, install, and configure all the network equipment.

Warm Site   A warm site falls between hot and cold, both in its expense and in the time needed to restore the network to full functionality. A warm site typically contains all the necessary building infrastructure and some or all of the hardware necessary to rebuild the network, so the time to restore functionality is substantially shorter than that of a cold site and longer than that of a hot site. In some instances, organizations ship their outdated equipment to a warm site for use in a backup data center. If a hot site's restore time is measured in minutes and a cold site's in weeks, a warm site restoration would likely take days.

Hot Site   A hot site is a redundant data center that is fully equipped and ready for use, with building infrastructure, service connections, and all networking hardware installed and configured. Bringing the site online requires only a transfer of the latest data. Constructing and maintaining a hot site is typically an enormous expense, but in the event of a disaster, the alternative site can be brought online in a matter of minutes.

These cold, warm, and hot site definitions refer to physical data centers, but an increasingly popular alternative to these is a cloud site. A *cloud site* is a virtual data center created in a cloud network hosted by a service provider. Compared to any physical site option, a cloud site is far less expensive to build and maintain because all the facility and infrastructure costs are absorbed by the service provider. Some providers have prepackaged virtual data center services available for just this purpose.

Multiple ISPs and Diverse Paths

For many organizations, their Internet connection is their life's blood; they cannot function without it. Therefore, just as redundancy can be applied to individual devices or to the company network, outside service connections can and should be redundant as well.

One form of Internet redundancy is to install at least two separate connections to the *Internet service provider (ISP)*, preferably using different routers and different carriers. This creates *diverse paths* to the Internet and provides some protection against router and carrier failures. However, if the ISP's own network should fail, then both connections will go down. A better solution is to connect the network to *multiple ISPs*, ideally those that do not share the same upstream providers. It is even possible to combine the two methods by installing multiple connections to each ISP.

First-Hop Redundancy Protocols

As discussed earlier in this chapter, incorporating redundant routers into a network design requires the use of a specialized protocol called a *first-hop redundancy protocol (FHRP)*.

An FHRP creates a virtualized router with its own IP and MAC addresses. Using those addresses, all communication with the redundant physical routers goes through the virtual router. Since all of the physical routers are configured to respond to the virtual router's addresses, any one can perform the essential routing functions.

The two most commonly used FHRPs are *Virtual Router Redundancy Protocol (VRRP)*, which is based on an open standard, and Hot Standby Router Protocol (HSRP), which is proprietary. Both work using the active-passive design, though they use different terms, with one router designated as the primary router (in VRRP) or the active router (in HSRP) and the other as a standby or backup router.

Other Concepts

High availability technologies often involve allowable time measurements for specific events. Some of these time measurements are described next.

Mean Time To Repair (MTTR)

Mean time to repair (MTTR) is a technical specification indicating the average time—usually in hours—that it takes to repair a specific device, component, or service. MTTR values are typically factored into the negotiations for service-level agreements (SLAs) so that the expected repair or replacement times for specific elements do not generate delays that result in a violation of contract terms.

Mean Time Between Failure (MTBF)

Mean time between failure (MTBF) is a technical specification typically used to quantify the resilience of hard disk drives. Calibrated in hours, the MTBF value specifies the average amount of time the disk is expected to operate without a failure. Typical MTBF values can reach into the millions, however, which should make it clear that they are estimated values and not the result of real-time testing.

Recovery Time Objective (RTO)

Recovery time objective (RTO) is essentially a measurement of how much network down-time the organization can tolerate before the affected business process is restored. Administrators typically use this value when designing a network's fault tolerance and high availability posture. For example, a lower RTO value might mean the difference between maintaining a backup data center as a hot site or a warm site.

Recovery Point Objective (RPO)

The *recovery point objective (RPO)* specifies the maximum length of time allowable between a disaster resulting in data loss and the last time the data was backed up. Usually measured in hours, the RPO typically determines how often network backups should occur. For example, if the data is backed up once per day, then the RPO could conceivably be as long as 24 hours. If the organization determines that the RPO must be no more than 12 hours, then backups must occur more frequently, at least twice a day.

NETWORK DEVICE BACKUP/RESTORE

Backups are an essential fault tolerance element of any network, whatever the size. The type of backup medium for a network depends on the amount of data that needs protection and the amount of time available to perform the backups.

The traditional medium for network backups is magnetic tape, but tape backups are slow, and the technology is expensive. Backing up to hard disks is increasingly popular because it is faster and provides random access to files without having to search through a tape. Cloud backups provide an offsite data storage solution, which might or might not be practical depending on the amount of data involved and the speed of the network's Internet connection.

While data backups are important, a high availability plan should also include backups of device configurations and states. In a disaster recovery situation, servers, routers, switches, and other devices might have to be installed and configured before any data is restored. This can be a lengthy process that greatly extends the time needed to restore the network to its full functionality.

The *configuration* of a device can often be saved as a simple text file in the case of a router or switch. Many router and switch products include some mechanism for backing up the configuration file to a server or removable storage device. Without this file, administrators replacing the switch might have to reconfigure each port individually.

In the case of a server, network backups can preserve the data, but replacing the server in the event of a disaster by simply restoring the data from a backup can be problematic. The data, as preserved in the backup, expects the server to have a specific hardware configuration, which might not be exactly the same in a replacement computer. For this reason, many backup products are able to back up the full system *state*, which makes it possible to perform a complete restoration without having to reinstall and reconfigure the operating system and the applications.

CERTMIKE EXAM ESSENTIALS

▶ High availability extends into the data center infrastructure, which must include a properly conditioned power supply, HVAC environmental support, and adequate fire suppression capabilities.

▶ Redundant systems can typically operate in an active-active mode, in which both devices are always operating and balancing the load, or an active-passive mode, in which one device operates while the other remains in a standby state until needed.

▶ Redundant data centers can exist in different states, depending on the organization's operational requirements and budget. Hot sites are ready for use in minutes, warm sites in days, and cold sites in weeks or months.

Practice Question 1

Ralph is deploying a new server in his company's data center. The server has redundant power supplies, so Ralph wants to make the whole installation as fault tolerant as possible. The building has a backup generator connected to its AC circuit with an automatic failover switch. Ralph plugs both of the server's power supplies into a UPS and plugs the UPS into an AC socket.

Using this configuration, which of the following failures can the server tolerate and keep running indefinitely? (Choose all correct answers.)

A. A power supply failure
B. A UPS failure
C. An AC power failure
D. A generator failure

Practice Question 2

Alice has been asked to design a network for a new branch office that has redundant Internet connections with the fullest possible fault tolerance. Which of the following elements must Alice incorporate into her design to meet her goal?

A. Different ISPs
B. Different WAN connections
C. Different routers
D. All of the above

Practice Question 1 Explanation

A. is correct because if one power supply in the server fails, the other one can keep the server running.
B. is incorrect because both power supplies are plugged into the same UPS. If the UPS should fail, the server will have no power source and will shut down.
C. is correct because, in the event of an AC power failure, the UPS can supply battery power until the generator starts up and takes over.
D. is correct because, if the generator should fail, the server can continue running as long as the AC power supply remains online.

Correct Answers: A, C, and D

Practice Question 2 Explanation

A. is incorrect because although different ISPs provide a degree of fault tolerance, other elements are needed to achieve the full fault tolerance Alice needs to complete her task.
B. is incorrect because while different WAN connections to the ISP provide a degree of fault tolerance, other elements are needed to achieve the full fault tolerance Alice needs to complete her task.
C. is incorrect because while using different routers for the connections to the ISP provides a degree of fault tolerance, other elements are needed to achieve the full fault tolerance Alice needs to complete her task.
D. is correct because the full fault tolerance that Alice needs requires redundancy in every part of the Internet connections, including the routers, the WAN connections, and the ISPs.

Correct Answer: D

Domain 4.0: Network Security

Network Security is the fourth domain of CompTIA's Network+ exam. In it, you'll learn how networking professionals build and maintain secure networks and facilities that are hardened against a variety of attacks. This domain has five objectives:

4.1 Explain common security concepts.

4.2 Compare and contrast common types of attacks.

4.3 Given a scenario, apply network hardening techniques.

4.4 Compare and contrast remote access methods and security implications.

4.5 Explain the importance of physical security.

Questions from this domain make up 19% of the questions on the Network+ exam, so you should expect to see approximately 17 questions on your test covering the material in this part.

CHAPTER 16

Security Concepts

Objective 4.1: Explain common security concepts.

This chapter examines some of the security concepts implemented on a typical enterprise network. The Network+ exam expects candidates to be familiar with these basic concepts.

In this chapter, you'll learn everything you need to know about Network+ objective 4.1, including the following topics:

▶ **Confidentiality, integrity, availability (CIA)**
▶ **Threats**
▶ **Vulnerabilities**
▶ **Exploits**
▶ **Least privilege**
▶ **Role-based access**
▶ **Zero trust**
▶ **Defense in depth**
▶ **Authentication methods**
▶ **Risk management**
▶ **Security information and event management (SIEM)**

CONFIDENTIALITY, INTEGRITY, AND AVAILABILITY

The fundamental security goals of an enterprise network are to maintain the *confidentiality, integrity, and availability (CIA)* of the organization's data. This is known as the *CIA triad*. The elements of the triad are defined as follows:

Confidentiality   The prevention of data access by anyone other than authorized personnel, using tools such as physical locks, authentication mechanisms, data encryption, and firewall barriers

Integrity   A mechanism that ensures that data has not been modified, either accidentally or deliberately by unauthorized individuals, while being transmitted over the network or stored on a server. The mechanism is typically a digital signature containing hashes and checksums

Availability   The continued accessibility of the data under all circumstances, including deliberate attacks and natural disasters, using fault tolerance and high availability mechanisms such as backups, RAID arrays, server farms, and other redundant components

THREATS

In enterprise networking, a *threat* is anything that could possibly endanger the network itself or its data. The word threat has connotations of malicious attackers deliberately targeting the network, but there are many other types of threats that are just as damaging.

Threats to a network can be classified as external or internal. *External threats* are those originating from outside the firewall and the company facilities. In most cases, access to the network comes in through the Internet connection, but an external threat can also enter a company building and physically disrupt the network by vandalism, theft, or sabotage. External threats also include natural disasters, such as hurricanes and earthquakes. Protection against external threats includes firewalls and access control for the cyberthreats and physical barriers against intrusion, such as key card entry systems, cameras, and guards.

Internal threats originate behind the firewall and the company facilities. These threats are often harder to detect and can be even more malicious. Disgruntled employees might already have the physical or digital network access they need to cause trouble, whether they come about it legitimately or not. Even if the employees are no longer with the company, they are considered an internal threat because that is how they gained their network access privileges.

Internal threats also include accidental occurrences that cause network damage, which can range from shared passwords to inadvertent file deletion to coffee spilled on electronics to fire in the data center. Protection against internal threats begins with careful allocation of access permissions, both digital and physical, and auditing of both successful and unsuccessful accesses to sensitive data and facilities.

VULNERABILITIES

In an enterprise network, *vulnerabilities* are security weaknesses, whether in hardware, software, or even personnel, which enable unauthorized exposure of data or other resources, and which have not been addressed by any sort of compensating control, countermeasure, or safeguard. Where hardware is concerned, a vulnerability can be as simple as an unlocked data center door. In software, vulnerabilities are the basis for an arms race, with attackers seeking them and protectors plugging them. Personnel vulnerabilities typically take the form of individuals with access permissions they do not need and should not have.

Addressing vulnerabilities is one of the primary reasons most software products are updated on a regular basis. However, tracking vulnerabilities and collaborating with others to define and resolve them can be difficult because people might experience the same vulnerability in different ways, making classification a problem. To address this problem, it was necessary to devise a means of identifying and tracking vulnerabilities.

Common Vulnerabilities and Exposures

Common Vulnerabilities and Exposures (CVE) is a registry for known vulnerabilities in publicly released software products. Entries in the registry are assigned a unique CVE identifier, such as CVE-2022-34720, which is the number for a Windows Internet Key Exchange (IKE) Extension Denial of Service Vulnerability, by a *CVE Numbering Authority* (CNA). Once a vulnerability is identified and classified and can be referenced by CVE number, the process of defining, tracking, and mitigating the vulnerability is much easier.

Zero-Day

Zero-day is a term used to describe a vulnerability that has become public knowledge and for which a countermeasure has not yet been devised or released. The term refers to a problem that administrators have zero days to fix because there is no remedy available. A *zero-day attack* is a network infiltration that occurs during that period between the discovery or announcement of the vulnerability and the release of a patch or workaround.

EXPLOITS

If a vulnerability is a weakness, then an *exploit* is the means by which someone can take advantage of that vulnerability. In most cases, an exploit takes the form of a script or other code that is designed to take advantage of a vulnerability to gain access to sensitive resources. More serious than just the existence of a zero-day vulnerability, a *zero-day exploit* is a proven means for infiltrating a system using a vulnerability that has not yet been documented or mitigated.

LEAST PRIVILEGE

Least privilege is a security principle stating that individuals should have the network and data access they need to perform their jobs and no more than that. Many applications and operating systems leave their administrative functions open by default, which enables both users and intruders to access controls that can damage the system or the network.

For example, users who have administrative privileges on their workstations can conceivably alter configuration settings that might render the computer unusable. This is not a catastrophe, but it adds to the workload of the first-line IT workers. Even worse, however, those same users might fall victim to a phishing or social engineering attack and grant an intruder access to their systems, providing that intruder with the same administrative access.

To apply the principle of least privilege, administrators should grant users only the permissions they need. For example, users should receive read-only access to files unless modifying them is part of their job. The principle becomes more complicated with supervisors and IT personnel who do need administrative access at times. These users should have two accounts, one with administrative privileges and one with basic user privileges, and they should only use the administrative account when they need to perform administrative tasks. The less often the administrative privileges are used, the less likely they will be compromised.

ROLE-BASED ACCESS

Role-based access is a technique designed to simplify the permissions assignment process, enabling administrators to apply the least privilege principle more easily. The process of assigning users the permissions they need to work while denying them everything else can be lengthy and time-consuming, especially when there are dozens or hundreds of users to configure.

Rather than configure each user account individually, administrators can create a group or other element that is dedicated to a single role or job, and which possesses all of the permissions needed to perform that job. Then, by adding the users who perform that job to the group or assigning them the role, the users inherit all the permissions they need. When a user leaves the job or the company, simply removing them from the group revokes the permissions they no longer need.

ZERO TRUST

The traditional security model for a network calls for people connected to the network to be treated as trustworthy and those outside the network to be non-trustworthy. With the increasing number of network threats and vulnerabilities today, this model is increasingly naive. *Zero trust* is a security principle similar to least privilege, in that all users start with no access to the network at all and then are granted only the permissions they need to perform their required tasks.

Zero trust means that everything users do on the network they do because they have been authenticated and authorized for each particular task at the time access is required. This generally means that authentication traffic on the network increases, users have to supply access credentials more often, and there are more IT help desk requests from people with login problems, but this is the price of security.

DEFENSE IN DEPTH

The principle of *defense in depth* calls for there to be multiple layers of security between protected resources and potential intruders. Ideally, the layers should consist of different types of security. For example, before a user can receive an email message, it might have to pass through a firewall, then be subject to access control barriers, and then finally be decrypted. Multiple barriers of different types make a system inherently more secure.

This section describes some of the security mechanisms that an enterprise network might use as part of its defense in depth.

Network Segmentation Enforcement

When a network consists of a single segment, every computer has theoretical access to every other computer. However, by splitting the network into multiple segments, it is possible to control access among them by using a technique called *network segmentation enforcement*.

There are different means of segmenting a network; it can be done physically by separating the devices in different locations and regulating access between them. However, a more common solution is to segment the network at the data link layer by creating virtual local area networks (VLANs) in the switches and using port security to control access to them. This means that, apart from any other security mechanisms that might be in place, users must be authenticated before they can even gain access to a particular VLAN segment.

Perimeter Network

A *perimeter network*—also called a *screened subnet* or a *demilitarized zone (DMZ)*—is a separate part of an enterprise network that houses the servers requiring a presence on the Internet, such as web and mail servers. The perimeter network is located between the company's protected inner network and the open Internet.

Typically, there are two firewalls, an internal one at the interface between the perimeter network and the inner network and an external one between the perimeter network and the Internet. In the case of a web server located on the perimeter network, the external firewall would usually be configured to allow only web request traffic through from the Internet. The internal firewall might allow the web server to communicate with back-end servers on the internal network, such as a SQL server, but other interaction with the internal network is highly restricted.

It is also possible, in some cases, for a single *next-generation firewall (NGFW)* separating the enterprise network from the Internet to implement the perimeter network and all its necessary rules internally. This eliminates the need for a potentially complicated cable installation to create the perimeter network.

Separation of Duties

Separation of duties is a security principle that is intended to prevent any one person from possessing too many administrative privileges. The concept is not that employees are untrustworthy, but rather that defense in depth calls for a division of duties. For example, accessing a safe deposit box in a bank requires two people with two different keys, one from a bank official and one from the box owner. Neither one is suspected of wrongdoing, but the division of labor prevents unauthorized entry to the box by either party.

Just as different types of security mechanisms add to the protection of the network, separating administrative duties prevents IT personnel from accidentally or deliberately compromising the security of the network.

Network Access Control

Network access control (NAC) is a security mechanism that frequently works with the 802.1X authentication protocol to screen users as they connect to the network. Some of the common NAC screening criteria include the update status of the operating system and applications, whether the computer has an antivirus product installed with updated virus signatures, and whether the system is running a properly configured firewall. If the systems are not in compliance with the NAC policies, then NAC can prevent the users from authenticating and deny them access to the network.

Honeypot

A *honeypot* is a system with no significant access to sensitive data or services that is designed to be a tempting target for potential attackers. By setting up a single system or a group of systems (called a *honeynet*) that is ripe for penetration, administrators can gather intelligence about attackers and the means they might use to gain access to the network. In addition, the honeypot can divert the intruder's attention from the actual network targets. One strategy—called a *tarpit*—is to configure the honeypot or honeynet to run as slowly as possible, so as to keep the intruder occupied pursuing a false target.

AUTHENTICATION METHODS

Authentication is the process of verifying the identity of a person, device, or application attempting to access a protected resource. The process can be simple and self-contained, with accounts maintained by an application for its own use, but enterprise networks typically use a directory service of some type to store user accounts. Users might be authenticated many times in the course of a typical computer work session, sometimes invisibly and at other times requiring them to supply credentials to verify their identities. There are many protocols and concepts that can be involved in the authentication process, including those described in this section.

Multifactor

Multifactor authentication is when a system requires more than one proof of an individual's identity. A typical authentication requires users to supply an account name and a password. For a system that has implemented multifactor authentication, the users will have to furnish another proof. Depending on the system, the proofs required for a multifactor authentication can fall under the following categories:

- ▶ **Something you know:** A piece of information that no one else knows but you, such as a password or PIN
- ▶ **Something you have:** A physical device, such as a key fob or swipe card, that you must present at the time of authentication
- ▶ **Something you are:** A physical trait or characteristic that is unique to you, such as your fingerprint, voice, or face

The most commonly used multifactor authentication mechanisms today call for a password (something you know) plus a fingerprint scan (something you are) or a code sent to the user's smartphone (something you have). As long as the factors used for authentication are from different categories, the system should be more secure than a typical single-factor authentication system.

Authentication, Authorization, and Accounting

Authentication, authorization, and accounting (AAA) is a model for a centralized service that stores user accounts and handles the authentication and authorization processes for other devices on the network. The accounting function keeps a record of users' activities. Some products add auditing capabilities, leading to the use of the abbreviation AAAA.

There are two primary AAA products in use today, as follows:

- ▶ **TACACS+:** Based on a 1980s protocol that provided reauthentication services for network users, *Terminal Access Controller Access-Control System (TACACS+)* was developed in the 1990s to be a full-featured authentication, authorization, and accounting (AAA) server. TACACS+ uses TCP for its transport communications and encrypts all user data before transmission.
- ▶ **RADIUS:** Originally designed in the 1990s to authenticate dial-in users for ISPs, the *Remote Authentication Dial-in User Service (RADIUS)* is a standards-based protocol that provides AAA functions for a variety of network applications, including wireless LANs, remote access connections, and standard cabled networks.

Single Sign-On

Single sign-on (SSO) is an authentication technique that allows users to sign on once with their credentials and then access other protected resources automatically using those same credentials. This prevents the users from having to repeatedly supply credentials whenever they access a new resource.

On today's networks, there are often many different applications and services that require authentication before users can access them. When users have to log into each one individually, they can easily become frustrated with maintaining passwords for multiple user accounts. This can lead the users to create passwords that are overly simple, write down passwords in obvious places, or circumnavigate the company password policies in other ways.

To implement single sign-on, enterprise networks typically use a centralized directory service, such as Active Directory. Once users authenticate to their Active Directory accounts the first time, they are issued a digital token that provides them with access to the other resources they are authorized to use. After the initial sign-on, subsequent authentications and authorizations are transparent to the user.

LDAP

Lightweight Directory Access Protocol (LDAP) is an application layer protocol most commonly used to carry directory service information between clients and servers. Based on the earlier Directory Access Protocol (DAP), which was used with the now-obsolete X.500 directory service in the 1980s, LDAP is currently the underlying communication protocol for Microsoft's Active Directory directory service.

Kerberos

Kerberos is an authentication protocol used by the Active Directory directory service for communications with clients, servers, and domain controllers. Based on the three-headed hellhound of Greek mythology, Kerberos carries authentication traffic from both the clients and the servers to a domain controller, which is the central clearinghouse for Active Directory authentication. Both clients and servers request and receive tickets from the domain controller, which enable them to authenticate each other. The domain controller renews the tickets periodically, as needed, so the clients and servers can continue to communicate.

Kerberos uses strong encryption for all of its communications, but even so, it never transmits passwords or secret keys over the network. Instead, the authenticating system and the domain controller both use a symmetric cipher to generate secret keys from the user passwords they have on file. Then, they use those keys to encrypt and decrypt messages to each other. If a message encrypted by one system using the secret key can be decrypted successfully by the other system with its own key, then they both must have generated their keys using the same password, and the authentication is successful.

Local Authentication

Local authentication, as the name implies, is an identity verification process that is implemented and executed all on a single system. The operating system stores the user accounts and passwords, which the authenticating user specifies to gain access to the system. No network communication is involved, so there is no danger of passwords being compromised from network traffic.

The problem with local authentication is that each system requires its own set of user accounts. When users want to change their passwords, someone must change them on every system where each user has an account. Typically, local authentication functions only as a fallback that allows users to log on to their computers, even when the network is down.

802.1X

802.1X is a standard published by the IEEE defining an authentication method for controlling access to networks by manipulating switch port security settings. An 802.1X transaction involves three parties: a supplicant, an authenticator, and an authentication server.

The *supplicant*, which is a user or a device requesting access to a resource, sends an access request and its credentials to the *authenticator*, which is typically a switch, but can also be a wireless access point or a virtual private network (VPN) server. The authenticator then forwards the credentials to an *authentication server*, which typically runs TACACS+ or RADIUS and verifies the supplicant's credentials. If the authentication is successful, the authentication server informs the authenticator, which grants the supplicant the requested access.

One of the main advantages of 802.1X is that it enables switches and other devices to offload their authentication processing to a dedicated authentication server, lessening the burden on the switches themselves.

Extensible Authentication Protocol

Extensible Authentication Protocol (EAP) is not really a protocol at all, but rather a framework for a protocol that extends the 802.1X framework to support a variety of authentication mechanisms, including swipe cards, fingerprints, and other forms of biometrics, as well as passwords. There are many protocols that use the EAP framework, including Protected Extensible Authentication Protocol (PEAP), which encapsulates EAP within an encrypted TLS tunnel, and Extensible Authentication Protocol-Transport Layer Security (EAP-TLS), used on wireless networks.

RISK MANAGEMENT

In IT, *risk management* is the process of identifying potential dangers to the network, prioritizing those dangers, and taking steps to minimize or eliminate them. An enterprise network should have a formal risk management program in place that performs regular assessments of the network's security posture.

One of the primary elements of a comprehensive risk management program is to perform *security risk assessments* on a regular basis. These are tests used to evaluate the network's resistance to known risks, such as the following:

Threat Assessment   Administrators must remain aware of the new threats that appear regularly and the dangers they pose to the network. There are many websites that track the latest threats and describe their characteristics.

Vulnerability Assessment   A scan, typically performed by a third-party software product, which evaluates the potential vulnerabilities of a network by identifying open ports, missing software updates, configuration anomalies, and other weaknesses.

Penetration Testing   A test in which a third party—acting as an intruder—attempts to exploit the weaknesses in the network's security posture under ordinary operating conditions and access its protected resources. In many cases, for a more realistic assessment, the test intruder is provided with no prior knowledge of the network and the company's IT personnel are not told that the test is pending.

Posture Assessment   Often occurring along with a penetration test, a posture assessment is a test of how the IT department reacts to a network attack.

Business Risk Assessments   Beyond the existence of vulnerabilities, a business risk assessment evaluates those vulnerabilities with regard to the dangers they pose to the organization's business interests. This enables the administrators to better prioritize the vulnerabilities and refine their reaction plans.

Process Assessment   An examination, with an eye to network security, of the business processes that company workers perform on a regular basis.

Vendor Assessment   An examination of the security posture of the organization's vendors and other business partners, including what access they have to the organization's network and data resources as well as their own security procedures.

SIEM

Security Information and Event Management (SIEM) is an umbrella term used for products that combine the functions of *security information management (SIM)*, which provides long-term log storage and analysis, and *security event management (SEM)*, which provides real-time monitoring of network devices. Available as software, hardware, or a managed service, an SIEM product can gather log files from various network devices, such as firewalls and switches; collate the information; and then evaluate it by comparing the data with known threat behaviors. If the SIEM product detects a threat, it can typically notify an administrative contact in various ways. Some products can even take action to remediate a threat.

CERTMIKE EXAM ESSENTIALS

▶ The CIA triad defines the three basic security goals for an enterprise network: confidentiality, integrity, and availability.

▶ Defense in depth is a security principle that calls for multiple layers of security between the protected material and its potential threats. Some of the associated concepts are network segmentation enforcement, perimeter networks, NAC, and honeypots.

▶ Authentication is one of the most critical security elements in an enterprise network. It can involve many different concepts and technologies, including multifactor authentication, AAA, single sign-on, LDAP, Kerberos, 802.1X, and EAP.

Practice Question 1

Ralph is designing the network for his company's new branch office. The office will be running a custom application that frequently needs updating. Ralph's director has instructed him to set up the network so that users cannot connect to it unless their workstations have been updated with the latest patches for the custom application. Which of the following technologies must Ralph use to achieve this goal?

A. LDAP

B. SIEM

C. RADIUS

D. NAC

Practice Question 2

Alice is working the IT help desk when she receives a call from the Director of Human Resources, informing her that an employee had just been terminated and had to be escorted out of the building by Security. The director instructed her to disable all of the employee's accounts, change the passwords for all network devices to which the employee had access, and have the data center doors rekeyed. Alice was surprised to receive these instructions because company employees had been terminated before without these precautions.

Which of the following terms best describes the director's specific concern in asking Alice to do these things?

A. Social engineering

B. Internal threats

C. War driving

D. External threats

Practice Question 1 Explanation

A. is incorrect because Lightweight Directory Access Protocol (LDAP) is used for Active Directory communication, not for enforcing configuration standards.
B. is incorrect because Security Information and Event Management (SIEM) is a security product that provides long-term log storage and analysis and real-time monitoring of network devices.
C. is incorrect because Remote Authentication Dial-in User Service (RADIUS) is a centralized authentication, authorization, and accounting service; it does not enforce configuration standards.
D. is correct because Network Access Control (NAC) is a technology that enforces configuration standards that systems must meet before they can connect to the network.

Correct Answer: D, NAC

Practice Question 2 Explanation

A. is incorrect because social engineering is a form of attack in which an innocent user is persuaded by an attacker to provide sensitive information via email or telephone.
B. is correct because the director's concern is that the disgruntled employee might take advantage of their access to company resources to sabotage the network. When individuals take advantage of information gathered during their employment, it is called an internal threat.
C. is incorrect because war driving is an attack method that consists of driving around a neighborhood with a computer scanning for unprotected wireless networks.
D. is incorrect because an external threat is one originating from a non-employee.

Correct Answer: B, Internal threats

CHAPTER 17

Network Attacks

Objective 4.2: Compare and contrast common types of attacks.

This chapter examines some of the network attack types that commonly affect a typical enterprise network. The Network+ exam expects candidates to be familiar with these basic security threats.

In this chapter, you'll learn everything you need to know about Network+ Objective 4.2, including the following topics:

▶ **Technology-based**
▶ **Human and environmental**

TECHNOLOGY-BASED ATTACKS

Attacks on an organization's network or its data typically take one of two forms: technological, in which an intruder uses an Internet connection to access the network, and physical, in which an intruder uses personal communication to gain access to protected resources.

Some of the most common types of technological attacks are described in this section.

Denial-of-Service (DoS)

A *denial-of-service (DoS)* attack is one in which an intruder floods a server or a network with traffic, slowing down its response time and sometimes preventing legitimate clients from connecting. While any type of traffic directed at the target will slow it down, some DoS attacks use legitimate requests to target a server's processor, as well as its network connection. Another type of DoS attack, called an *amplified DoS attack*, sends carefully formulated request messages to a legitimate DNS server, which causes the server to flood the intended victim with dozens of responses for each request.

While there are plenty of small-scale DoS attacks, in which an intruder uses one computer to generate traffic and direct it toward the target system, the truly dangerous ones are called *distributed denial-of-service (DDoS)* attacks. This type of attack involves one intruder, but many computers, referred to as *zombies* because they are running an application called a *bot* that can execute instructions at the behest of an attacker, such as instructions to bombard a particular target with traffic. DDoS attacks are virtually unlimited in scale and have been known to bring the largest networks to a standstill.

Bots

A *bot* is a software application or routine that operates remotely once deployed on a computer. An army of bots obeying commands from a single controller is called a *botnet*. Many bots are benign and perform useful services, but like any automated system, they can be made to perform malignant acts.

In a typical attack scenario, the attacker uses viruses or other means to deploy an army of bots on the computers of unsuspecting victims. The bots communicate over the Internet with a *command and control server*, which is run by the attacker, who can use it to command the bots to initiate a DDoS attack or perform other malicious acts. The target of the attack is then bombarded with traffic from dozens or hundreds of bots at once.

On-Path Attack

Formerly known as a *man-in-the-middle attack*, an *on-path attack* is a technique in which an intruder intercepts data packets as they travel over the network, reads and perhaps modifies the contents of the packets in some fashion, and then sends the modified packets on their way to their intended destination. There are any number of ways that an attacker can take profitable advantage of this arrangement.

> **EXAM TIP**
>
> When the Network+ exam objectives provide alternative names for a particular skill, as with the terms *on-path* and *man-in-the-middle*, their intention is for the exam candidate to be familiar with both, and to know that they represent the same technology.

DNS Poisoning

The Domain Name System (DNS) provides name resolution services to clients all over the world. When a client sends a query containing a computer or domain name to its DNS server, the server responds with the IP address associated with the queried name. *DNS poisoning* is a practice in which an attacker uses nefarious means to alter the DNS record for a particular name with a bogus IP address. The DNS server then begins responding to queries with the wrong IP address, sending clients to the wrong destination.

DNS poisoning was frequently used at one time to send traffic to web servers that duplicated the appearance of the real ones. However, DNS security has since been enhanced, and the exploits that made DNS poisoning easy have been remediated.

VLAN Hopping

VLAN hopping is a technique that allows an attacker to bypass the access control measures implemented in the network switches and access protected systems on another VLAN. Virtual LANs (VLANs) are logical networks—that is, networks that administrators create in switches by grouping ports together. VLANs behave much like physical networks composed of computers and cables and switches. Normally, a system on one VLAN cannot access other VLANs unless an administrator grants the permissions it needs to do so.

A VLAN can include ports on multiple switches. The switches use a technique called trunking for their inter-switch communications. Trunking requires that each packet be tagged with a VLAN identifier. VLAN hopping is a technique in which an individual adds a second tag to their packets. This *double tagging* can fool the switches into thinking the packets come from a different VLAN, enabling the attacker to access a VLAN for which they do not have permissions.

ARP Spoofing

Address Resolution Protocol (ARP) is a data link layer protocol that performs IP address to MAC address resolutions. When a system broadcasts an ARP request message containing an IP address, the host using that IP address must return a reply message containing its MAC address.

By generating ARP reply messages containing a false MAC address—a process called *ARP spoofing*—an attacker can poison the requestor's ARP cache with incorrect addresses, causing traffic to be redirected to a different destination. Directing an ARP spoofing attack at both parties of a transaction is one way to achieve an on-path (man-in-the-middle) situation.

Rogue DHCP

Because the Dynamic Host Configuration Protocol (DHCP) relies on broadcast messages on IPv4 networks, the entire network receives all of the DHCP messages. DHCP servers are configured to respond to broadcasts from clients and furnish them with IP addresses and other configuration settings.

A *rogue DHCP* server is an unauthorized server deployed on the network by an attacker for the purpose of supplying bogus IP addresses to clients. This is a form of DoS attack because, when the client systems configure themselves using the incorrect IP addresses, they are suddenly cut off from the network. Today, a technique called DHCP snooping built into switches can protect against rogues by filtering out unauthorized DHCP traffic.

Rogue Access Point

A *rogue access point (AP)* is an unauthorized wireless access point that someone has connected to the network. This might be an innocent attempt by employees to create their own wireless network, or it might be a deliberate attack. Whether innocent or malicious, a rogue access point—especially one that is not secured—is essentially providing free access to the company network to anyone.

Evil Twin

An *evil twin* is a type of attack in which a rogue access point is configured to kidnap wireless clients from the legitimate network and add them to the attacker's network. In addition to gaining unauthorized access to the company network, an attacker can use a rogue AP with DHCP functionality to allocate incorrect IP addresses to clients.

By configuring the rogue AP with the same SSID as the company network and setting it to use a different channel, and then jamming the channel the real APs are using, the attacker causes the clients to connect to the only AP available to them, that of the attacker. The rogue AP then uses DHCP to assign the clients IP addresses on the attacker's network, leaving them open to a peer-to-peer attack.

In addition, by supplying a false default gateway address, the rogue AP can cause wireless clients to send all of their outgoing traffic to the attacker's server for analysis, rather than to the actual default gateway router.

Ransomware

Ransomware is a term used to describe a form of malware that causes an infected computer to lock up, preventing all user access and displaying an official-looking screen stating that the computer can only be unlocked by paying a fine. While the screen might imply that the computer had been locked down by a U.S. government law enforcement agency, the source of the malware is never official and paying the fine (usually by some form of digital currency) might or might not result in the computer being unlocked.

Some ransomware doesn't actually lock the computer; it just displays its threat as a full-screen graphic and prevents any user input from changing the graphic and returning to the standard desktop. Other, more serious, threats actually encrypt all of the data on the victim's computer, forcing them to pay if they want the data decrypted.

Password Attacks

A *password attack* is a technique for accessing secured resources by guessing the password of a privileged account. Password attacks are typically just a matter of trying one password after another, but there are specialized techniques for automating and accelerating the process, including the following:

> ▶ **Dictionary:** An application that uses a preexisting dictionary—actually a database—of commonly used passwords and tries them against the account one by one

▶ **Brute-force:** An application that attempts to penetrate a password by using every conceivable permutation of its characters, including the substitution of upper- and lowercase characters, numerals, and symbols

The primary administrative guard against password attacks is the ability to limit the number of incorrect password guesses before the account is locked down for a period of time. Another counter to password attacks is simply to use longer and more complex passwords. The more characters there are in a password and the larger the character set, the greater the number of character permutations there are to guess, which further complicates the attack process.

MAC Spoofing

MAC spoofing is an attempt to access a protected resource by using the media access control (MAC) address of a system with privileged access to that resource. On cabled networks, MAC addresses are hard-coded into the computers' network interface adapters, making them relatively difficult to spoof. However, on a virtual machine, changing the MAC address of a network interface is a simple matter, which makes MAC spoofing that much easier.

MAC spoofing can be an effective method of defeating switch port security, which often uses MAC address filters to specify the devices that are permitted to access the network through a particular port. Spoofing can also enable an attacker to assume the identity of a registered device and use the MAC Authentication Bypass (MAB) protocol to avoid firewall security filters.

IP Spoofing

IP spoofing is a form of digital impersonation in which an individual modifies the Source Address field in the IP headers of their outgoing packets. This field is supposed to contain the IP address of the sending system; by changing it, individuals can make it appear as though the packet originated from somewhere else. By altering their transmissions in this way, people can send attack messages anonymously. DoS attacks, for example, frequently use IP spoofing to conceal the identities of the perpetrators. It is sometimes also possible to use IP spoofing to impersonate a host with elevated privileges and gain access to protected resources.

Deauthentication

Typically used to facilitate an evil twin attack, *deauthentication* is the misuse of the 802.11 *deauthentication frame*, a documented feature of the protocol that causes wireless clients to disconnect from their current access point. The clients, once disconnected, seek out another available access point, which might happen to be a rogue AP set up by the attacker. Once the client is connected to the rogue AP (the evil twin), the attacker can make use of it in various ways.

Malware

Malware is a general term for any software that is designed to perform unauthorized operations on a computer, including viruses, worms, Trojans, adware, spyware, and ransomware, among others. Because it is a catchall term, the effects of malware can range from merely annoying to catastrophic. Protection against many forms of malware is typically included in most of the so-called antivirus products, which usually protect against much more than viruses.

HUMAN AND ENVIRONMENTAL ATTACKS

In the IT world, the attackers and the defenders wage a technological war that is constantly escalating. However, some attackers prefer to stick to the tried and true by taking advantage of human weaknesses that never seem to change. Some of these human and environmental attacks are described in this section.

Social Engineering

Although the name sounds technological, *social engineering* does not require any technology, except maybe a telephone. Social engineering is an attack technique that consists primarily of simply asking people for information that is supposed to be confidential.

Many people, when they are at work, are inclined to be helpful. So, when someone calls them, saying they are from the IT department and that there is a problem with their user account, they often believe it and willingly tell the person their username and password. Even in a time when people are wary of being victimized, techniques like this often work surprisingly well. The only counter to social engineering is user education regarding the approaches the attacker might take and the types of information that the users should not disclose.

Phishing

Phishing is an attack technique in which the attacker sends official-looking emails, texts, or other communications to potential victims, which are designed to lure them into clicking a link, calling a telephone number, or responding to the email. The objective is to collect confidential information from the victims.

A phishing email might be an exact replica of an official email from a known correspondent, such as a government agency or a bank, asking the recipient for important information and providing a link to their official web site. The only difference from an actual email is that the link has been changed to send the recipients to an alternative website, one that might look just like an official site but that is run by the attacker.

The bogus site typically includes a form that asks the user for all kinds of personal information, such as banking and credit card account numbers. For the victims who supply the requested information, the damage that the attacker can do with it is no less than catastrophic. As with most forms of social engineering, the only defense against phishing is vigilance and user education.

Tailgating

Tailgating is a technique for gaining physical access to a restricted area protected by an access control system. Swipe cards and other access control devices typically unlock a door for a few seconds, time enough for the user to walk through. Tailgating is a practice in which an unauthorized user takes advantage of those few seconds that the door is unlocked and slips through with the authorized user. The standard counter to tailgating is an *access control vestibule (or mantrap)* with door locks timed so that unauthorized users cannot slip through unnoticed.

Piggybacking

When an unauthorized person slips through a protected entrance with an authorized person, there is always a question of whether the authorized user was complicit in the act. The term *tailgating* typically refers to unauthorized entrance with an unsuspecting user. When an authorized user deliberately allows an unauthorized person through the door, the term *piggybacking* is more common.

In this situation, an access control vestibule is no counter because the authorized user is presumably willing to hold the doors open for the unauthorized user. Cameras or security guards are therefore the preferred counter for this type of security breach.

Shoulder Surfing

Shoulder surfing refers to a type of social engineering in which an attacker stands behind a seated user and looks over their shoulder, trying to see either the user's hands typing a password or credit card number or any confidential information appearing on the screen. The only real counter to shoulder surfing is for the user to be vigilant about entering confidential information when someone is looming behind them.

CERTMIKE EXAM ESSENTIALS

▶ Enterprise networks today are susceptible to a variety of technological attacks, including denial-of-service (DoS), on-path, DNS poisoning, VLAN hopping, and evil twin.

▶ Attackers often penetrate network security by configuring one system to impersonate another, a technique called spoofing. For various purposes, attackers might use ARP spoofing, MAC spoofing, or IP spoofing. Attackers might even spoof entire devices by connecting their own rogue DHCP servers or rogue access points to the network.

▶ Human-based attacks are typically techniques for duping innocent users into revealing confidential information, a process called social engineering. Phishing and shoulder surfing are variations on this method, using emails and eavesdropping to gather information.

▶ Techniques for defeating physical barriers include tailgating, which involves an unsuspecting authorized user, and piggybacking, in which an authorized user deliberately admits an unauthorized person.

Practice Question 1

Ralph is a new hire in the IT department at his company. His supervisor has called him into a meeting with the directors of the company and informed him that there have been several document security incidents in recent months due to social engineering. He asks Ralph to formulate a plan for addressing the social engineering problem and preventing further document security incidents.

Ralph assures his supervisor that it will not be a problem to produce such a plan. Ralph does this because he is assuming that he will have time to do some research and find out what social engineering is, which he doesn't know. Before the meeting ends, however, Ralph's supervisor asks him to outline the basic idea of his plan for the directors right then. Ralph attempts to stall, but he is pressed to provide an answer to the directors on the spot. Which of the following solutions should he propose?

A. Install an antivirus software product on all user workstations.

B. Implement a program of user education and revised corporate policies.

C. Install an additional firewall between the internal network and the internet.

D. Use IPsec to encrypt all network traffic.

Practice Question 2

Alice receives an email from her bank informing her that her checking account has been frozen due to suspected fraudulent activity. To confirm the charges that are fraudulent, the email provides a link to the bank's website, where Alice can review a list of the suspicious transactions. Alice clicks the link and logs on to the bank site with her username and password, plus the PIN that the bank recently implemented for added security. She is taken to a web page that appears to be that of her bank, but it is not. Which of the following types of attacks is Alice likely to be experiencing?

A. VLAN hopping

B. Evil twin

C. Spoofing

D. Phishing

Practice Question 1 Explanation

A. is incorrect because social engineering is not a virus or a form of malware, so an antivirus product will have no effect on the problem.

B. is correct because social engineering is the practice of obtaining confidential data by contacting users and impersonating someone with a legitimate need for that data. No technological solution can prevent it; the only way is to educate users of the potential dangers and establish policies that inform users what to do when they experience a social engineering attempt.

C. is incorrect because social engineering does not involve the network or its traffic in any way. Therefore, a firewall cannot block it.

D. is incorrect because social engineering does not involve the network, so encrypting the network traffic using IPsec will have no effect on the problem.

Correct Answer: B

Practice Question 2 Explanations

A. is incorrect because VLAN hopping is a means of gaining access to a protected VLAN by inserting extra tags into network packets.

B. is incorrect because evil twin is a type of attack that uses a rogue access point to kidnap wireless clients.

C. is incorrect because spoofing is the process of modifying network packets to make them appear as though they are transmitted by or addressed to someone else.

D. is correct because Alice has probably fallen victim to a phishing attack. The email was likely false, with a link that brought Alice not to her bank's website, but to the attacker's own duplicate site. By supplying her account credentials to log on, she has given them to the attacker, including the newly implemented PIN. The attacker can now gain access to Alice's genuine bank account.

Correct Answer: D, Phishing

CHAPTER 18

Network Hardening
Objective 4.3: Given a scenario, apply network hardening techniques.

This chapter examines some of the network hardening techniques that administrators frequently implement on a typical enterprise network. The Network+ exam expects candidates to be familiar with these basic security threats.

In this chapter, you'll learn everything you need to know about Network+ Objective 4.3, including the following topics:

▶ Best practices
▶ Wireless security
▶ IoT access considerations

BEST PRACTICES

In a security context, *network hardening* refers to settings or practices that increase the security of the network in specific ways. There are many hardening techniques that administrators use to add protection to various elements of the network. Some of them are so basic that they should be automatic, such as changing default passwords, whereas others require more consideration and planning. The following sections describe some of the best practices in network hardening—that is, the techniques that are most commonly employed by enterprise network administrators.

Secure SNMP

The *Simple Network Management Protocol (SNMP)*, as described in Chapter 13, "Network Availability," consists of a central console that communicates with agents scattered all over the network. The agents send status information to the console, and the console sends configuration changes to the agents. Until SNMP version 3, there was no security at all for the console/agent communications. Anyone who discovers the community name for an SNMP version 1 or 2c implementation can send GET or SET commends to a network device and retrieve its information or reconfigure its settings.

SNMP version 1 and 2c servers can operate in read-only or read/write mode. It is common for read-only servers to use the default community name *public* and read/write servers to use the name *private*. If it is not possible to upgrade to SNMP version 3, administrators should at least change the default community names.

SNMP version 3 improves the protocol's security by adding support for password authentication, encryption, and message integrity. While even SNMP version 3 is not without security deficiencies, it is far more secure than the earlier versions.

Router Advertisement (RA) Guard

Router Advertisement (RA) messages are generated by the Neighbor Discovery Protocol (NDP) on IPv6 networks to advertise network address prefixes. IPv6 hosts, once they have the prefix for their network, can generate their own IPv6 addresses. However, the RA messages are subject to being spoofed, enabling an intruder to divert host traffic and capture it for inspection.

Router Advertisement (RA) Guard is a feature built into some switches that allows an administrator to specify the switch ports that are allowed to transmit RA messages. By designating the ports connected to the routers and other switches on the network as RA ports, they can perform router advertisements in the normal manner. All of the other ports—presumably including the ones to which potential intruders are connected—are blocked from transmitting RA messages.

Port Security

Port security is a feature found on most managed switches that allows administrators to restrict the MAC addresses that can connect to individual switch ports. This is to prevent people from plugging unauthorized devices, such as hosts, wireless access points, or other switches, into a port that provides access to protected resources.

Port security is implemented in different ways, depending on the manufacturer of the switch. One common technique is for a switch to restrict each of its ports to the sender's MAC address in the first packet received through that port. Not only can no other MAC address connect to that port, but the administrator can also prevent multiple addresses from connecting, as when an intruder plugs another switch or access point into the port.

Dynamic ARP Inspection

Dynamic ARP inspection (DAI) is a technique designed to prevent Address Resolution Protocol (ARP) spoofing. *ARP spoofing* is a type of attack in which an intruder generates fraudulent messages that cause hosts to change the IP address-to-MAC address mappings in their ARP caches, a process known as *ARP poisoning*.

DAI, implemented in switches, is a feature that reads the incoming ARP request messages and compares their IP-to-MAC address mappings to the mappings in the binding table created on the switch by the DHCP snooping process. The mappings in the binding table are presumed to be correct because they come from trusted DHCP servers. Any mappings in ARP request messages that do not agree with those in the binding table are presumed to be fraudulent, and the messages are discarded.

Control Plane Policing

The control plane in a router or switch carries non-data traffic to and from other routers and switches; it is one of three standard communication planes, along with the data plane and the management plane. *Control plane policing (CPP or CoPP)* is a rate limiting feature in some routers and switches that uses quality of service (QoS) policies to prevent the control plane from being inundated with irrelevant traffic, such as that produced by denial-of-service (DoS) attacks.

Private VLANs

A *private VLAN* is a microsegment within another VLAN, essentially a VLAN within a VLAN. Administrators create virtual local area networks (VLANs) by applying a VLAN designation to a group of switchports on one or more switches. When the administrator creates a private VLAN within an existing VLAN, the private VLAN becomes the *secondary* to the existing LAN's *primary*.

There are two types of private VLANs, as follows:

▶ **Isolated:** Connected devices can communicate only with a router port, not with each other.
▶ **Community:** Connected devices can communicate with each other, as well as with a router port.

Private VLANs are a means of creating separate microsegments in which selected devices can be isolated with limited communication.

Disable Unneeded Switchports

Unused switchports, especially those that are connected to wall plates in common areas, should be disabled at the switch. Many administrators omit this practice for the sake of convenience, but an open wall plate into which anyone can connect a host, switch, or access point is an invitation to attack.

Disable Unneeded Network Services

Services and daemons provide benefits to users, but they are also open doors into the network. Any services that are not in active use should be disabled, just as an unused door should be locked. On a TCP/IP network, services and daemons are associated with TCP/IP ports. Intruders can easily detect ports that are open to incoming traffic using scanning software. Once detected, the ports become targets for the intruder's exploitation.

For necessary services, their TCP/IP ports must be left open, and it is up to administrators to protect them with firewalls and other means. However, for any ports that are left open by services or daemons not actively being used, administrators should take action by disabling the services and closing the port to any incoming traffic.

> **EXAM TIP**
>
> The term *port* has multiple definitions in the IT universe. A TCP/IP port is a logical endpoint through which an application communicates with the network. Switches also have ports, which are physical cable connectors that provide links to hosts and other network devices. Candidates for the Network+ exam should be aware of the term's uses.

Change Default Passwords

Virtually all network devices require users or administrators to log on before they can access its administrative interface. While some devices require a user to create a password during the first connection, many have default usernames and passwords set by the manufacturer.

In these cases, the first thing the administrator should do when setting up the device is change the default password and, if possible, the username as well. If intruders know the default username for a device, they can begin to work on cracking the password immediately. If the administrator has changed the default username, then intruders have to guess that as well as the password.

Password Complexity/Length

When specifying a password for a device or an account, the objective is to make the process of guessing the password as long and difficult as possible. The longer the password is, the greater the number of possibilities there are for an attacker to guess and the longer it takes to crack it.

As shown in Table 18.1, adding to the length of a password increases the number of possibilities dramatically, as does adding basic symbols to the alphanumeric character set. Just increasing the password length by two characters, from eight to 10, increases the crack time from hours to months.

TABLE 18.1   Effects of password length on possibilities and crack time

Number of characters	Letters & numbers	Letters, numbers, & basic symbols	Offline crack time (with symbols)
6 characters	2.2 billion	109 billion	1.1 seconds
8 characters	2.9 trillion	521 trillion	1.45 hours
10 characters	3.7 quadrillion	2.4 quintillion	9.47 months
15 characters	227 sextillion	3.88 octillion	1.2 billion years

All passwords are a trade-off between security and convenience, but administrators should consider these figures when configuring passwords for network devices and creating password policies for the network's users.

Enable DHCP Snooping

DHCP snooping is a feature found on many switches that is designed to prevent rogue DHCP servers from connecting to the network and allocating incorrect IP addresses to clients. These incorrect IP addresses can prevent the clients from accessing the real enterprise network, sending them instead to an alternative network run by the attacker responsible for the rogue. By itself, this is a form of denial-of-service attack, but it can also be the opening salvo of an on-path (or man-in-the-middle) attack.

The DHCP snooping feature enables administrators to designate certain switch ports as trusted for DHCP server traffic. DHCP packets arriving at the switch through a nontrusted port are silently discarded. The switch also analyzes (or snoops) the DHCP packets arriving through the trusted ports and uses the information inside to create a table of legitimate IP address-to-MAC address mappings called a *binding table*.

Change Default VLAN

By default, switches are equipped with a single VLAN—usually called VLAN1—to which all of the switchports are assigned at the factory. The default VLAN is permanent and unchangeable, so potential attackers know it is there, where it presents a tempting target. Therefore, even if the administrators do not plan to segment the network using VLANs, they should create at least one new VLAN (hopefully not called VLAN2) and move all of the switchports into it. Any attackers must then discover the VLAN before they can target it, which makes the target that much less tempting.

Patch and Firmware Management

Operating systems, applications, and network devices all require software updates from time to time, but it is up to the administrators of the network to create a *patch management* policy that specifies when and if to apply the updates. The most critical types of updates for operating systems and applications are those that address the latest security issues.

Attackers and software developers are involved in a never-ending arms race, and it is important to apply the developers' responses to the latest exploits. This is particularly true when a software manufacturer releases an emergency security update outside of their normal release schedule. Updates containing bug fixes are the next priority, followed by updates containing new features.

Network device manufacturers sometimes release *firmware updates*, which modify the read-only software stored in a hardware device's nonvolatile memory, or driver updates, which modify the hardware's interaction with the operating system. These are the types of updates that often cause hesitation among network administrators. When a device is functioning properly, some administrators adhere to the "if it ain't broke, don't fix it" rule and wait until there is a compelling reason to apply an update.

Some enterprise networks have a policy of testing updates in a sandbox environment before applying them to production devices. Products like Microsoft's Windows Server Update Services (WSUS) enable administrators to download, evaluate, and test update releases and then deploy them to the entire network at a selected time.

Access Control List

Access control lists (ACLs) are systems of permissions that restrict access to network resources. Administrators can use ACLs to allow or deny access to a resource based on specific criteria. Operating systems and applications use ACLs to identify the users who can log on and access specific resources.

In the network infrastructure, routers and firewalls use ACLs to filter the traffic entering and leaving a network by examining its IP addresses. Routers can use ACLs to create protected network segments within the enterprise. Firewalls use ACLs to restrict the traffic coming in from the Internet and going out to it.

Role-Based Access

Configuring access control lists for user accounts can be complicated and time-consuming when there are many permissions to assign for many different users. One method for streamlining the process is to create roles, which are combinations of the permissions needed to perform specific jobs. *Role-based access* allows administrators to configure a set of permissions once and then assign them to multiple users.

Many operating systems and applications include preconfigured roles. They are usually quite general, however, such as an operating system that offers only administrator and user roles. When network administrators create their own roles, they can customize them with greater granularity to accommodate specific jobs and users.

Firewall Rules

A firewall is a barrier between two networks, either between two internal networks or between an internal network and the Internet. Administrators create *firewall rules* in the form of ACLs that specify what traffic is allowed to pass through the barrier and what traffic is denied access to the network.

The most common approach to configuring firewall rules is to create allow permissions for the traffic that should be admitted to the network. After the allow permissions, the administrator creates an *implicit deny* rule, which blocks all other traffic that has not been explicitly allowed by the previous rules.

Another approach is to create a rule that allows all traffic into the network except that which has been blocked by *explicit deny* rules. For Internet firewalls, this is usually not a practical approach because it requires administrators to anticipate all possible attacks and create rules that block all of the traffic those attacks direct at the network. For firewalls between internal networks, the explicit deny approach might be feasible.

WIRELESS SECURITY

Hardening a wireless network requires different tools and procedures from wired networks. Some of the concepts used to secure wireless networks are described in this section.

MAC Filtering

Just as the managed switches on cabled networks have a port security feature that limits network access to specific hosts, wireless access points (WAPs) can do the same thing. The mechanism used on both devices is called MAC filtering. On a wireless network, *MAC filtering* is essentially a list of the clients' MAC addresses, maintained on the WAP, which specifies the only hosts that are permitted to connect to the network.

The administration of MAC filtering can be time-consuming when there is a large number of clients. In some cases, administrators must discover the MAC addresses of the client devices and enter them into the WAP's MAC address table manually. Any wireless clients that attempt to connect to the network must be listed in that table before they are permitted access. MAC addresses are also easily spoofed, which makes MAC filtering less valuable as a security measure.

Antenna Placement

One of the security threats inherent in wireless networking is unauthorized persons connecting to the network, sometimes even from outside the company premises. An intruder can sometimes sit outside in the parking lot with a laptop and receive enough of a network signal to establish a connection.

One way to avoid this threat is for administrators to carefully consider the network's *antenna placement*. The standard antennas on wireless access points are omnidirectional, so placing them too close to an outside wall can allow the signal to propagate outside the building. Moving the antennas nearer to the center of the interior space can limit the strength of the signal that reaches outside. Another possibility is to use semidirectional antennas near the outer walls, such as patch antennas, which point their coverage to the interior space and limit the amount of signal that reaches the parking lot.

Power Levels

Another way to prevent wireless signals from propagating outside of the premises is to move the access point or adjust its transmission *power levels*. Performing a site survey can tell administrators exactly where the signals are too weak inside the facility or excessively strong outside. Moving the access point around is one way to address these problems. Another way, available as a feature on some access points and wireless LAN controllers, is to adjust the overall power level of the unit.

The 802.11h wireless LAN standard includes a feature called *Transmission Power Control (TPC)*, which automatically reduces the transmission power of the AP on a 5 GHz network when other networks are detected nearby. This is designed to prevent interference with the signals from other networks.

Wireless Client Isolation

By default, most wireless networks allow clients connected to an access point to communicate with each other, as well as to the wired network and the Internet. This kind of peer-to-peer access is appropriate for a residential network on which everyone is trusted. However, on a business network, peer access can be a security risk.

The ability to access the other wireless clients just provides potential intruders with a much larger attack surface to target. Some access points include a feature called *wireless client isolation*—or a similar name—that allows administrators to disable peer access between the wireless clients connected to the access point. The clients can still access the wired network and the Internet, but they cannot connect to each other.

Guest Network Isolation

Guest network isolation is another WAP feature similar to wireless client isolation in that it disables peer access. The difference in this feature is that the WAP disables peer access only for the clients connected to the guest network.

Many WAPs support a guest network feature, which can provide temporary users with limited network access. The guest network is essentially a separate network segment. Clients connected to it are granted access to the Internet, but nothing more. Guest network clients cannot access other wireless clients or the wired network to which the WAP is connected, unlike the primary wireless LAN, which is unaffected.

Preshared Keys (PSKs)

A *preshared key (PSK)* is an alphanumeric text string most commonly used for encrypting wireless network traffic protected by the Wi-Fi Protected Access (WPA) and WPA2 security protocols. Protocols that use PSKs typically use them for symmetrical encryption, in which the same key both encrypts and decrypts data. This is in contrast to systems that use public key cryptography, which uses pairs of keys, public and private.

WPA and WPA2, in their PSK modes, also use the same preshared key for all of the network users connecting to the wireless access point, which means that any network user can compromise the security of the entire system by sharing the PSK with unauthorized people. For more information on WPA and WPA2, see "Encryption Standards" in Chapter 12, "Wireless Standards."

Enterprise Authentication

Because the use of a single key preshared with all of the network users is inherently insecure, all but the smallest SOHO networks typically use some form of enterprise-based authentication that does not rely on PSK encryption. There are several alternatives to PSK, including the enterprise version of WPA/WPA2 and EAP, as discussed in the following sections.

WPA/WPA2 Enterprise

In addition to its PSK mode, WPA and WPA2 have an Enterprise mode, which does not rely on preshared keys. WPA/WPA2 Enterprise uses the 802.1X authentication protocol with a separate authentication server, usually running Remote Authentication Dial-In User Service (RADIUS).

EAP

Extensible Authentication Protocol (EAP) is not really a protocol at all, but rather a framework for a protocol. EAP extends the 802.1X framework to support a variety of authentication mechanisms that can provide a network with different levels of hardening, including swipe cards, fingerprints, and other forms of biometrics, as well as passwords. There are many protocols that use the EAP framework, including Protected Extensible Authentication Protocol (PEAP), which encapsulates EAP within an encrypted TLS tunnel, and Extensible Authentication Protocol – Transport Layer Security (EAP-TLS), used on wireless networks.

Geofencing

Geofencing is a technique for limiting access to a network, system, or service based on the geographic location of the client, as specified by global positioning system (GPS) or radio-frequency identification (RFID) chips. There are several ways in which networks can use this technology. Users within a specified virtual boundary can be permitted access to the network and denied access when they cross outside of the boundary. The system can generate alerts when an unauthorized device crosses the boundary into the protected area. It is also possible to configure mobile devices intended for use only within the boundary to self-erase their data if someone takes them outside of the boundary.

Captive Portal

A *captive portal* is a web page, as shown in Figure 18.1, where wireless network users must authenticate—or at least identify themselves—before they are granted access to the network. Most businesses that provide free wireless Internet access—such as coffee shops and fast-food restaurants—configure their networks to send users to a captive portal when they first attempt to establish a network connection.

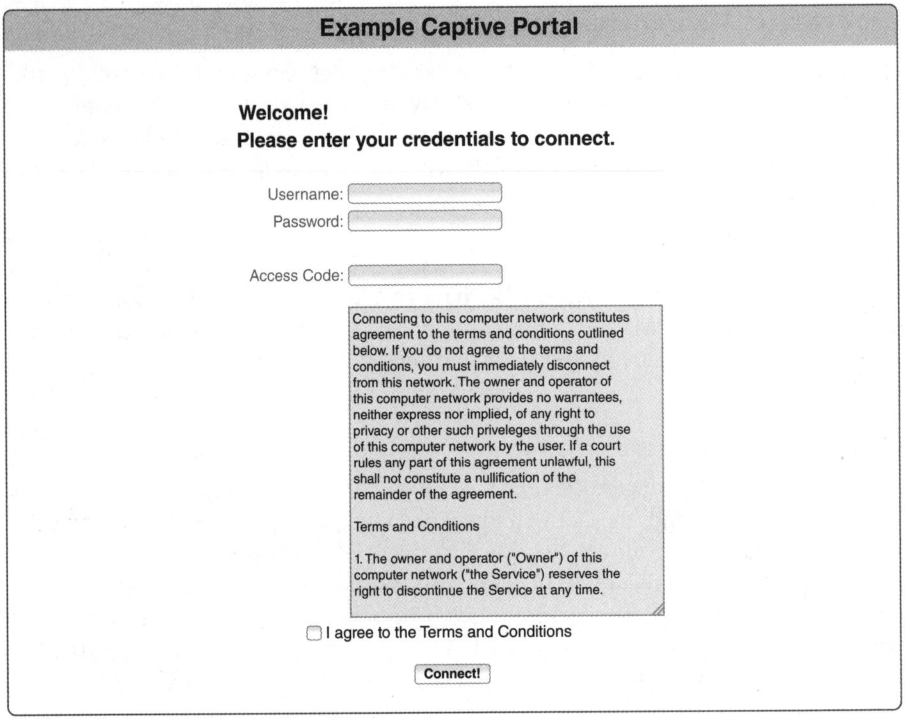

Example Captive Portal

Welcome!
Please enter your credentials to connect.

Username: [_____]
Password: [_____]

Access Code: [_____]

Connecting to this computer network constitutes agreement to the terms and conditions outlined below. If you do not agree to the terms and conditions, you must immediately disconnect from this network. The owner and operator of this computer network provides no warrantees, neither express nor implied, of any right to privacy or other such privileges through the use of this computer network by the user. If a court rules any part of this agreement unlawful, this shall not constitute a nullification of the remainder of the agreement.

Terms and Conditions

1. The owner and operator ("Owner") of this computer network ("the Service") reserves the right to discontinue the Service at any time.

☐ I agree to the Terms and Conditions

[Connect!]

FIGURE 18.1 A captive web portal

A captive portal, at the very least, requires users to agree to an end-user license agreement by specifying their email addresses. Businesses that charge users for Internet access, such as hotels, sometimes use a captive portal for the e-commerce transactions or to specify existing account credentials.

IoT ACCESS CONSIDERATIONS

The *Internet of Things (IoT)* refers to hardware devices—such as lights, thermostats, cameras, and other home automation devices—that are capable of connecting to a TCP/IP network, most often to provide users with remote administration of the device. IoT devices are frequently wireless and connect to a network using Wi-Fi, Bluetooth, or a similar technology.

IoT devices have IP addresses like any other network client, which makes them vulnerable to attack. The devices themselves typically do not have much in the way of security mechanisms and often can easily be infected with a bot and turned into a zombie. Protection for the devices and for the network must usually come from an outside source, such as a firewall.

CERTMIKE EXAM ESSENTIALS

▶ Many network hardening techniques are means for reducing the network's attack surfaces, such as disabling unneeded switchports and services, creating more secure VLANs, implementing ACLs and firewall rules, and using strong passwords.

▶ Attackers can often gain unauthorized access to a network by taking advantage of regular administration traffic, such as that generated by SNMP, ARP, NDP, and DHCP. Closing these avenues off to potential attackers is a key element of network hardening.

▶ Wireless networks have unique security issues, many of which administrators address by manipulating and configuring features on the WAPs, such as MAC filtering, client and guest network isolation, and geofencing.

Practice Question 1

Alice is responsible for the security of the 23rd floor Wi-Fi networks in her company's office building. Recently, there have been some security incidents that were traced to unauthorized wireless network accesses on the 23rd floor. Alice's floor contains the company's buyers, so there are frequently salespeople in the office who need Internet access for their mobile devices. The buyers' offices all contain wireless printers, so they can print out orders for the salespeople on the spot, and to accommodate the salespeople, Alice uses the WPA2 protocol for security with a preshared key, which the receptionists supply to the salespeople as they enter. Alice knows that this is less than secure, and she suspects that it might be the source of the security breaches.

Which of the following steps should Alice take to increase the security of the 23rd-floor Wi-Fi network while accommodating the salespeople and without inconveniencing the buyers?

A. Implement MAC filtering on the WAPs.
B. Create an isolated guest network.
C. Move the WAP antennas.
D. Change the preshared key daily.

Practice Question 2

One Monday morning, Ralph is working the IT helpdesk when he starts receiving calls and emails from users who cannot access the network. This is a familiar type of call for Ralph, but there are far too many of them at once to be a result of user error. Ralph inspects several of the workstations experiencing the problem and is surprised to discover that they all have IP addresses on a network that is not one of the company subnets.

Ralph tries manually changing the addresses to correct ones, and the workstations connect to the network without a problem. Investigating further, Ralph notices that the incorrect addresses are still being assigned by a DHCP server. He concludes that someone must have connected another DHCP server to the network, which his supervisor tells him is called a rogue.

Which of the following would be the easiest way to locate and neutralize the rogue DHCP server?

A. Capture a network traffic sample and analyze the DHCP message contents.
B. Map the locations of the misconfigured workstations.
C. Reconfigure the switchports to which the legitimate DHCP servers are connected.
D. Reconfigure all of the workstations to use manually assigned IP addresses.

Practice Question 1 Explanation

A. is incorrect because it would not be practical to use MAC filtering on a network with so many temporary users.

B. is correct because creating an isolated guest network for the salespeople would prevent them from accessing any network resources other than the Internet connection.

C. is incorrect because moving the antennas does nothing to address Alice's suspected cause of the security problems.

D. is incorrect because changing the preshared key adds no security when Alice has to distribute the new key to the salespeople each day.

Correct Answer: B

Practice Question 2 Explanations

A. is incorrect because, although the contents of the DHCP messages can disclose the address of the rogue server, they cannot tell Ralph where it is located, nor can they neutralize it.

B. is incorrect because a DHCP server's clients can be located anywhere on the network. The locations of the affected workstations are no indication of the server's location.

C. is correct because many switches include a DHCP snooping feature that allows administrators to designate certain switchports as connected to legitimate DHCP servers. The switches then discard DHCP traffic arriving over any other switchports.

D. is incorrect because, while using manually assigned addresses would solve the problem, the process would be far too time- and labor-intensive.

Correct Answer: C

CHAPTER 19

Remote Access
Objective 4.4: Compare and contrast remote access methods and security implications.

This chapter examines some of the remote access techniques that administrators frequently implement on a typical enterprise network. The Network+ exam expects candidates to be familiar with these basic concepts.

In this chapter, you'll learn everything you need to know about Network+ Objective 4.4, including the following topics:

▶ **Site-to-site VPN**
▶ **Client-to-site VPN**
▶ **Remote Desktop Connection**
▶ **Remote Desktop Gateway**
▶ **SSH**
▶ **Virtual network computing (VNC)**
▶ **Virtual desktop**
▶ **Authentication and authorization considerations**
▶ **In-band vs. out-of-band management**

VIRTUAL PRIVATE NETWORKS

A *virtual private network (VPN)* is a means for connecting computers or networks together using a secure tunnel carried by an unsecured network, such as the Internet. This means that all of the packets containing the VPN traffic are encrypted and encapsulated within standard IP packets so that they can be safely transmitted over an unsecured network.

Client-to-Site VPN

The primary use for a VPN is to provide a client workstation with access to a VPN server at a remote site, which in turn provides access to the site's network. The typical *client-to-site VPN* scenario is that of a user at a remote location connecting to a company network using the Internet. All that is required at the user end is the client software and an Internet connection. At the server end is a device that listens for incoming connection requests from the Internet. This device can be a router or a VPN server software product running on a computer, but there are also specialized devices called *VPN concentrators* that can handle connections from many clients at once. This spares the servers and routers the additional burden of processing those connections.

It is also possible to create VPN connections using other carriers, such as wide area network (WAN) or even local area network (LAN) connections. For example, some administrators take advantage of VPN security by using them within a facility to connect to and manage their servers.

Site-to-Site VPN

VPNs have also become a popular solution for site-to-site connections. For many years, leased lines and other WAN connection types were the standard for links between sites at distant locations. However, leased lines are expensive and inflexible; their cost is based on the length of the connection, and the customer pays for a set amount of bandwidth day and night, whether or not they use it.

By contrast, a site-to-site VPN connection requires only that each site have a VPN server and a connection to a local Internet service provider (ISP). The cost is much lower than that of a leased line or any other WAN technology, and increasing the VPN's bandwidth only requires a change in the contract with the ISPs at both sites.

Clientless VPN

A remote access VPN connection typically requires a VPN client software product. The VPN client is responsible for establishing and maintaining one end of the tunnel. However, VPN products are now available that use the Secure Sockets Layer/Transport Layer Security (SSL/TLS) encryption capabilities built into current web browsers to create the client end of the tunnel. No special software installation is required at the client end of the tunnel, and a web-based user interface enables remote users to access resources on the network at the server end.

Split Tunnel vs. Full Tunnel

When a VPN client connects to a remote VPN server, it creates a new logical network connection. However, the client's original (unencrypted) connection to the Internet is still in place. VPN clients typically provide two options for the use of these connections, as follows:

▶ **Split tunnel:** In a split tunnel client, both of the network connections remain active, with all company traffic going through the VPN tunnel connection, while the system uses its original, unprotected connection for Internet access. This reduces the traffic passing through the VPN tunnel but presents a potential security hazard if the Internet connection is unprotected.

▶ **Full tunnel:** In a full tunnel client, only the VPN tunnel connection remains active, with all client traffic going to the remote network. The client therefore accesses the Internet through the remote network, providing it with the additional security monitoring and protection of the company infrastructure.

Remote Desktop Connection (RDC) (see Figure 19.1) is a graphical application that enables a client user at one location to connect to a host computer at another location and control it

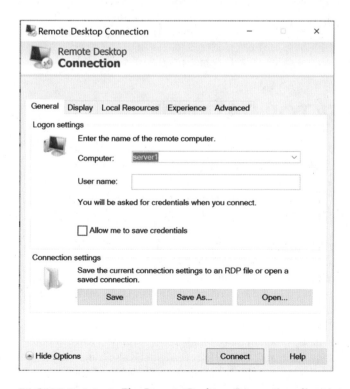

F I G U R E   1 9 . 1   The Remote Desktop Connection client interface

as though the user was seated in front of it. Once connected, everything the client user does occurs on the host machine; the client and the host exchange only keyboard, mouse, and display traffic.

RDC is a tool, originally created by Microsoft, that uses a proprietary *Remote Desktop Protocol (RDP)* to carry traffic between the client and the host. RDC enables administrators to access their servers from anywhere, telecommuters to access their company workstations, and troubleshooters to work on users' problems without traveling.

All Microsoft operating systems since Windows XP in 2001 have included an RDC client, and there are now client ports available for virtually every other popular operating system, including those for smartphones and other mobile devices. The server side of the RDC application for a single remote user is provided in the Pro versions of the current Microsoft operating systems. There is also a Windows Server role called Remote Desktop Services, which enables clients to access session desktops, virtual desktops, and RemoteApp applications on the host server's network.

> **EXAM TIP**
>
> Now called Remote Desktop Services, the server-based RDP product was called Terminal Services until the release of Windows Server 2008. Candidates for the Network+ exam should be aware that documentation might still be available under the earlier name.

REMOTE DESKTOP GATEWAY

Remote Desktop Gateway (RD Gateway) is a role service—that is, a subcomponent—of the Remote Desktop Services role in Windows Server. RD Gateway provides Remote Desktop clients with a secure, encrypted RDP connection to the server, through which they can access network resources. In addition, RD Gateway can work with other servers in the network to provide certificate-based authentication and authorization services for connecting users.

RD Gateway is designed to provide secure access to Remote Desktop servers and other resources on the host network without the need for a VPN server. The server running the RD Gateway role service is typically located on a perimeter network, where it is both accessible from the Internet and can access resources running on the internal network. Clients connecting to RD Gateway can access virtual desktops, Remote Desktop servers, and RemoteApp applications on the host network.

Telnet is a simple, character-based program that enables a user to connect to a computer at a remote location and execute commands there. However, Telnet is also completely insecure, sending passwords and other input in clear text. *Secure Shell (SSH)* is a character-based remote access protocol that differs from Telnet mainly in that SSH encrypts the connection between the client and the server. SSH also authenticates both the client and the server daemon before it permits the connection to be established.

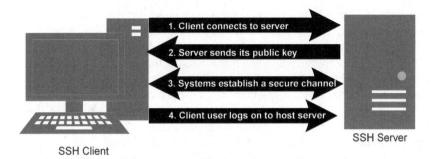

FIGURE 19.2 SSH secure channel establishment

Originally created for use on Unix/Linux systems, and despite using the same command-line interface, SSH is an enormous improvement over Telnet. This is primarily because SSH ensures the confidentiality and integrity of all of its client/server traffic using public key encryption, as shown in Figure 19.2, while Telnet transmits everything over the network in unencrypted form, including usernames and passwords.

VIRTUAL NETWORK COMPUTING (VNC)

Virtual Network Computing (VNC) is a graphical remote control application similar in function to Remote Desktop Connection, with the exception that VNC was designed from its inception to be platform independent. VNC requires the installation of a software product at both ends of the connection: a client and a server. There is also a protocol that carries the traffic between the client and the server called Remote Frame Buffer (RFB). Unlike RDC, the VNC software is not supplied with operating systems, nor is it free.

VIRTUAL DESKTOP

A *virtual desktop* is an operating system image, hosted on a server, that a user can access from a client device at any remote location. Like RDC, the virtual desktop and all of its applications run on the server. A typical virtual desktop arrangement uses a *Virtual Desktop Infrastructure (VDI)* at the server end, which hosts multiple desktop images for different users. The device from which the user accesses the virtual desktop functions only as a *thin client*, exchanging keystrokes, mouse movements, and display traffic with the server.

There are notable advantages to this arrangement. The user's device only needs resources sufficient to run the virtual desktop client software; any applications running on a user's virtual desktop actually execute on the VDI server, using the server's processors, memory, storage, and other resources. This means that virtually any device can function as a virtual desktop client, including devices that are not capable of running the desktop operating system themselves, such as smartphones and other mobile devices.

In addition, all of a virtual desktop user's applications, data, and configuration settings remain on the VDI server, protected by the enterprise infrastructure either in the company data center or in the cloud. Some organizations deploy all of their user workstations as virtual desktops. This enables users to access their fully configured desktops from anywhere. For example, a user can work in the office on a particular document until quitting time, then go home, leaving the document open on their virtual desktop, and later connect to the same desktop from their home computer and resume working where they left off.

Some organizations maintain a VDI in their own data centers, but others implement it in their own cloud infrastructure. Some cloud service providers also provide virtual desktops to customers by individual subscription, marketing the product as desktop as a service (DaaS).

AUTHENTICATION AND AUTHORIZATION CONSIDERATIONS

Many remote access solutions are available with security capabilities that vary widely, but all of them suffer from the same fundamental weakness: they all open a great big door to your network with flashing lights and a neon WELCOME sign. The nature of the protection that network administrators should provide at that door must be a critical part of any remote access server deployment.

Authentication is the basic credential check that all remote users should undergo before they gain any access to the host network. Many remote access server software products are capable of using other services on the network for authentication, such as RADIUS, TACACS+, and Active Directory. The authentication process for remote access users should be, if anything, more rigorous than that for on-premises users. Multifactor authentication, a practice that seemed extreme just a few years ago, is now commonplace, typically using a username/password and a one-time code sent to a smartphone or email address.

Authorization is the process of controlling access to specific network resources, often employing a system of permissions that enables administrators to precisely tune the access granted to specific users. The theory of least permissions, in which users are granted only the minimum access they need to perform their required tasks, applies to remote access even more strenuously than it does for an on-premises user.

IN-BAND VS. OUT-OF-BAND MANAGEMENT

Network devices, such as routers, have three categories of network traffic, called planes. The data plane and the control plane consist of the actual user traffic being processed by the device, while the *management plane* handles the traffic generated by administrators as they monitor and configure the device.

In most cases, network devices default to using the standard network interfaces for all three planes. In other words, the management traffic is mingled with the data and control traffic. This is known as *in-band management*, with the term *band* referring to the device's standard network interfaces. Under normal conditions, in-band management is a perfectly serviceable arrangement, but if there should be a fault that affects the device's network interfaces, then administrators might be left with no means of accessing the management plane to troubleshoot the problem.

For this reason, many network devices have an alternative means of accessing the management plane. Any mechanism that provides access to a device's management plane through means other than the standard network interfaces is called *out-of-band management*.

For many devices, their out-of-band management capabilities take the form of an extra network interface, such as an Ethernet or USB port, typically labeled Console. Administrators can plug a device into the Console port, such as a laptop, a terminal, or even a dial-up modem, and gain access to the device's command-line interface. In addition to providing monitoring and troubleshooting access, the Console interface provides the administrator with the management plane access needed to perform the initial setup and configuration of the device.

CERTMIKE EXAM ESSENTIALS

▶ A virtual private network is a secure connection between a client and a network or between two networks. Using the Internet or any other carrier, the VPN endpoints establish a secure, encrypted connection between called a tunnel.

▶ Remote control programs allow users to perform actions on a system at a distant location. Early applications, such as Telnet and SSH, are character-based and provide access to the command-line interface only. The more recent remote control products, such as Remote Desktop and VNC, are graphical, enabling users to take full control of a remote system.

▶ All types of remote access introduce serious security vulnerabilities to a network. The procedures for authenticating and authorizing remote access users should be more stringent than those for internal users.

Practice Question 1

Ralph is an IT consultant for a firm that has decided to permit employees to telecommute for the first time. He is responsible for designing a remote access solution that will enable users to access network resources, such as company email and customer databases, securely.

Ralph is evaluating some of the remote access solutions available to him, with a particular eye on those that are included with the Windows operating systems because his budget for the year is nearing its limit. He discovers that Windows includes remote access solutions called Secure Shell and Remote Desktop. After doing a bit more research, Ralph is not sure which of these two free solutions is preferable. It appears as though both require a client and a server, which enable client users to connect to a remote server and execute commands.

Ralph's questions were answered when he tested both programs and saw their interfaces. Which of the following options specifies the types of traffic that are exchanged by Remote Desktop clients and servers that are not exchanged by SSH?

A. Display information and mouse movements
B. Keystrokes and application data
C. Keystrokes and mouse movements
D. Display information and application data

Practice Question 2

As a test platform for a possible company wide deployment, Alice recently installed a VPN server on her company's perimeter network and has permitted a select few users to try it, client to site, using company laptops preconfigured by Alice with a full tunnel VPN client. During testing, all of the users report that web browsing is much slower when they are connected to the VPN server. When they disconnect, the browser speeds up again. Which of the following statements could explain why web browsing is so much slower when the VPN is connected? (Select all that apply.)

A. The VPN processing is slowing down the client computers.
B. The client's web browser is running on the VPN server.
C. The client is using the remote network's Internet connection.
D. The VPN tunnel restricts the amount of bandwidth available.

Practice Question 1 Explanations

A. is correct because Remote Desktop servers transmit display data, enabling the client to see a facsimile of the server's screen. Like SSH, Remote Desktop clients send keystrokes to the server, but they also send mouse movements along with keystrokes, which SSH does not.
B. is incorrect because neither Remote Desktop nor Secure Shell transmits application data over the network, and both programs send keystrokes.
C. is incorrect because both Remote Desktop and Secure Shell exchange keystroke information over the network. Only Remote Desktop sends mouse movements.
D. is incorrect because while Remote Desktop servers transmit display information to clients, neither Remote Desktop nor Secure Shell transmits application data over the network.

Correct Answer: A

Practice Question 2 Explanations

A. is correct because encryption and decryption are processor-intensive tasks, which could explain the performance degradation when the VPN is connected.
B. is incorrect because a VPN is just a network connection, albeit a well-protected one, and not a remote control solution.
C. is correct because when users connect to a remote network using a full tunnel VPN client, they become a participant on that network, which includes using the remote network's Internet connection. Therefore, all web requests and replies must pass through the VPN tunnel, incurring slight processing delays as data is encrypted and unencrypted.
D. is incorrect because the VPN tunnel does not restrict the bandwidth of a connection. The only restrictions are in the devices' connections to the Internet.

Correct Answer: A and C

CHAPTER 20

Physical Security

Objective 4.5: Explain the importance of physical security.

When the issue of IT security hazards comes up, many network administrators think first of Internet-based cyberattacks and software vulnerabilities. They might forget that an intruder can also walk through the front door and attack the network in person. Physical security is no less important than cybersecurity to an enterprise's overall security posture. This chapter examines some of the physical security mechanisms that administrators frequently implement on a typical enterprise network. The Network+ exam expects candidates to be familiar with these basic concepts.

In this chapter, you'll learn everything you need to know about Network+ Objective 4.5, including the following topics:

► **Detection methods**
► **Prevention methods**
► **Asset disposal**

DETECTION METHODS

The two main areas of physical security are the *detection methods* that allow administrators to monitor vulnerable network equipment and the *prevention methods* that block unauthorized access to that equipment. Detection devices tell administrators when and how an intrusion has occurred and can sometimes provide evidence of the intruder's identity. Some of the detection methods used to provide a network with physical protection are described in this section.

Camera

Video surveillance captures the most information of any of the standard detection methods, allowing network administrators to see events as they happen and record them for archiving. Unlike many detection methods that rely solely on numerical data, such as access auditing, *cameras* allow administrators to see not just that something was done, but also who did it.

Early video surveillance systems used analog closed circuit television (CCTV) cameras connected to a central recorder using coaxial cables. These were dedicated systems, separate from any other network. Today, video surveillance cameras typically connect to IP networks using Ethernet cables or Wi-Fi and save their information as digital video. This arrangement is not only less expensive than CCTV, since it can use existing equipment, but it can also take advantage of the network's own infrastructure. For example, *Power over Ethernet (PoE)* can provide the cameras with electricity over the network cable, and administrators can place the cameras' switchports into their own VLAN, keeping their traffic separate from the rest of the network.

Motion Detection

Motion detection equipment is described as any device capable of sensing the passage of a human through a specific area. The motion detectors that most people picture are the small boxes affixed to the wall containing passive infrared (PIR) sensors. Humans generate heat, and heat shows up on infrared, so these devices can sense changes in the infrared pattern of a room and generate a signal that triggers an alert or an alarm. There are also similar devices intended for larger areas that use microwaves instead of infrared.

In addition to infrared and microwave sensors, there are many other types of devices that can be considered motion detectors, including pressure pads under carpeting that detect footsteps, electric eye beams that signal an alarm when interrupted, and sound sensors that react to excessive noise. Unlike cameras, motion detectors can tell when someone enters a protected area, but they can't identify who that someone is.

Asset Tags

Asset tagging is the process of assigning unique identifiers to company-owned hardware assets to facilitate the tracking of each device, both in its physical location and in its life cycle. Simply put, asset tagging is a solution to the problem of how to identify one particular computer when the company has purchased hundreds of them.

Originally, asset tagging consisted of affixing a unique number to each device and using that number on all of its documentation, such as trouble tickets and service contracts. The products created to facilitate asset tagging have evolved over the years. The first solution was probably an indelible ink marker, but this would soon become impractical. Later, it became possible to purchase sets of adhesive metal plates with serialized asset numbers, which could be placed outside or inside the device's case. Later still, products with barcodes appeared.

Today, asset tagging technology manufacturers have greatly expanded the functionality of their products by creating tags using radio frequency identification (RFID) chips or other wireless tracking mechanisms. This can enable network administrators to not only identify devices, but actually track their locations within the facility.

Tamper Detection

Tamper detection is any mechanism that can indicate when a particular device, container, or facility has been opened by unauthorized persons. At its simplest, there are tamper detection tapes and stickers that administrators can place on computers or other devices in such a way that, when someone opens the device's case, the tape is broken.

Of course, mechanical tamper detection devices like this require someone to see the broken tape, which means regular inspection of network devices. Better than this are mechanisms that can generate a signal when they detect tampering and alert an appropriate administrator. Many servers have switches built into their cases that are tripped when someone opens it. The switch is typically connected to the motherboard so that the computer itself receives the tamper detection signal and can take action on it, such as generating an SNMP trap.

PREVENTION METHODS

It is important to be able to detect an attack or intrusion when it occurs, but it is far more preferable to prevent those incidents from happening before they occur. While some intrusion *prevention methods* involve the application of technology or hardware, others are more a matter of careful planning and communication, both with end users and with IT support personnel. This section describes some of the most commonly used attack prevention methods for enterprise networks.

Employee Training

While there are many types of attacks and intrusions that administrators can prevent by applying technology, it is important to remember that end users nearly always outnumber IT personnel. They can be the organization's first line of defense, as long as they know what to look for and what to do when a suspicious event occurs. *Employee training* is the answer to that.

Security training for end users consists largely of things they should look out for that can indicate an imminent attack, or even one in progress, such as phishing messages, social engineering contacts, tailgating attempts, and other suspicious behaviors. End users should also be informed about security-related policies and the reasons for them, such as mandatory password changes and multifactor authentication.

In the same way, IT personnel—and especially the first-line support people—should receive regular training to keep them updated about changing conditions and threats. The main problem with all of this training is keeping the attention of the users long enough for the message to penetrate. Videos, paper handouts, emails, and intranet websites can all help keep the information available, but relatively short meetings with small groups are often the best way to communicate security messages.

Access Control Hardware

The most common type of *access control hardware* is, of course, the key lock. But in a business environment, keys can easily be lent, lost, stolen, or duplicated, making them a less than secure form of access control. Many organizations still rely on key locks, and there are many combinations of doors, gates, and other devices available to fit various situations.

In addition to metal keys, many locking solutions call for a secondary access control mechanism. Some of the other common access control hardware solutions seen in business facilities are described next.

Badge Readers

A badge, like a key, is something you have, so it too can be lent, lost, or stolen. However, ID badges can perform several security functions. First, the badge, which typically includes a photograph, can identify the person wearing it. When appropriate for the organization's security requirements, it might be company policy to require the prominent display of ID badges, with security personnel and users trained to regard as suspicious any people not wearing them.

ID badges can also function as keys providing authorized entrance into secure areas equipped with *badge readers*, whether in the form of a swipe card, a touch reader, or a proximity switch. Replacing metal keys and locks with ID badges and badge readers can greatly simplify the process of managing access control. Administrators can rekey locks electronically, rather than physically replace the metal locks in a door, and deactivate the ID badges of departing employees, rather than have to collect metal keys from them.

To prevent unauthorized people from using a found or stolen ID badge to gain access to protected areas, entrances typically require a second authentication factor, something the user knows such as a PIN or password, in combination with the badge.

Biometrics

Biometrics have become an increasingly popular access control solution because they are based on something you are, such as a fingerprint, which cannot readily be lent, lost, or stolen (action movie severed finger cliches notwithstanding). Fingerprints are the most commonly used biometric indicator, usually in combination with a PIN or password.

Many smartphones and other mobile devices use biometric access control, and door entry devices with a fingerprint scanner and a keypad are relatively commonplace these days. However, retinal scans and palm prints are also possibilities, as is facial recognition, which requires no deliberate participation from the user. Cameras can scan people's faces as they approach a door and automatically open the lock for authorized users, allowing them to pass through the barrier with no delay.

Locking Racks

Network devices such as servers, switches, and routers are often mounted vertically in racks in a server closet or data center. Large data centers often contain rows of racks placed side to side and arranged in aisles. Depending on the hardware selected and the organization's security needs, the individual racks might be enclosed, with a locking door protecting each one. Even if the racks are located in a locked closet or data center, it is still a good idea to keep the racks locked and provide keys only to those people who need them. Granting a person access to the data center itself does not necessarily mean that the person needs access to all of the network equipment.

Locking Cabinets

In some large data centers, entire rows of equipment racks are enclosed within clear-walled cabinets or mesh cages, which are also lockable. Locking cabinets are particularly necessary in large facilities that house equipment belonging to multiple clients. The cabinets or cages might use metal keys, but any of the badge-based or biometric locking solutions discussed earlier can serve.

Access Control Vestibule

One method for gaining illicit entry into a secure area is simply to follow closely behind an authorized user as they go through the door, a technique known as *tailgating*. The best solution for preventing this type of intrusion (apart from user education, as noted earlier in this chapter) is a security guard checking IDs, but that is an expensive proposition that might not be feasible or practical in many situations.

Another effective solution—one that does not require guards—is an *access control vestibule*, also known as a *mantrap*. An access control vestibule is a short corridor with a secured door at each end, located at the entrance to a sensitive area. The doors are designed so that each one requires some form of authentication, and when the door at one end of the vestibule is open, the door at the other end is locked. This prevents multiple people from passing through the vestibule at once. Live or video monitoring of the people passing through the vestibule can add further security.

An access control vestibule is typically used only for entrances to facilities requiring high security, but the vestibule can also combine its security function with other necessary functions, such as environmental preparation solutions. For example, entrance to a clean room or biohazard zone might require clothing changes, showers, and other preparation, which can occur in the vestibule along with the identification and authorization of the user.

Smart Lockers

Smart lockers, which are commonly used for package deliveries by e-commerce retailers, can serve as a secure means to distribute anything to specific users in a company facility, such as loaner laptops and other devices, or even packages.

The lockers are connected to the Internet (or an internal network), so they can authenticate users. When something is delivered to a locker, the system sends an email or text message to the intended recipient with instructions containing some means of identifying them, such as a PIN or a barcode. Supplying that information to the control panel in the bank of lockers causes the correct door to unlock, providing the user with access to its contents.

ASSET DISPOSAL

In a properly organized IT department, network hardware devices have a documented life cycle that specifies when they should be inspected and maintained as well as when they should be replaced, retired, and disposed of.

The process of decommissioning a network device of any appreciable value typically involves company departments other than IT. The disposition of the device, as a financial asset of the company, must be accounted for in tax and other records. There might also be local ordinances to consider regarding the environmentally safe disposal of particular types of devices.

Asset disposal is also a serious security problem. IT personnel must be absolutely certain that any hardware leaving the company's possession contains no usable or recoverable data. There are likely to be different retirement protocols for different types of products. Some of these are described in this section.

Factory Reset/Wipe Configuration

For some types of network devices, the only data they contain are the configuration settings for the device. Managed switches, for example, have individual configuration settings for each port, as well as those for the device as a whole. Those settings can contain the IP addresses and MAC addresses associated with each port, information that could be used to mount an attack against the network.

When retiring this type of device, the configuration settings must be erased before disposal. Many switches and routers network devices have a built-in feature to do this, variously called *factory reset* or a *wipe configuration*. This feature typically returns the device to its original default configuration, eliminating the settings applied by its current owners.

However, the implementation of this particular feature is up to the individual manufacturer, so there is no guarantee that a factory reset renders the previous configuration settings unrecoverable. IT personnel should check with the manufacturer of a device before relying on a reset to render a product safe for disposal.

Sanitize Devices for Disposal

For some types of devices, a factory reset or configuration wipe is a sufficient method of *sanitizing* a device for disposal. However, for computers or other devices that have hard disk drives or other storage media, a factory reset is definitely not sufficient. Windows operating systems, for example, have a reset feature that can optionally delete the user's files from the computer's hard drive, but it takes no steps to permanently delete them.

When someone deletes files on a hard drive, they are not actually erased. The drive simply deletes the filenames from its file allocation table, leaving the actual data in place and flagging the storage space as available for use. The data can therefore be recovered unless someone takes steps to remove it permanently. IT departments deal with a variety of storage media, and the requirements for sanitizing them can differ widely, as follows:

▶ **Hard disk drives:** Sanitizing (or purging) magnetic media requires that every bit of data be overwritten with 1s and 0s. There are software tools designed to do this, including some that comply with the traditional Department of Defense (DoD) 5220.22-M standard, which calls for three overwrite passes: one with zeroes, one with ones, and one with random ones and zeroes. Magnetic media can also be sanitized by degaussing with a powerful magnet that removes all data.

▶ **Solid-state drives:** As a relatively recent development, solid-state drives (SSDs) require special consideration because it is not possible to simply overwrite them, as with magnetic media. The DoD 5220.22-M standard does not address the issue of SSDs. A newer standard published by the National Institute of Standards and Technology (NIST) as SP 800-88 does address a wider variety of data types. In most cases, SSD manufacturers provide proprietary commands for wiping the data from their drives.

Of course, the ultimate sanitization method for any medium is to destroy it. Shredding, crushing, chemical solvents, and high temperatures are some of the options used for various media types.

CERTMIKE EXAM ESSENTIALS

▶ Networks are as susceptible to physical attacks as they are vulnerable to cyberattacks.

▶ Detection methods allow network administrators to learn when an intrusion or attack has occurred. Video surveillance with well-placed cameras is one of the most efficient detection methods, but there are also motion detectors that generate alerts when an unauthorized entrance to a protected area occurs.

▶ Prevention methods are designed to make it more difficult for attackers to penetrate the network's security. These methods can range from training employees to spot suspicious behavior to installing elaborate locking and authentication systems involving ID badge readers or biometric scanners.

Practice Question 1

Ralph is attending a department meeting convened to discuss increasing the security of the corporate data center. There had been an incident recently in which a former employee gained entrance to the data center after hours and stole certain items. The IT department had been told in no uncertain terms that nothing like this must ever happen again, and it had been decided that there must be some means of detecting intruders in the data center after hours. Ralph was writing down the ideas suggested by the other people at the meeting and ended up with a list like the following:

    Motion detection
    Video surveillance
    Biometrics
    Smartcards

Which of the suggested solutions are viable means of detecting afterhours intruders in a network data center? (Select all that apply.)

A. Motion detection
B. Video surveillance
C. Biometrics
D. Smartcards

Practice Question 2

Alice is responsible for the physical security of the company data center, and she has recently noticed several employees enter the data center without swiping their ID badges by slipping through the door on the heels of another person. The incidents Alice saw were just for the sake of convenience, but she doesn't like that it's even possible to tailgate another person that way.

To address the problem, Alice has the entrance to the data center modified into a double doorway. The two doors, both equipped with swipe card readers, have a short corridor between them, and one door must be closed before the other one can open. Which of the following terms describe this arrangement? (Select all that apply.)

A. Server closet
B. Mantrap
C. Honeypot
D. Access control vestibule

Practice Question 1 Explanation

(A) is correct because motion detection can detect the movement of a person in the empty data center after hours.

(B) is correct because properly monitored video surveillance can detect a person in the empty data center after hours.

(C) is incorrect because biometric devices are a means of preventing intrusion, not detecting an intrusion as it occurs.

(D) is incorrect because smartcards are a means of preventing intrusion, not detecting an intrusion as it occurs.

Correct Answer: A and B

Practice Question 2 Explanation

(A) is incorrect because a server closet is a small, locked room containing servers or other equipment that does not need a double doorway entrance.

(B) is correct because an entrance arrangement in which people must pass through one door and close it before they can open the second door is called a mantrap or access control vestibule.

(C) is incorrect because a honeypot is an unprotected website left as a tempting target for intruders; it has no physical entrance to protect.

(D) is correct because an entrance arrangement in which people must pass through one door and close it before they can open the second door is called an access control vestibule or mantrap.

Correct Answer: B and D

Domain 5.0: Network Troubleshooting

Network Troubleshooting is the fifth domain of CompTIA's Network+ exam. In it, you'll learn how IT professionals use standard procedures to troubleshoot issues on wired and wireless networks. This domain has five objectives:

5.1 Explain the network troubleshooting methodology.

5.2 Given a scenario, troubleshoot common cable connectivity issues and select the appropriate tools.

5.3 Given a scenario, use the appropriate network software tools and commands.

5.4 Given a scenario, troubleshoot common wireless connectivity issues.

5.5 Given a scenario, troubleshoot general networking issues.

Questions from this domain make up 22% of the questions on the Network+ exam, so you should expect to see approximately 20 questions on your test covering the material in this part.

CHAPTER 21

Network Troubleshooting Methodology

Objective 5.1: Explain the network troubleshooting methodology.

Troubleshooting is the process of identifying a problem and formulating a solution to that problem. In a network environment, there are many variables that can be potential sources of trouble, and the process of finding the source and addressing it can be complicated. For this reason, it is important that the troubleshooting process be conducted methodically and scientifically so that other IT personnel can track what has been done about the problem and what is expected to be done.

In this chapter, you'll learn everything you need to know about the troubleshooting methodology defined in Network+ Objective 5.1, including the following topics:

- ▶ **Identify the problem**
- ▶ **Establish a theory of probable cause**
- ▶ **Test the theory to determine the cause**
- ▶ **Establish a plan of action to resolve the problem and identify potential effects**
- ▶ **Implement the solution or escalate as necessary**
- ▶ **Verify full system functionality and, if applicable, implement preventive measures**
- ▶ **Document findings, actions, outcomes, and lessons learned**

IDENTIFY THE PROBLEM

The first step in troubleshooting is identifying exactly what the problem is. In a network environment, this can often be the most difficult part of the process. The troubleshooter frequently has to gather information from multiple sources and weigh that information to determine what is pertinent to the problem-solving process. This section describes the various steps in this information-gathering process. However, the steps are not necessarily performed in the order shown here.

Gather Information

In this step, the troubleshooter functions like a forensic investigator at a crime scene, collecting all evidence that could possibly help the troubleshooting process. Initially, this might include error messages, log entries, and descriptions of what happened. Going beyond this, it might be necessary to note network and device conditions at the time of the problem, collect core dumps and log files, and speak to users about their experiences of the problem.

Question Users

Gathering information from end users is a skill that IT personnel develop over time. Users might know something about networking, or they might know nothing at all. IT people have to learn the right questions to ask to glean pertinent information from users about the problem at hand.

Some users might know very little about how the network functions, or even that there is one. Questioning these users requires some skill in describing what is happening in their computers without confusing them with too much detail. For example, an IT tech might instruct a user on how to locate their computer's IP address, but there's no need to describe the details of IP addressing.

Perhaps more difficult to handle are the users who do know a little about networking and insist on trying to diagnose the problem themselves. The trick here is to not let the user digress from the immediate problem or get caught up in lengthy explanations of why the user's diagnosis is incorrect.

Identify Symptoms

Identifying the symptoms of a problem helps IT technicians to determine the severity of the issue and its scope. While there might just be one user reporting a problem right now, it is important to determine whether other users are affected as well. This not only helps the troubleshooter locate the source of the problem, but also helps the IT department to establish appropriate service priorities. Obviously, an issue that affects an entire network must be assigned a higher priority than one that affects a single user.

For example, in the case of a network slowdown, the following questions can help troubleshooters identify the symptoms of a problem:

- ▶ Are all of the user's applications affected or just some of them? Which ones?
- ▶ Is the network slowdown continuous or intermittent? When or under what conditions do slowdowns occur?
- ▶ Are other users experiencing the same problem? What other users?
- ▶ How far does the problem extend outward from the initial complaint? Is the entire network affected or just the immediate area?

Determine if Anything Has Changed

One of the most important questions that IT personnel might ask of end users is whether anything in their computer hardware, software, or configuration settings has changed recently. A new piece of hardware or software or a change in configuration settings can easily be the cause of many common problems.

However, getting users to admit to these changes can sometimes require additional interrogation. As a result, IT people should be familiar with the log files and other places where these types of changes are documented so that they can determine for themselves what recent modifications might have been made.

Duplicate the Problem, if Possible

One of the more common experiences for IT helpdesk personnel is being told by users that they have received an error message. When asked what the error message said, users frequently have no idea. When this occurs, the next step is to try to reproduce the error by having users repeat their actions. A problem that can readily be duplicated is much easier to troubleshoot than one that appears intermittently.

Approach Multiple Problems Individually

A problem does not necessarily have only one cause. For example, users reporting a significant reduction in network transmission speed does not mean that there is just one problem causing the bottleneck. There can be several contributing factors, so IT technicians should not stop troubleshooting when they detect one cause of a problem. There might be others, so a properly methodical troubleshooting procedure should proceed until all possible causes have been examined.

When a troubleshooter does detect multiple problems that each require remediation, the best practice is to approach the problems individually, creating a separate trouble ticket for each one. This ensures that each of the problems receives its due attention and also allows supervisors to delegate the various issues to different personnel.

ESTABLISH A THEORY OF PROBABLE CAUSE

After identifying the problem, the next step in a scientific troubleshooting method is to hypothesize a theory of the problem's possible cause. The first probable cause a troubleshooter comes up with might not be the correct one, however. At this point, it is still just a theory. In fact, it might be necessary to repeat this step several times and test several possible causes.

Question the Obvious

When hypothesizing about the possible causes of a problem, it is important not to neglect the most obvious ones. In the case of a network communication failure on a particular workstation, for example, before initiating a detailed protocol analysis of the network's traffic, a troubleshooter should make sure that the network cable isn't unplugged and that other, equally simple, causes have not been overlooked.

Consider Multiple Approaches

To theorize a probable cause, troubleshooters should work methodically through a process that investigates all of a problem's possible causes. There are several approaches that break down the networking process for examination, including the following:

- ▶ **Top-to-bottom/bottom-to-top OSI model:** Proceeding methodically through the layers of the OSI model, either upward or downward, is one way to perform a comprehensive examination of the networking process in relation to the problem. As troubleshooters gain experience, they typically develop instincts about the general location of a particular type of problem, which enables them to decide whether it would be more efficient to proceed through the OSI model from the top down or the bottom up.
- ▶ **Divide and conquer:** In some cases, the troubleshooter's instinct might point to a possible cause somewhere in the middle of the OSI model. Instead of wasting time by starting from the top or bottom layer and working toward the middle, a *divide and conquer* approach might be preferable, in which the troubleshooter starts from the suspected layer and works up or down from there. In the same way, a troubleshooter might be able to divide a process into multiple subprocesses and examine each one individually.

TEST THE THEORY TO DETERMINE THE CAUSE

Once a troubleshooter has a theory of probable cause, the next step is to perform tests that confirm or disprove the theory. Note, however, that this step in the process is devoted to testing the efficacy of the theory only. This is not the time to actually address the problem.

For a simplistic example, a troubleshooter might be investigating why a particular server is not available on the network and arrive at the theory that the server might be powered down. To test the theory, the troubleshooter might go to the server closet and see that the server is indeed powered down.

However, this does not mean that the troubleshooter should resolve the problem by switching the server back on right then. There could be any number of reasons someone else powered the server down, and resolving the problem requires a carefully planned course of action including investigating these reasons. Even in a simple situation like this, troubleshooters should follow a prescribed method.

Depending on the results of the testing, the troubleshooting process should continue in one of the following ways:

If the theory is confirmed, determine the next steps to resolve the problem.   Testing a theory of probable cause is usually more complicated than just visually inspecting a component. The test should be carefully planned and executed. After confirming a theory of probable cause, the troubleshooter can go on to the next step: creating a plan for resolving the problem.

If the theory is not confirmed, reestablish a new theory or escalate.   When testing indicates that the troubleshooter's hypothesis is incorrect and the suspected cause is not the source of the problem, then the troubleshooter must repeat this step of the process by devising another theory of probable cause and testing it. If the theory is incorrect and the troubleshooter is not able to come up with another possible cause, then it is time to escalate the problem within the IT department or consult a third party.

EXAM TIP

The network troubleshooting methodology described in this objective provides high-level guidance, but it does not include the specific details of how the troubleshooter should go about identifying the problem, establishing a theory of probable cause, and testing that theory. However, candidates for the Network+ exam are expected to be familiar with the tools and procedures for doing these things, as discussed in the previous chapters.

ESTABLISH A PLAN OF ACTION TO RESOLVE THE PROBLEM AND IDENTIFY POTENTIAL EFFECTS

After a troubleshooter successfully identifies the cause of a problem, they can proceed to create a detailed plan of action for resolving it. In the previous example, the actual solution to the problem might be simply switching on the server that was found to be powered down. However, in a methodical troubleshooting process, it is important to consider all the possible side effects the solution might have on the rest of the network.

Before switching the server on, the troubleshooter must determine why it is off in the first place. Was it powered down deliberately by another technician, or did some operative condition cause it to power down by itself? If someone else in the IT department is working on that server, there should be records of that process that specify what is happening.

If there is no apparent reason why the server is powered down, then the troubleshooter might have to check the logs on the server itself to determine what happened. If there is a server malfunction that shut the computer down, then this would lead to the creation of an entirely new trouble ticket for the malfunctioning server. The entire troubleshooting process would then repeat from the beginning.

It is also important for the troubleshooter to consider all possible ramifications of the resolution process and incorporate them into the plan of action. In many situations, fixing one problem can conceivably cause another one, and troubleshooters must try to anticipate these possibilities. If a troubleshooter suspects that a dangerous side effect of the solution might occur that would affect network productivity, the plan of action should call for the solution to be implemented during non-business hours. There should also be a detailed rollback plan in place in case the solution ends up being worse than the original problem.

Here again, this step in the troubleshooting process calls only for the planning of the solution, not its implementation. In many cases, troubleshooters might have to seek approval from supervisors before the actual implementation can occur. It might also be necessary to seek permission from (or at least notify) other departments when a service interruption is expected.

IMPLEMENT THE SOLUTION OR ESCALATE AS NECESSARY

With a plan of action in place and all the necessary approvals and permissions secured, the troubleshooter can proceed to implement the solution to the original problem. As in the example mentioned earlier, the implementation of the solution might be as simple as flipping a server's power switch. However, it can also be much more complex and require additional IT resources, such as help from other technicians, replacement hardware components, or assistance from outside service providers.

In some cases, the actual implementation of a particular solution might be beyond a troubleshooter's job description and require the case to be escalated to a more senior technician for implementation. For example, a troubleshooter's plan of action might include some changes to the configuration of certain switchports in the data center. If the troubleshooter is not authorized to access the switches or make those changes, then they will have to escalate the implementation—or at least part of it—to someone who is authorized.

VERIFY FULL SYSTEM FUNCTIONALITY AND, IF APPLICABLE, IMPLEMENT PREVENTIVE MEASURES

After implementing a solution, the next step is to try to reproduce the original problem to determine whether the solution was effective. If the problem still exists, then the troubleshooter will have to go back and try another theory of probable cause.

Whether or not the solution is successful, the troubleshooter must attempt to recognize the full effect of the attempted solution by checking that all functions related to the original problem are operative. If the solution is not effective, then the best practice might be to reverse the changes to avoid any side effects of the modifications.

If the solution addresses the problem successfully, the troubleshooter should also consider the possibility of the same problem occurring again. If possible, the troubleshooter might propose additional modifications as preventive measures. For example, if the troubleshooter determines that the server in the previous example shut itself down due to a driver issue and installing an updated driver resolves the problem, then it might be a good idea to install the same update on any other servers using that driver.

DOCUMENT FINDINGS, ACTIONS, OUTCOMES, AND LESSONS LEARNED

Documenting the troubleshooting process and its results is something that should occur throughout the procedure, not just at the end. In an enterprise network environment, it is important for there to be a record of what the troubleshooter has learned and done. This enables other IT personnel to learn what problems have occurred and what solutions have been tried. In the event that the problem reasserts itself or another related problem occurs, the records can prevent other troubleshooters from having to repeat the same steps. When troubleshooters first start working on a problem, part of their information gathering process should include checking for any documentation of prior occurrences.

The documentation should include as much detail as possible about the problem, its symptoms, and its effects on the network, as well as an account of the entire troubleshooting process, including all of the information discovered and actions taken by IT personnel. A troubleshooting procedure might not all be completed at once, and not necessarily by the same person. Proper documentation enables anyone in the IT department to take over the process, if necessary.

CERTMIKE EXAM ESSENTIALS

▶ Network troubleshooting can often be an instinctive process, but in an enterprise environment, it should proceed methodically, according to a documented series of steps.

▶ The troubleshooting method defined in the Network+ objectives consists of the following steps: identify the problem, hypothesize a theory of probable cause, test the theory, design a plan of action to solve the problem, implement the plan, verify the results, and document the entire troubleshooting process.

Practice Question 1

Alice is working the helpdesk in her company's IT department in Atlanta. A user calls to report that they are trying to send email to a colleague in the Chicago office but are unable to do so. Alice begins her trouble-shooting process by trying to identify a probable cause of the problem. She asks the user to try sending some other emails: to another user in Chicago, to a local Atlanta user, and to an Internet user outside the company. Then Alice checks the user's IP configuration settings and tests their local network connectivity. Finally, she has the user confirm that the computer is properly plugged into the wall plate.

Which of the following methodologies is Alice using to establish a theory of probable cause?

A. Question the obvious
B. Divide and conquer
C. OSI top-to-bottom
D. OSI bottom-to-top

Practice Question 2

Ralph is troubleshooting a network problem that has been submitted by multiple users. He has come up with a theory specifying a possible cause of the problem and sets about performing a test to confirm his theory.

Depending on the results of the test, positive or negative, which of the following would likely be the next step in Ralph's troubleshooting process? (Choose two answers.)

A. Create a plan of action to resolve the problem.
B. Begin replacing components that might contribute to the problem.
C. Repeat the process of establishing a theory of probable cause.
D. Reinterview the users experiencing the problem to question the obvious.

Practice Question 1 Explanation

A. is incorrect because although Alice does check the obvious by having the user confirm that the network cable is plugged in, that technique does not account for the other elements in her troubleshooting process.
B. is incorrect because the divide and conquer approach would not begin at the top of the OSI model and work its way down.
C. is correct because Alice begins her process at the top of the OSI model (the application layer) by checking the system's email capabilities and ends it at the bottom by checking the computer's physical layer connection to the network.
D. is incorrect because Alice's process begins by checking the system's email capability, which is an application layer function at the top of the OSI model, not the bottom.

Correct Answer: C

Practice Question 2 Explanation

A. is correct because if the test confirms Ralph's theory of probable cause, the next step would be to devise a plan of action to address the cause and resolve the problem.
B. is incorrect because while replacing components by guesswork could conceivably resolve the problem, it would more likely be a waste of time and hardware.
C. is correct because if the test indicates that Ralph's first theory of probable cause is disproved, the next logical step is to devise another theory.
D. is incorrect because obvious solutions should have already been considered during the creation of the first theory.

Correct Answers: A and C

CHAPTER 22

Troubleshooting Cable Connectivity

Objective 5.2: Given a scenario, troubleshoot common cable connectivity issues and select the appropriate tools.

This chapter examines some of the fundamental network cable trouble-shooting concepts and introduces the tools that IT technicians typically use when working with cables. The Network+ exam expects candidates to be familiar with these basic networking functions.

In this chapter, you'll learn everything you need to know about Network+ Objective 5.2, including the following topics:

- ▶ **Specifications and limitations**
- ▶ **Cable considerations**
- ▶ **Cable application**
- ▶ **Common issues**
- ▶ **Common tools**

SPECIFICATIONS AND LIMITATIONS

Cabled networks have basic specifications that administrators typically use to select an appropriate platform for their users' needs. These specifications impose limitations on the network that are among the chief causes of communication issues.

Throughput

Throughput is a measurement of the amount of data transmitted across the network during a given time interval. Usually measured in bits per second (bps), the throughput is a measurement of the actual data flowing through the network. When the throughput measurement approaches the network's speed, the network is approaching saturation. This causes latency to increase, as well as the potential for dropped packets.

Speed

A network's *speed* is its theoretical maximum transmission rate, usually measured in bits per second (bps). Actual networks almost never achieve this theoretical maximum, so administrators designing networks should always choose physical layer specifications with speeds at least double that of their anticipated throughput needs. For example, a Gigabit Ethernet network is rated at 1,000 megabits per second (Mbps). While occasional bursts of traffic might reach that speed momentarily, there are many variables in networking that will prevent the average network from achieving and maintaining its maximum possible speed.

> **EXAM TIP**
> Speed and throughput measurements are typically supplied in bits per second (bps) or multiples of that, such as megabits per second (Mbps) or gigabits per second (Gbps). Note the distinction between the abbreviations for megabits per second and gigabits per second—Mbps and Gbps, with a capital M or G and a lowercase b—and megabytes per second and gigabytes per second: MBps and GBps. Network+ exam candidates should be aware of the differences in the abbreviations and how they are used.

Distance

Distance is the maximum cable length that a particular physical layer implementation can support while functioning properly. In many cases, networks have distance limitations to avoid the signal degradation caused by attenuation, the weakening of a signal as it travels through a network medium. Ethernet networks also require distance limitations because a frame must reach the destination system before it completely leaves the sending system. If a cable segment is too long, late collisions can occur, which is a serious problem.

CABLE CONSIDERATIONS

While there are standards-based specifications for various network types that administrators should adhere to when installing new cables, there are also specific environmental concerns that can dictate the type of cable they use. Sources of interference and installations within air ducts or other air circulation channels are both concerns that can affect the type of cable needed for the installation.

Shielded and Unshielded

Twisted pair cables are available in shielded and unshielded varieties. Most twisted pair network installations use the *unshielded twisted pair (UTP)* version, in which individual pairs of wires are twisted together and enclosed in a sheath. The *shielded twisted pair (STP)* versions—which are always more expensive than UTP—are intended for environments in which there is a great deal of electromagnetic or other types of interference present. This can include locations with industrial equipment or other sources of EMI.

Depending on the cable type, the shielding, which can be made of a metal foil or braided wire, can be wrapped around the entire bundle of wires, around the individual wire pairs, or both. In addition to preventing EMI from reaching the copper wires, the shielding is a conductor that can be attached to a ground.

Plenum and Riser-Rated

Standard UTP cables are sometimes called *riser-rated* because they are intended to run between floors without traversing an air space. The air circulation spaces inside a building, whether inside of ductwork or not, are called *plenums*. There are special plenum-rated cables that are designed to run through the air spaces.

The difference between riser-rated and plenum cables is that the plenum variety is encased in a sheath made of a material that does not outgas toxic vapors when it burns. Riser-rated cables have a polyvinyl chloride (PVC) sheath that, if it burns in an air space, produces toxic fumes.

Plenum cables are more expensive than riser-rated ones, and they might be more difficult to install. The plenum cable's fire-retardant sheath is less flexible than that of the standard PVC sheath on a riser-rated cable, which means that the plenum cable has a larger bend radius that prevents it from stretching around corners as easily.

CABLE APPLICATION

Most UTP cables are wired "straight through," meaning that each pin in the connector at one end is wired to the same pin at the other end. These cables typically take one of two forms. They are either permanently installed cable runs in the walls or ceilings that connect wall plates to a patch panel in a server closet or data center, or they are patch cords that connect computers and other devices to wall plates and patch panel ports to switches.

There are, however, other applications for specialized types of cables, as described in this section.

Rollover Cable/Console Cable

Routers typically have a command-line interface (CLI) for configuring the device, but they do not have screens or keyboards. However, they do traditionally have a console port into which an administrator can plug a terminal or laptop and access the CLI. Modern routers can have a variety of interfaces for the console port, but earlier models used the venerable RS-232 serial interface, usually with a DB-9 D-shell connector. Before USB, this was the interface that people used to connect an external modem to their computers. Current routers might have an RJ-45 console port supporting the rollover wiring configuration, a standard Ethernet RJ-45 port, or even a mini-USB port.

A *rollover cable*, also known as a *console cable*, is a variation on the standard twisted pair design that eliminates both the twists and the pairs. A rollover cable is typically flat, not round like a UTP cable, and colored a light blue. At one end is a standard RJ-45 connector and at the other is either a DB-9 connector, as shown in Figure 22.1, or another RJ-45 and an EIA/TIA adapter that converts it to a DB-9.

DB9 (Female)

RJ45 (Male)

FIGURE 22.1 A rollover cable

Unlike UTP cables, the eight wires in a rollover cable are eight different colors, and the cable uses a nonstandard wiring scheme. Pin 1 at one end connects to pin 8 at the other end, pin 2 to pin 7, and so forth.

Crossover Cable

For communication between network devices to occur, the signals a device sends out through the transmit pairs of the cable must arrive at the receive pairs of the destination device. Standard Ethernet cables are wired straight through, so the crossover circuit that connects the transmit to the receive pairs is located in the network switch.

When a user wants to connect two computers directly to each other with an Ethernet cable, however, there is no switch to provide the crossover circuit, so the user must connect the devices with a special crossover cable. In a *crossover cable*, the transmit pairs at each end are wired to the receive pairs at the other end. Crossover cables can also connect two switches or two routers together, if needed, but most of the devices made today have some means of toggling the crossover circuit in the device.

Power over Ethernet

Devices such as video cameras, VoIP telephones, and wireless access points all can benefit from being connected to a cabled network. One of the problems with all three of these devices is the need to supply them with power when they are often located in places with no convenient outlets.

Power over Ethernet (PoE) is an IEEE 802.3 standard defining a method by which standard Ethernet cables can carry power, as well as data, to connected devices. As shown in Table 22.1, the original 2003 PoE standard was capable of supplying 15.4 watts of DC power, but the standard has matured to the point at which it can now supply up to 71.3 watts.

T A B L E 2 2 . 1 Power over Ethernet Specifications

Name	Standard	DC power	Max current
PoE	IEEE 802.3af-2003	15.4 watts	350 mA
PoE+	IEEE 802.3at-2009	25.5 watts	600 mA
PoE++ (Type 3)	IEEE 802.3bt-2018	51 watts	600 mA
PoE++ (Type 4)	IEEE 802.3bt-2018	71.3 watts	960 mA

COMMON ISSUES

Troubleshooting cable connectivity issues can be complicated by the large number of things that can conceivably go wrong with cables. Some of the common conditions that a troubleshooter might encounter are described in this section.

Attenuation

Attenuation is the tendency of a signal to weaken as it travels through a network medium. This is one of the reasons all physical layer specifications for networks have a maximum allowable cable length, which installers should not exceed. If a cable is too long, the signals can degrade excessively and cause errors. All types of networks are subject to attenuation, but to different degrees.

There are cable testers available of various types that can measure the length of a cable segment. Overlong segments due to poor installation can be a possible cause of intermittent errors. Unfortunately, often nothing can be done except to pull a new cable that can support the distance.

As a general rule, signals attenuate much faster on copper cables than they do on fiber optic, so copper cannot support distances as long as fiber can. The standard distance limitation for most UTP Ethernet networks is 100 meters, but some types of fiber-optic cable can run for miles.

Interference

In networking, the term *interference* can refer to electromagnetic interference (EMI) or radio frequency interference (RFI), both of which can be disturbing influences on network communication. EMI and RFI are typically caused by electrical or electronic equipment in proximity to the network cables, such as light fixtures, wireless phones, or radio equipment. There are natural sources of interference as well, such as solar flares.

Measuring the levels of interference on a cable run should be part of the network installation process, but it is possible for interfering equipment to be added after the cables are in place. When this occurs, cable testers can be used to detect and quantify various types of interference. Unfortunately, the only solutions for interference caused by other equipment are to either move the cable and the equipment farther apart or replace the cable with shielded twisted pair (STP).

Decibel (dB) Loss

The signal strength on a cable is measured in decibels (dB). *Decibel loss* is a value representing the ratio of a signal's strength at its source to its strength at its destination. As noted earlier, all cable types suffer from attenuation to some degree; the decibel loss measurement is a means of quantifying that effect. Decibel values are logarithmic, meaning that the signal strength decreases exponentially as the decibel loss value increases. If a 10 dB loss means that the signal at the destination is one-tenth of its original strength, then a 20 dB loss means the signal is one-hundredth of its original strength.

Incorrect Pinout

Inside a twisted pair cable are eight or more wires, grouped in pairs, with each pair consisting of a signal wire and a ground wire. At each end of the cable is a connector that plugs into the computer, wall plate, or patch panel. The connector presses each of the eight wires in the cable to a copper pin, according to one of the pinout patterns defined in the ANSI/TIA-568-D standard, as discussed in Chapter 3, "Cables and Connectors." When the connector is plugged into the socket, an electrical circuit is created between the two cable ends.

Inside a UTP cable connector, eight pins are connected to the cable's eight wires. For a standard Ethernet cable to be wired straight through, and for a proper circuit to be established, each pin at one end of the cable must be connected to its corresponding pin at the other end.

An *incorrect pinout*, in which the individual wires are mixed up inside the connector, can manifest as a variety of errors, including open circuits, short circuits, and crosstalk. These errors can slow down network traffic or prevent a connection entirely. A simple tool like a tone generator can locate incorrect pinouts by a manual process, but high-end cable testing tools can test all of the wires at once and specify the type of error that has occurred.

Bad Ports

When a device cannot connect to the network, many IT technicians swap out patch cables early in their troubleshooting process. Bad cables do happen, but though much less common, bad ports can happen also, either through misconfiguration or hardware damage. Remember that there are four RJ45 ports involved in a typical network cable run—in the computer, the wall plate, the patch panel, and the switch—and any one of them can conceivably malfunction. Therefore, when swapping cables, it might be a good idea to swap ports as well, just in case.

Open/Short

Opens and shorts are wiring faults usually resulting from cables that are faulty, damaged, or incorrectly installed. An *open circuit* is one in which signals are not reaching the destination, usually because of a break in the medium. In a twisted pair cable, an open circuit typically occurs when one or more of the wires within the sheath is severed. A *short circuit* is a condition in which two conductors are touching, causing signals to be incorrectly diverted. For example, frayed insulation on the wires inside a cable can cause the copper conductors to touch, resulting in a short that can interrupt the connection. Many types of cable testing equipment are available that can detect a wiring problem, but higher-end models can identify the type of problem and even specify its exact location in the cable.

Light-Emitting Diode (LED) Status Indicators

Most network interfaces have one or more *light-emitting diode (LED)* indicators that provide information about the connection. A link status indicator—usually colored green—indicates that there is a connection between two network devices. The indicator might blink to indicate the active transmission or receipt of data. Some multispeed devices have other LEDs that can indicate the speed at which the connection is running, based on negotiation with the connected device.

When a link status LED is out, then there is no connection to the other device, even if they appear to be properly connected. The LEDs are physical layer indicators, so if the link state LED is dark, there is usually a fault somewhere in the cables or connectors involved.

Incorrect Transceivers

Higher-speed network interfaces, especially those for fiber-optic cables, often support interchangeable plug-in transceivers. This allows administrators to choose the correct transceivers for the type (single mode or multimode) and wavelength of the cable. The transceivers at both ends of a cable run must match for any connection between the devices to be established. Many plug-in transceivers are similar in appearance, so it can be easy to mix them up. When a fiber-optic link fails to connect, checking for the correct transceiver at both ends should be a basic troubleshooting step.

Duplexing Issues

Originally, all Ethernet connections were *half-duplex*, meaning that only one of the connected systems could transmit at a time. This was because the protocol used a single wire pair for both transmitting and receiving data. Beginning with Fast Ethernet (100Base-T), the protocol included a *full duplex* mode, which uses separate wire pairs for the TX (transmit) and RX (receive) connections. This enables the connected systems to transmit and receive data simultaneously, increasing the theoretical transmission speed of the link to 200 Mbps.

Virtually all Ethernet networks today run in full duplex mode. When establishing a connection, the network interface adapters negotiate the best possible speed and duplex mode. Typically, *duplexing issues* result when one or both of the connected devices has a manually configured duplex setting. If one device is set to half duplex and the other to full duplex, the result will be a large number of collisions and errors, degrading the network performance dramatically.

Administrators typically allow workstations to autonegotiate their duplex and speed settings. However, it is more common for them to manually configure the interfaces on switches and routers, in which case a duplex mismatch could occur by accident. When troubleshooting a slow Ethernet network with excessive collisions, duplexing settings are one of the configuration settings to check early in the process.

Transmit and Receive (TX/RX) Reversed

As noted earlier, UTP Ethernet cables are supposed to be wired straight through, with the crossover circuit implemented in the switch. If, through some installation error, the *transmit (TX)* and *receive (RX)* wires in a cable connector are reversed, then there will be two crossovers on the circuit, which cancel each other out. In theory, two crossovers will prevent the devices from establishing a connection.

This is a theory because the effect of the additional crossover on the network depends on the capabilities of the switch. Some switches have a feature called auto-MDIX that enables them to detect the presence of a crossover on a circuit and adjust themselves accordingly by disabling their internal crossover. This is designed to enable switch-to-switch connections. In other switches, there might be a toggle for the internal crossover circuit or a dedicated uplink port that can function as a workaround until the cable installation error is corrected.

Dirty Optical Cables

When installing fiber-optic cables, it is important for the cable ends to be thoroughly cleaned before they are joined to a connector. Fiber-optic signals are beams of light, and anything that inhibits the passage of light through the fibers increases the attenuation on the link and causes a degraded signal. If there is sufficient dirt or grease on the fiber splices, the connection between the devices can drop intermittently, a condition called *flapping*.

Cleaning fiber-optic cable ends requires no special equipment, just care on the part of the installer. Standard glass cleaners and microfiber cloths can be used to prepare the cable ends for connectors.

COMMON TOOLS

Cable troubleshooting requires specialized tools, some of which can be extraordinarily expensive. However, there are often relatively inexpensive alternatives that provide at least basic functionality. Some of the tools that cable troubleshooters commonly use include the following:

Cable Crimper   A plier-like device used to attach connectors to the ends of bulk cable lengths by squeezing the connector closed onto the cable. There are crimpers for different cable and connector types, as well as devices with interchangeable bits.

Punchdown Tool   A device for attaching twisted pair cable ends to connectors for wall plates and patch panels. The installer lays the wires out in the correct slots on the connector and uses the punchdown tool to press each wire down. In one motion, the tool removes the insulation from the end of the wire, presses it into the slot, and trims off the end.

Tone Generator and Locator   A basic, inexpensive tool for identifying specific wires within a twisted pair cable. After connecting the tone generator to one of a cable's wires, touching each wire at the other end of the cable with the locator will eventually produce a tone from the selected wire. As a basic troubleshooting tool, the tone generator and locator has its uses, particularly when more elaborate cable testing equipment is not available. However, using the tool for any sort of a large cabling project is time-consuming and impractical.

Loopback Adapter   A testing device that consists of a plug that redirects the transmit signal from a cable or connector back into its receive input. Most commonly used today on fiber-optic cables, plugging the loopback adapter into one end of a cable run allows for an OTDR (see the next item) at the other end to test the entire cable run at once. There are also loopback adapters for Ethernet devices, which can test whether their transmit and receive circuits are functioning, but they are rarely needed these days.

Optical Time-Domain Reflectometer (OTDR)   A high-end testing device for fiber-optic cables that uses light pulses sent through the fibers to measure the length of the run, locate fiber breaks, and measure signal loss. There is also a similar device for copper cables called a time-domain reflectometer (TDR).

Multimeter   A testing device that measures electrical voltages, continuity, and resistance. Although not used for testing network cables, testing power levels of AC and DC sources is sometimes necessary in network troubleshooting.

Cable Tester   A generic name for a group of devices that connect to a cable and read its specifications. Low-end analog cable testers send impulses on each wire pair in the cable and use LEDs to indicate whether the pairs are properly connected to the other end. High-end cable testers are digital devices that can display a much larger list of specifications and compare the readings to the published requirements for a specific cable type. Sometimes called a *cable certifier*, this type of device tests the cable and displays a list of Pass/Fail results for the cable type.

Wire Map   A *wire map tester* is a relatively inexpensive cable testing tool that consists of two devices that connect to the ends of a twisted pair cable. The tester examines each wire in the cable and can detect opens, shorts, and transposed wires. All newly installed cable runs should be tested in this way, at minimum, but the tool is also useful for testing patch cables and troubleshooting nonfunctioning cable runs. High-end cable testers include the same functionality, but they are far more expensive, and a wire map tester is a reasonably priced alternative.

Tap   An active or passive networking tool that enables administrators and troubleshooters to physically access the packets on a specific network connection and capture traffic samples for analysis.

Fusion Splicers   A fiber-optic cable installation device that splices two lengths of fiber together end-to-end with exacting precision and high temperatures.

Spectrum Analyzers   A network analysis tool that monitors the utilization of a specific range of audio, optical, or radio frequencies. The tool is most commonly used to monitor channel utilization and sources of interference on Wi-Fi networks.

Snips/Cutters   They are not expensive, and they are not dedicated networking tools, but a good pair of wire cutters or snips will probably be the most frequently used tool in the cable troubleshooter's toolbox.

Cable Stripper   A scissors-like wiring tool that has, instead of a straight blade for cutting, a V-shaped blade designed to remove the insulation from a wire without damaging the copper conductor at its core.

Fiber Light Meter   A fiber-optic cable testing device that measures the signal loss of a cable run based on its measurement of a reference light source applied to the other end of the cable.

CERTMIKE EXAM ESSENTIALS

▶ Network cables have specifications that installers should observe and troubleshooters should check, including throughput, which measures the actual amount of traffic on the network; speed, which is the maximum possible transmission rate; and distance, which specifies the maximum length for a cable segment.

▶ When evaluating cable types for a network installation, IT people must also consider whether the environment calls for STP, cables that are shielded against outside interference, or plenum-rated cables, which have a sheath that does not outgas toxic fumes when it burns.

▶ Network troubleshooters often encounter cabling faults, such as opens, shorts, and reversed transmit and receive wires on copper networks, and dirty optical cables, decibel faults, and incorrect transceivers on fiber-optic networks.

Practice Question 1

A third-party cable contractor has just finished installing CAT 6 UTP cabling in a new office space for Ralph's company, and Ralph is responsible for checking their work. He connects a wire map tester to each new cable run and finds one that has a short circuit. Which of the following procedures would most likely be the simplest way to resolve the problem?

A. Move the cable away from any potential sources of electromagnetic interference.
B. Use a different pinout on both ends of the cable.
C. Reinstall the cable run using CAT 6a UTP.
D. Replace the connectors at both ends of the cable run.

Practice Question 2

Alice is working as an IT technician for a firm that has just completed a move to new office space in a building that is prewired for twisted pair Ethernet. All of the other network components have been brought from the old location. Once the IT team had installed the Gigabit Ethernet equipment and connected it to the building's cable runs, Alice was responsible for setting up a group of workstations as a test network. The network's performance was poor, however.

After analyzing some captured packets, Alice discovered that there were many Ethernet frames being retransmitted. Next, she inspected the cable runs in the drop ceilings and measured them. The cables did not exceed the maximum allowable length for the network, nor were there any major sources of electromagnetic interference near them. Which of the following could conceivably be the problem causing the dropped frames and poor network performance?

A. The existing cable is not rated for use with Gigabit Ethernet.
B. The transceivers at the cable ends are mismatched.
C. The cables have RJ11 connectors installed instead of RJ45 connectors.
D. Some of the cable runs are using T568A pinouts and some are using T568B.

Practice Question 1 Explanation

A. is incorrect because a short circuit is a wiring fault that cannot be caused by electromagnetic interference.
B. is incorrect because a short circuit is a wiring fault that can happen using any pinout. Changing the pinout would entail replacing the connectors as well, which would probably resolve the problem, but this is not the simplest resolution.
C. is incorrect because a short circuit is a wiring fault that can happen on any grade of cable. Replacing the cable would entail replacing the connectors as well, which would probably resolve the problem, but this is not the simplest resolution.
D. is correct because a short circuit is a wiring fault usually indicating that a connector pin at one end of a cable run is connected to two pins at the other end. Replacing the connectors will most likely correct the problem.

Correct Answer: D

Practice Question 2 Explanation

A. is correct because it is the only option that could be a source of the problem. Some older buildings might still have CAT 3 cable installed, which was used in the original Ethernet twisted pair specification. CAT 3 cable is unsuitable for use with Gigabit Ethernet and can result in the poor performance that Alice's test network is experiencing.
B. is incorrect because all of the transceivers were part of the Gigabit Ethernet equipment moved from the old location and should not be mismatched.
C. is incorrect because if the cables had RJ11 connectors, a Gigabit Ethernet network would not function at all.
D. is incorrect because cables using different pinout standards will not cause degraded performance as long as each run uses the same pinout at both ends.

Correct Answer: A

CHAPTER 23

Network Software Tools and Commands

Objective 5.3: Given a scenario, use the appropriate network software tools and commands.

This chapter examines some of the network tools and commands that IT personnel use when troubleshooting. The Network+ exam expects candidates to be familiar with these tools.

In this chapter, you'll learn everything you need to know about Network+ Objective 5.3, including the following topics:

▶ **Software tools**
▶ **Command-line tools**
▶ **Basic network platform commands**

SOFTWARE TOOLS

In addition to the hardware tools described in Chapter 22, "Troubleshooting Cable Connectivity," network troubleshooters typically have an arsenal of software tools available to them as well. Some of the most useful of these tools are described in this section.

Wi-Fi Analyzer

A *Wi-Fi analyzer* is a software product that scans the standard wireless network frequencies and displays information about the networks it detects in the immediate area. The functionality is incorporated into many more elaborate and expensive tools, but free versions are also available for mobile platforms.

Used primarily to examine wireless network traffic levels, a Wi-Fi analyzer typically displays a list of the networks it finds, with additional information about each one, such as the following:

SSID   Specifies the name by which the network is identified

Signal Strength   Specifies the power level of the signal (in decibel-milliwatts or dBm) relative to the user's own access point

Channel   Identifies the channel that the network is using in the current frequency band

Channel Width   Specifies the width (in MHz) of the channel the network is currently using

MAC Address   Specifies the hexadecimal MAC address of the network's access point

Encryption Protocol   Specifies the protocol that the network is using to encrypt and decrypt its transmissions

Some products also include graphical displays that provide a visual indication of the traffic on each channel.

Protocol Analyzer/Packet Capture

The terms *protocol analyzer* and *packet capture* refer to tools that go by several different names. Packet capture tools, also referred to as *sniffers* or network monitors, allow technicians to capture a sample of the network's traffic and save it to a buffer for later analysis. A protocol analyzer interprets the captured traffic and displays it for examination. The process of capturing network traffic is dependent on the tool used, the network segment to which the tool is connected, and the capabilities of the network interface adapter in the computer performing the capture.

On a standard workstation performing a packet capture, the capture tool can only access packets destined for that workstation. However, many switches support port mirroring, which makes it possible for one switchport to function as a mirror image of another port, allowing an administrator to capture the traffic from the mirrored port. To capture more than a workstation's own traffic, its network adapter must support *promiscuous mode*, which enables it to process incoming traffic destined for any MAC address.

EXAM TIP
Depending on the product, some protocol analyzers allow the user to view all of a packet's contents, including its payload data. This data could include passwords and other sensitive information in clear text. IT technicians should be aware of the potential security hazards their tools represent when they are abused.

The protocol analyzer is a tool that uses a series of parsers to interpret the data for each protocol represented in a packet. For example, Figure 23.1 shows a protocol analyzer display of a packet containing an ICMP Echo Request message. On the Ethernet line, the tool has interpreted an Etype code from the Ethernet header, indicating that the frame contains an IP datagram. In the same way, the tool has interpreted the IP header's Next Protocol field to indicate that the IP datagram contains an ICMP message. Each line in the display is expandable, enabling the technician to examine each protocol in detail.

```
Frame Details
 ┌Frame: Number = 3, Captured Frame Length = 74, MediaType = ETHERNET
 ⊞ Ethernet: Etype = Internet IP (IPv4),DestinationAddress:[00-0C-29-65-E4-5C],SourceAddress:[00-0C-29-5B-29-D2]
 ⊞ Ipv4: Src = 10.0.0.11, Dest = 10.0.0.12, Next Protocol = ICMP, Packet ID = 2823, Total IP Length = 60
 ⊟ Icmp: Echo Request Message, From 10.0.0.11 To 10.0.0.12
    ┌Type: Echo Request Message, 8(0x8)
    ├Code: 0 (0x0)
    ├Checksum: 19718 (0x4D06)
    ├ID: 1 (0x1)
    ├SequenceNumber: 85 (0x55)
    └ImplementationSpecificData: Binary Large Object (32 Bytes)
```

FIGURE 23.1   An ICMP packet displayed in a protocol analyzer

Bandwidth Speed Tester

Many people are familiar with web-based Internet speed testing tools that work by performing downloads from and uploads to a server belonging to the user's Internet service provider (ISP). By measuring the amount of data sent and received in a specified amount of time, the tool can display the speed of the Internet connection, downstream and upstream.

There are also *bandwidth speed testing* tools that IT troubleshooters can use to measure the throughput of an internal network connection. The software tool includes both a client end and a server end, which when installed exchange traffic much in the same way that an Internet speed tester does. The benefit of a tool like this is that it enables technicians to quantify the speed of the network and compare it to readings taken earlier so that when users report that the network is slow, it is possible to determine objectively if this is true.

Port Scanner

A *port scanner* is a software device that sends a series of query messages to a specified server and listens for responses. The messages contain queries targeted at each of the server's ports, and the responses indicate which of the targeted ports are open to traffic and which are blocked by a firewall. A properly secured server should have no open ports except those required by its applications, and a port scanner is a convenient method for testing this. A port scanner is also a quick and easy way to determine if an application associated with a particular port is functioning.

iPerf

iPerf is a client/server application that can measure the actual throughput achievable on a particular network connection. The tool is worth mentioning because it is open source and has been ported to many platforms, including Windows, mobile operating systems, and various Linux and Unix distributions. This provides a highly versatile test platform for troubleshooters.

After installing the iPerf client and server, the user selects the protocols and ports the tool will use to generate the traffic it sends to the server. The client floods the connection with as much traffic as it can handle, and the server calculates its throughput.

NetFlow Analyzers

NetFlow is a standard defining a tool that gathers information about the traffic processed by a network interface and sends it to a central console for analysis. There are many NetFlow implementations available, but most are based on a standard monitoring architecture that consists of three elements:

> ▶ **Exporter:** Collects information about a device's incoming and outgoing traffic, including IP addresses, ports, and protocols, and forwards it to a collector
> ▶ **Collector:** Receives, collates, and stores network traffic data it receives from exporters on the network
> ▶ **Analyzer:** Uses the traffic data supplied by the collector to create reports and visualize network traffic conditions, often using charts and graphs

Many routers and switches include built-in standards-based NetFlow exporter support, and console products might combine the collector and analyzer functions into a single application.

Trivial File Transfer Protocol (TFTP) Server

Unlike the File Transfer Protocol (FTP), the *Trivial File Transfer Protocol (TFTP)* requires no authentication and does not provide a user interface. TFTP is a server application that provides files to clients on request.

TFTP servers are usually freeware products and have multiple uses. Workstations that use the Preboot Execution Environment (PXE) to automate their initial setup obtain an IP address from a Dynamic Host Configuration Protocol (DHCP) server and then download a boot loader file from a TFTP server. In the same way, administrators often use a TFTP server as a source for router and switch upgrade downloads and for backing up network device configurations.

Terminal Emulator

Back in the days of mainframe computers, all of a computer's processors, memory, and storage were located in one place, and users accessed the computer with a terminal, which could be located elsewhere. A terminal is strictly an input/output device with no intelligence of its own. Today, there are still some network devices, especially switches and routers, that need a terminal to access their command-line interfaces (CLIs), so administrators use a program called a *terminal emulator*, which enables a computer or other device to function as a simple terminal. The terminal emulator connects to the device using either a direct cable connection or a network protocol, such as Telnet, or more commonly, Secure Shell (SSH).

IP Scanner

An *IP scanner* is a device similar to a port scanner, except that it sends messages to a range of IP addresses and listens for replies. This enables technicians to determine which addresses are in use. However, some IP scanners use ICMP Echo Request messages, as the ping tool does, which might be filtered out by firewalls, rendering the scanner ineffective.

COMMAND-LINE TOOLS

Most operating systems include a collection of simple network configuration and trouble-shooting tools that run from a CLI. Some tools, such as ping, function in pretty much the same way on all platforms. In other cases, there are tools that perform the same tasks on different platforms but that have different names, such as traceroute and tracert. Some of the most commonly used tools of this type are described in this section.

Ping

Ping is a simple tool that sends Echo Request messages to a specified hostname or IP address and listens for Echo Reply messages from the target. The messages use the Internet Control Message Protocol (ICMP), and there are command-line parameters that allow the user to customize the messages sent.

A successful ping test consisting of requests and replies indicates that the target system and its TCP/IP interface are up and running. However, many system administrators allow their firewalls to block incoming Echo Request traffic because it can conceivably be used to mount denial-of-service (DoS) attacks. Therefore, a failed ping test does not necessarily mean that the target system is not functioning.

Ipconfig/Ifconfig/Ip

Ipconfig (on Windows) and *ifconfig* and *ip* (on Unix/Linux) are all command-line utilities that display information about a system's network interfaces. On Windows, running `ipconfig -all` from the command line displays detailed IP addressing information for each of the computer's interfaces, similar to the following:

```
Windows IP Configuration
    Host Name . . . . . . . . . . . . : WORK13
    Primary Dns Suffix  . . . . . . . :
    Node Type . . . . . . . . . . . . : Hybrid
    IP Routing Enabled. . . . . . . . : No
    WINS Proxy Enabled. . . . . . . . : No
Wireless LAN adapter Wi-Fi:
```

```
Connection-specific DNS Suffix  . :
Description . . . . . . . . . . . : Intel(R) Dual Band Wireless-AC 8265
Physical Address. . . . . . . . . : E4-70-B8-43-21-E4
DHCP Enabled. . . . . . . . . . . : Yes
Autoconfiguration Enabled . . . . : Yes
Link-local IPv6 Address . . . . . : fe80::9873:dbd5:70c9:a5aa%14(Preferred)
IPv4 Address. . . . . . . . . . . : 192.168.1.21(Preferred)
Subnet Mask . . . . . . . . . . . : 255.255.255.0
Lease Obtained. . . . . . . . . . : Thursday, January 12, 2023 2:27:07 AM
Lease Expires . . . . . . . . . . : Tuesday, January 17, 2023 2:29:14 PM
Default Gateway . . . . . . . . . : 192.168.1.1
DHCP Server . . . . . . . . . . . : 192.168.1.1
DHCPv6 IAID . . . . . . . . . . . : 98857144
DHCPv6 Client DUID. . . . . . . . : 00-01-00-01-21-B2-B8-75-54-E1-AD-D5-96-16
DNS Servers . . . . . . . . . . . : 192.168.1.1
NetBIOS over Tcpip. . . . . . . . : Enabled
```

On a system using DHCP for its addressing, ipconfig is the easiest way to learn the address the system is using. It is also possible to use ipconfig to release and renew DHCP address assignments.

On most Unix and Linux distributions, the standard ipconfig equivalent is a command called ifconfig, which can display information about an interface and modify its configuration settings as well, something the ipconfig command cannot do. ifconfig uses a different format for its output, like the following:

```
eth0: flags=4163 <UP, BROADCAST, RUNNING, MULTICAST> mtu 1500
inet 192.168.1.45 netmask 255.255.255.0 broadcast 192.168.1.255
inet6 fe80::215:5dff:fe00:f05 prefixlen 64 scopeid 0x20<link>
ether 00:15:52:00:0f:04 txqueuelen 1000 (Ethernet)
RX packets 53064 bytes 78325568 (78.3 MB)
RX errors 0 dropped 0 overruns 0 frame 0
TX packets 3325 bytes 243054 (243.0 KB)
TX errors 0 dropped 0 overruns 0 carrier 0 collisions 0
```

The ip tool is another Unix/Linux utility that is replacing ifconfig on some distributions. The tool can display and configure interface settings, much like ifconfig, but it can also do a great deal more, including configuring static routes, multicasts, tunnels, and ARP tables.

Nslookup/Dig

Nslookup is a Domain Name System (DNS) tool, found on both Windows and Unix/Linux platforms, that allows users to resolve hostnames and domain names into addresses, both from the command line and interactively. By default, entering **nslookup www.contoso.com**

at the command line returns an IP address associated with that server name, according to the computer's default DNS server.

One of the most useful nslookup features for troubleshooters, however, is the ability to direct name resolution queries to a specific server. Sometimes, name resolution problems can result from DNS resource records not having propagated to all of the name servers on the Internet. By directing a query, you can determine whether a particular server has the latest information.

Dig is a Unix/Linux tool that is virtually identical to nslookup in its capabilities, although it displays its results differently. Dig does not have an interactive mode as nslookup does, which is why some Unix/Linux distributions include both.

Traceroute/Tracert

The path that a network packet takes on the way to its destination is called its *route*. The route consists of *hops*, which are individual trips the packet takes from router to router. Internet transmissions might have routes with 20 or more hops between the source and the destination.

The traceroute tool on Unix/Linux and the `Tracert.exe` program on Windows both display a list of the hops on the route to a specified destination. The tools do this by sending a series of ICMP Echo Request messages with successively larger values in the IP header's Time to Live field. This causes transmissions to fail at each hop and return error messages to the source. The error messages contain the IP address of the router at each hop, which the Windows `tracert` command lists in a display like the following:

```
Tracing route to www.fineartschool.co.uk [173.146.1.1] over a maximum of 30 hops:
1    <10 ms    1 ms  <10 ms   192.168.2.99
2    105 ms   92 ms   98 ms   qrvl-67terminal01.cpandl.com [131.107.24.67.3]
3    101 ms  110 ms   98 ms   qrvl.cpandl.com [131.107.67.1]
4    123 ms  109 ms  118 ms   svcr03-7b.cpandl.com [131.107.103.125]
5    123 ms  112 ms  114 ms   clsm02-2.cpandl.com [131.107.88.26]
6    136 ms  130 ms  133 ms   sl-gw19-pen-6-1-0-T3.fabrikam.com [157.54.116.5]
7    146 ms  129 ms  133 ms   sl-bb20-pen-12-0.fabrikam.com [157.54.5.1]
8    147 ms  149 ms  152 ms   sl-demon-1-0.fabrikam.com [157.54.173.10]
9    230 ms  225 ms  226 ms   tele-back-1-ge023.router.adatum.co.uk [157.60.173.12]
10   233 ms  220 ms  226 ms   tele-core-3-fxp1.router.adatum.co.uk [157.60.252.56]
11   236 ms  221 ms  226 ms   tele-service-2-165.router.adatum.co.uk [157.60.36.149]
12   220 ms  224 ms  210 ms   www.fineartschool.co.uk [206.73.118.65]
Trace complete.
```

Traceroute is an especially valuable tool on a large enterprise network because it can provide the troubleshooter with information about the routes packets are taking through the network. For example, in the sample display, notice the jump in the round-trip times from the 100s to the 200s when the route takes the packets from North America to servers in the United Kingdom.

Arp

As described in Chapter 11, "Switching," the *Address Resolution Protocol (ARP)* is a data link layer protocol that systems use to resolve IP addresses into media access control (MAC) addresses. The system then saves the resulting pair of addresses to an ARP table, which it saves in memory for reuse.

In addition to the protocol itself, there is also an arp utility in both Windows and Unix/Linux that allows users to display and modify the contents of the ARP table. Running `arp -a` from the command line, for example, produces a display like the following:

```
Interface: 192.168.1.21 --- 0xe
  Internet Address      Physical Address      Type
  192.168.1.1           28-80-88-1e-87-e5     dynamic
  192.168.1.11          84-b8-b8-2d-18-69     dynamic
  192.168.1.14          20-ef-bd-33-bc-e8     dynamic
  192.168.1.16          1c-1e-e3-b6-ae-42     dynamic
  192.168.1.23          9e-3d-cf-bf-c3-2d     dynamic
```

Netstat

Netstat is a Windows and Unix/Linux command that can display a variety of network statistics about a system's TCP and UDP connections. Running the command `netstat` with no parameters displays a list of the computer's currently open sessions, similar to the following:

```
Proto   Local Address           Foreign Address          State
TCP     127.0.0.1:49994         MZ13:60757               ESTABLISHED
TCP     127.0.0.1:59423         CL73:59424               ESTABLISHED
TCP     192.168.1.21:57617      52.56.69.2:https         ESTABLISHED
TCP     192.168.1.21:57633      140:https                TIME_WAIT
TCP     192.168.1.21:57638      40.96.190.18:https       TIME_WAIT
TCP     192.168.1.21:57662      40.97.186.226:https      ESTABLISHED
TCP     192.168.1.21:57674      a104-212-9-179:https     ESTABLISHED
TCP     192.168.1.21:57680      220:https                ESTABLISHED
TCP     192.168.1.21:57681      219.21.13.15:http        ESTABLISHED
TCP     192.168.1.21:57684      52.46.181.98:https       ESTABLISHED
```

```
TCP    [fe80::9873:dbd5:70c9:a5aa%14]:445      BK09:56332            ESTABLISHED
TCP    [fe80::9873:dbd5:70c9:a5aa%14]:55341    CK15:ms-wbt-server    ESTABLISHED
TCP    [fe80::9873:dbd5:70c9:a5aa%14]:57700    LM44:wsd              TIME_WAIT
```

With command-line parameters added, netstat can also display the system's listening ports, Ethernet packet counts, and TCP/IP packet counts for IP4 and IP6.

Hostname

Hostname is a simple utility found on most Windows and Unix/Linux systems that returns the name of the current computer, or host. There are no command-line parameters or other functions. However, when IT technicians are working with remote sessions to multiple systems at once, sometimes they need a quick reminder of which one they are currently accessing.

Route

Route is a Windows and Unix/Linux utility that provides access to a system's routing table. All TCP/IP hosts have a routing table, as described in Chapter 10, "Routing and Bandwidth Management," whether or not they are functioning as a router connecting networks.

The route print command in Windows (or route -n in Unix/Linux) displays the contents of the system's routing tables for IP4 and IP6. In addition to displaying the routing tables, the route utility can also allow administrators to add, modify, and delete routing table entries.

Telnet

Telnet is a communications protocol that allows a user to connect to a remote computer and execute commands there. In addition to the protocol itself, Telnet also includes a simple CLI with which a user can initiate the connection. Telnet is installed by default on virtually all Unix/Linux distributions. On Windows workstations, a Telnet client is included with the operating system, but users must turn it on in the Windows Features dialog box before they can use it.

Telnet can help troubleshooters to determine if a system on the network is operating, but it is important to remember that everything telnet transmits over the network is in plain text, including passwords. The Secure Shell SSH program is similar to telnet, but it transmits data in encrypted form.

Tcpdump

The *tcpdump* tool, found only on Unix and Linux platforms, can capture packets as they are transmitted and received over a particular network interface and display them. With command-line parameters, users can filter the packets to save only those using a specified IP address or a port number associated with a specified application layer protocol.

Nmap

Nmap is a network scanner application originally created for Linux but that has since been ported to other platforms, including Windows and some Unix distributions. By sending out a series of targeted messages over the network, nmap can generate a list of hosts discovered on the network, as well as open ports.

For example, Figure 23.2 shows the results of an nmap command that lists a series of open ports on the system being tested, including port 22 for the SSH server and port 80, the well-known port for HTTP web servers, such as Apache.

```
craig@ubuntu1:~$ nmap -A scanme.nmap.org
Starting Nmap 7.93 ( https://nmap.org ) at 2023-01-18 19:54 UTC
Nmap scan report for scanme.nmap.org (45.33.32.156)
Host is up (0.10s latency).
Other addresses for scanme.nmap.org (not scanned): 2600:3c01::f03c:91ff:fe18:bb2f
Not shown: 993 closed tcp ports (conn-refused)
PORT      STATE    SERVICE       VERSION
22/tcp    open     ssh           OpenSSH 6.6.1p1 Ubuntu 2ubuntu2.13 (Ubuntu Linux; protocol 2.0)
| ssh-hostkey:
|   1024 ac00a01a82ffcc5599dc672b34976b75 (DSA)
|   2048 203d2d44622ab05a9db5b30514c2a6b2 (RSA)
|   256 9602bb5e57541c4e452f564c4a24b257 (ECDSA)
|_  256 33fa910fe0e17b1f6d05a2b0f1544156 (ED25519)
80/tcp    open     http          Apache httpd 2.4.7 ((Ubuntu))
|_http-title: Go ahead and ScanMe!
|_http-favicon: Nmap Project
|_http-server-header: Apache/2.4.7 (Ubuntu)
135/tcp   filtered msrpc
139/tcp   filtered netbios-ssn
445/tcp   filtered microsoft-ds
9929/tcp  open     nping-echo    Nping echo
31337/tcp open     tcpwrapped
Service Info: OS: Linux; CPE: cpe:/o:linux:linux_kernel
```

FIGURE 23.2 Output of an nmap command on a Linux system

BASIC NETWORK PLATFORM COMMANDS

Originally created for use on Cisco routers and switches, some generic network platform commands have since been adopted by other network device manufacturers as well. In most cases, devices from other manufacturers respond to these commands.

show interface

The show interface (or show interfaces) command displays a list of the network interfaces in the device with statistics about each one. The listing typically includes the interfaces' current status, their addresses, their configuration settings, and packet counters for traffic sent and received, as shown in the following excerpt:

```
Ethernet 0 is up, line protocol is up
    Hardware is MIM Ethernet, address is 0000.0c00.740c (bia 0000.0c00.740c)
```

```
    Internet address is 131.108.28.8, subnet mask is 255.255.255.0
    MTU 1500 bytes, BW 10000 Kbit, DLY 100000 usec, rely 255/255, load 1/255
    Encapsulation ARPA, loopback not set, keepalive set (10 sec)
    ARP type: ARPA, ARP Timeout 4:00:00
    Last input 0:00:00, output 0:00:00, output hang never
    Last clearing of "show interface" counters 0:00:00
    Output queue 0/40, 0 drops; input queue 0/75, 0 drops
    Five minute input rate 0 bits/sec, 0 packets/sec
    Five minute output rate 2000 bits/sec, 4 packets/sec
        1134576 packets input, 448351251 bytes, 0 no buffer
        Received 351125 broadcasts, 0 runts, 0 giants
        0 input errors, 0 CRC, 0 frame, 0 overrun, 0 ignored, 0 abort
        5331142 packets output, 496317239 bytes, 0 underruns
        0 output errors, 422 collisions, 0 interface resets, 0 restarts
```

show config

The show running-config command on many routers and switches displays the configuration currently in the device's memory. To display the configuration stored in the device's
nonvolatile memory, use the command **show startup-config**. The output of these
commands, like the listing that follows, takes the form of a batch file, a series of commands
that an administrator could execute on the device interface.

```
enable
config terminal
card 2
type en4port1G
no shutdown
ib sm subnet-prefix fe:80:00:00:00:00:00 priority 0
interface gateway 2
ip address 192.168.1.1 255.255.255.0
interface ethernet 2/1
ip address 192.168.4.1 255.255.255.0
interface ethernet 2/2
ip address 192.168.3.1 255.255.255.0
arp ib 192.168.2.2 gid fe:80:00:00:00:00:00:00:02:c9:00:00:13:68:c3
qpn 2 2/0
arp ib 192.168.2.3 gid fe:80:00:00:00:00:00:00:02:c9:00:00:16:a
f:d3 qpn 2 2/0
```

show route

The show ip route command on many network devices displays the routing table currently in memory in a format similar to the following:

```
Codes: I - IGRP derived, R - RIP derived, O - OSPF derived
       C - connected, S - static, E - EGP derived, B - BGP derived
       * - candidate default route, IA - OSPF inter area route
       E1 - OSPF external type 1 route, E2 - OSPF external type 2 route
Gateway of last resort is 131.119.254.240 to network 129.140.0.0
O E2 150.150.0.0 [160/5] via 131.119.254.6, 0:01:00, Ethernet2
O E2 192.68.132.0 [160/5] via 131.119.254.6, 0:00:59, Ethernet2
O E2 130.130.0.0 [160/5] via 131.119.254.6, 0:00:59, Ethernet2
E    128.128.0.0 [200/128] via 131.119.254.244, 0:02:22, Ethernet2
E    192.65.129.0 [200/128] via 131.119.254.244, 0:02:22, Ethernet2
E    131.131.0.0 [200/128] via 131.119.254.244, 0:02:22, Ethernet2
E    192.75.139.0 [200/129] via 131.119.254.240, 0:02:23, Ethernet2
E    141.140.0.0 [200/129] via 131.119.254.240, 0:02:23, Ethernet2
```

By default, the show ip route command displays the IPv4 routing table. To display the IPv6 table, use the show ipv6 route command.

CERTMIKE EXAM ESSENTIALS

▶ Network troubleshooters often use a variety of software tools to discover information about the network and its performance. Wi-Fi analyzers scan and detect wireless frequencies to display the nearby access points, whereas protocol analyzers capture network traffic samples and interpret them. Port scanners and IP scanners display the open ports and IP addresses used on the network. Both of these functions can be incorporated into more elaborate and expensive testing devices.

▶ Most operating systems come equipped with a set of command-line tools, many of which network troubleshooters can use to resolve, or at least isolate, problems. These tools include ping, which confirms that another system is running; traceroute, which lists the routers on the path to a destination; nslookup, which performs DNS name resolutions; and route, which displays and modifies routing table entries.

Practice Question 1

Ralph is working the IT helpdesk when he starts receiving calls from users who can't access web pages on the Internet. They are receiving error messages that say that destination port UDP 53 is unreachable. He soon concludes that there is a name resolution problem, so Ralph starts looking at the network's DNS server, which is located on a screened subnet (or perimeter network) on the other side of a router. Using the nslookup utility, Ralph attempts to resolve a name by sending queries to the DNS server, but the attempt fails. He then performs a ping test using the DNS server's IP address, which is successful. Ralph concludes from these results that the server running the DNS service is operating, but the DNS service itself is not. Which of the following are possible causes of the problem? (Select all correct answers.)

A. Ralph's workstation has TCP/IP host configuration settings that are improperly configured.

B. The DNS server has TCP/IP host configuration settings that are improperly configured.

C. The router connecting the screened subnet to the internal network is not running DNS and therefore cannot forward DNS messages.

D. The DNS service on the server is not running.

E. There is a firewall between the screened subnet and the internal network that is blocking the DNS server's UTP 53 port.

Practice Question 2

Alice is attempting to determine why there has recently been an increase in traffic on her network, as well as a perceptible degradation of its performance. After capturing a sample of the network's traffic, Alice begins to examine it in a protocol analyzer. One thing she notices immediately is that there is a great deal of ICMP traffic on the network. At first, Alice suspects that there might be a DoS attack occurring, but she rules out that possibility. Next, she wonders if the ICMP traffic might be caused by her and her colleagues' frequent use of TCP/IP troubleshooting tools. Which of the following are network testing tools that Alice and her colleagues commonly use to perform their tests by sending and receiving Internet Control Message Protocol (ICMP) messages? (Choose all correct answers.)

A. Netstat

B. Ping

C. Ipconfig

D. Tracert

E. Route

Practice Question 1 Explanation

A. is incorrect because the ping test indicated that Ralph's TCP/IP client is running properly. In addition, there are other users experiencing the same problem, so the cause cannot be Ralph's workstation.

B. is incorrect because the ping test indicated that the TCP/IP client is running properly on the DNS server.

C. is incorrect because a router does not need to be running DNS to forward packets to the server.

D. is correct because although the DNS server computer and its TCP/IP client are operating, the DNS service is not responding to queries.

E. is correct because a firewall can block access to specific ports while leaving the rest of the computer operable.

Correct Answer: D and E

Practice Question 2 Explanation

A. is incorrect because netstat displays information gathered from the system's network interfaces; it does not use ICMP messages.

B. is correct because ping tests IP connectivity by sending ICMP Echo Request messages to a target and receiving Echo Reply messages (or ICMP error messages) back.

C. is incorrect because a Gigabit Ethernet network would not function at all with only two wire pairs connected.

D. is correct because tracert identifies the routers on a path to a destination by sending a series of ICMP Echo Request messages with incrementing TTL values. Each router in turn on the path experiences a packet failure and returns an ICMP error message to the sender.

E. is incorrect because the route utility only displays and modifies the system's own routing table; it does not use ICMP messages.

Correct Answer: B and D

CHAPTER 24

Troubleshooting Wireless Connectivity

Objective 5.4: Given a scenario, troubleshoot common wireless connectivity issues.

This chapter examines some of the specialized issues and procedures involved in troubleshooting wireless networks. The Network+ exam expects candidates to be familiar with these concepts.

In this chapter, you'll learn everything you need to know about Network+ Objective 5.4, including the following topics:

▶ **Specifications and limitations**
▶ **Considerations**
▶ **Common issues**

SPECIFICATIONS AND LIMITATIONS

As discussed in Chapter 12, "Wireless Standards," wireless networking technologies have specifications and limitations that govern how a network should be designed and installed. These same specifications, discussed in the following sections, are in many cases the starting point for the wireless network troubleshooting process as well.

Throughput

Throughput is the rate at which a network device can actually transmit data, as opposed to the theoretical speed ratings specified by wireless standards and hardware manufacturers. Wireless networks have many more variables than cabled networks that can affect their throughput.

Interference caused by the building's architecture is a relatively stable source of interference that technicians can plot and document as part of the network's initial site survey. However, there are many other potential sources of wireless interference that are transient, such as mobile users accessing the network from different places, users of other nearby networks on the same channel, and weather conditions.

However well the IT technicians survey the site of a wireless network during the design process, conditions can change in a moment, affecting its level of performance. This is why the troubleshooting process for a throughput problem on a wireless network must essentially start from the beginning each time a problem occurs. The troubleshooter must investigate the network conditions at that moment, which might be substantially different from those at any previous time.

Speed

A wireless network's rated *speed* is the theoretical maximum throughput of a device under ideal conditions. The one definite conclusion that an IT technician can make regarding a wireless network's theoretical speed is that the actual realized network will never achieve it. The IEEE 802.11 wireless standards all specify a speed rating for a network that conforms to the stated specifications. However, even without interference caused by issues such as conflicting devices and architectural barriers, normal network operating conditions can still prevent devices from achieving the network's rated speed.

When faced with what appears to be a slow wireless network, troubleshooters should be aware that failure to achieve the rated speed of the network is not necessarily an indication that something is wrong. The performance of the network should be compared with a baseline performance reading taken on the actual network at an earlier date, not with a theoretical maximum.

Distance

On a wireless network, signals tend to attenuate (weaken) and throughput to decrease as the *distance* between a device and its wireless access point (WAP) increases. Eventually, a wireless device that gets too far from the WAP will start intermittently dropping its network connection. However, on a wireless network, the question of how much distance from the WAP is too much is a difficult one to answer.

The specifications for cabled networks always have exact maximum cable length limitations. If a cable segment exceeds the maximum length, the number of signaling errors and packet retransmissions increases rapidly. However, on a wireless network, it is difficult to pinpoint a distance limitation based on protocol specifications. There are many more factors that can affect wireless connectivity than there are on a cabled network. Distance from the WAP is one factor, but there are also issues like the following:

- ▶ Which frequency band the network is using
- ▶ What type of antennas the devices have
- ▶ Where the antennas are located
- ▶ How the building is constructed
- ▶ How many other networks are using the same frequency and channel

As the 802.11 standards developed over the years, the potential distances that wireless network connections can achieve have increased due to technology improvements such as multiple input/multiple output (MIMO), so the selection of a wireless standard during the design process should be based in part on the distances the network must span.

RSSI Signal Strength

The *received signal strength indicator (RSSI)* is a means of quantifying the strength of the wireless network signal as it is received by a client device. Most phones and other devices display the signal strength as a number of bars, which is a less precise approximation of the actual RSSI signal strength value.

RSSI is not an absolute measurement against an established power scale. It is rather a relative measurement based on an arbitrary scale specified by the manufacturer of the device. Some wireless interface manufacturers use a scale of 0 to 100, whereas others have different value ranges. Many wireless network monitoring tools can measure signal strength using RSSI values, which provides troubleshooters with a more exact reading of the signal strength at a particular location.

EIRP Power Settings

Effective isotropic radiated power (EIRP) is a calculated measurement of the *radio frequency (RF)* power that can be emitted by an antenna in a single direction, based on its transmission strength and the antenna's gain. EIRP is measured in decibels over isotropic (dBi). The formula for calculating the EIRP is as follows:

$$EIRP = transmitter\ power - cable\ loss + antenna\ gain$$

An antenna with adequate gain makes it possible for the device to transmit at a lower power level, thus conserving battery life. Using EIRP values, troubleshooters can compare the relative power of emitters and adjust power levels as needed.

CONSIDERATIONS

Compared to cabled networks, wireless LANs have many more variables to consider that can affect the performance of the network. When designing or troubleshooting a network,

IT technicians should consider all the factors discussed in this section in relation to the network's functionality.

Antennas

Chapter 12 discusses the role of the antenna in wireless networking and some of the types of *antennas* that are available. In some cases, wireless networking problems can be attributed to the choice of antennas that WAPs use and their locations.

All wireless devices must have at least one antenna. While there are antenna replacement and enhancement products available for smartphones and other mobile devices, most troubleshooting efforts concentrate on the WAP antennas, which are more easily configurable or replaceable. When troubleshooting wireless transmission problems, consider the following aspects of the WAP antenna:

Placement   Resolving a wireless networking problem can sometimes be as easy as moving the access point antenna to a different location. If some of the wireless devices can readily access the network while others have trouble connecting, consider moving the antenna to a more central location. If unauthorized users outside the building are accessing the network, consider moving the antenna away from the outer walls.

Type   The location of an access point is also affected by the type of antenna it is using. Omnidirectional antennas can be located centrally because they transmit and receive in all directions. To restrict connectivity to a specific area, however, it is possible to use a directional antenna on a WAP and place it near a wall pointing inward. This can prevent unauthorized users outside the space from gaining access to the network.

Polarization   The orientation of a device's antenna specifies its *polarization*, which indicates the direction in which the signal is strongest. For the best transmission between a client device and a WAP, the two antennas should be oriented in the same way so their polarizations match. If one device is oriented vertically and the other horizontally, the signal strength can be substantially reduced.

Channel Utilization

As noted in Chapter 12, the 2.4 GHz and 5 GHz frequencies used for Wi-Fi networks are divided into channels. Access points are configured to use a particular channel or to select one automatically. As with any network, too much traffic on a medium can cause its performance to degrade. When there are too many client devices accessing the same channel, the network slows down and some users might be unable to connect.

When a network has too much traffic on one channel, troubleshooters can address the problem in various ways, including the following:

Configure the devices to use a different channel.   While this might seem like an obvious solution, the usage of the Wi-Fi channels tends to fluctuate constantly. Most wireless devices select a channel automatically by default, and many administrators permanently reconfigure their devices to use nonoverlapping channels. However, constantly scanning the frequencies and reconfiguring the network devices to use the least occupied channel at the moment is generally not a practical solution.

Configure access points to use different channels.   When a network has more heavy-use client devices than a single channel can support, one solution is to use multiple WAPs configured to use different channels with the same SSID.

Use a different frequency.   In a location where the 2.4 GHz band is regularly over-populated with other networks, some administrators move their equipment to the 5 GHz band instead, which tends to have less traffic (though this may change). In some cases, moving to the 5 GHz band might require equipment replacement, which would make it a less attractive solution.

AP Association Time

Every wireless client device, when connecting to an access point, must first authenticate itself and then associate itself with the WAP. Not until both processes are complete can the client access the network. Access points typically log the *AP association time*, the time required to perform each client connection, and can supply that information to admin-istrators using SNMP or other means. When association times get noticeably longer as a trend, it could be an indication that the access point is being overburdened with traffic. If the authentication/association process takes too long, the client device will eventually time out and disconnect. Troubleshooters working on a problem in which wireless clients spon-taneously disconnect from the network should check this statistic.

Site Survey

Site surveys should be a critical part of every wireless network's design, deployment, main-tenance, and troubleshooting processes. A pre-design survey provides information about the space to be served and should include scans that show other wireless networks and potential sources of interference in the area. Once the network equipment is installed, another survey can serve as a baseline for future comparisons.

Wireless networks are more volatile than cabled networks. For many organizations, adding new client devices, reconfiguring the office space, installing new equipment, and accommodating new sources of interference are all commonplace occurrences. For this reason, it is a recommended practice to repeat the site surveys on a regular basis. When problems appear, the records of the site surveys can help troubleshooters to identify trends that might be possible causes.

COMMON ISSUES

As noted earlier, there are many things that can go wrong on a wireless network. Some of the problems that occur most frequently are discussed in this section.

Interference

A source of interference on a wireless network can be anything that affects the successful transmission of a signal. Interference can cause a client device connection to slow down, drop the connection intermittently, or not connect at all. Assuming that the problem client was once functioning properly, a sudden increase in interference can be caused by new equipment installed nearby, such as cordless phones or a microwave oven, or intervening walls or furniture that was not there before, or any number of other sources.

There are two main ways to address excessive interference on a wireless network: either remove the source of the interference or move the problem client. Moving the client device away from the source of the interference should work, as would moving the client closer to the access point.

Channel Overlap

As explained in Chapter 12, the channels in the 2.4 GHz band overlap with each other, meaning that a device using one channel can interfere with another device on the adjacent channel. Mathematically, there are only three channels a 2.4 GHz wireless network can use and avoid *channel overlap* interference entirely: channels 1, 6, and 11. Many administrators configure their devices to only use these three channels for that reason.

The problem with this strategy is that it only applies to the 2.4 GHz band and only with some of the 802.11 standards. On 802.1g networks, for example, the nonoverlapping channels are 1, 5, 9, and 13.

The other issue that affects channel overlap is the ability to bond channels together to create a single, larger channel. Creating wider bonded channels means that there are fewer channels available. A 5 GHz 802.11ac network, for example, can support the bonding of up to eight 20 MHz channels, thus splitting the entire 5 GHz band into only two 160 MHz channels. Wider channels complicate the overlap situation as well. Troubleshooters should be conscious of the channel bonding strategy being used on the wireless network and consider channel overlap as a possible cause of interference.

Antenna Cable Attenuation/Signal Loss

External antennas are typically connected to wireless access points using coaxial cables, and it is important to minimize the signal loss between the antenna and the WAP. The antenna connection is as susceptible to attenuation as any other network medium, especially in the higher frequencies. Choose an antenna cable with low signal loss and install it carefully, with properly crimped connectors and a gentle bend radius.

RF Attenuation/Signal Loss

Radio frequency (RF) signals are as susceptible to attenuation as any other signals. The farther from the access point a client device is located, the greater the signal loss and the weaker the signals will be. As a result of the weakened signals, the 802.11 standards call for a reduction in the speed of the connection. If the signals grow too weak, the client will be unable to connect to the network at all.

Troubleshooters can measure the RSSI at the client device location to quantify the signal loss in decibels (dB). Higher frequencies are more subject to attenuation than lower ones, so a 5 GHz network is likely to attenuate more over the same distance than a 2.4 GHz network. To address an excessive loss of signal due to attenuation, troubleshooters can do any of the following:

- ▶ Move the client device and the WAP closer together.
- ▶ Add another WAP closer to the client.
- ▶ Replace the antenna on the access point with one more suitable to the environment.

Wrong SSID

The *service set identifier (SSID)* is the name by which a wireless network is identified by client devices. When a wireless device starts, it searches the frequencies for nearby SSIDs and displays them as a list from which the user can choose. Selecting the wrong SSID from the list or typing an incorrect SSID will attempt to connect the device to a neighboring network.

In the case of properly secured networks, the device will fail to authenticate to the wrong network and no connection will be established. In the case of unprotected networks, however, the device will connect to the wrong SSID, and it might take some time for the user to recognize that they are not connected to their usual network.

Incorrect Passphrase

On a wireless network that uses a preshared key for authentication, mistyping the key will cause the connection attempt to fail. Passphrases are case sensitive, and they are often masked in the interface, making it easy for users to mistype them without noticing.

As noted in Chapter 21, "Network Troubleshooting Methodology," troubleshooters should always question the obvious. When a user reports that they are unable to connect to the network, the troubleshooter should make sure they are typing the correct passphrase before exploring more complicated possibilities.

Encryption Protocol Mismatch

Encryption protocol issues are one of the most common problems faced by wireless network troubleshooters. For a client device to connect to a WAP, both must be configured to use the same encryption protocol. As with an incorrect passphrase, an *encryption protocol mismatch* will prevent the client from establishing a connection to the network. For example, a user might easily select the Wi-Fi Protected Access (WPA) security protocol instead of WPA2. Despite being different versions of the same protocol, the two are not compatible, and the connection attempt will fail.

For troubleshooters, the easiest way to determine whether a connection problem is due to a security issue is to temporarily configure the client device and the WAP with no security at all. If the client can successfully connect to an open network, but not to a secured one, then the problem is definitely related to the selection and configuration of the security protocol.

Depending on the client device interface, it might be necessary for the user or the troubleshooter to delete (or forget) the SSID connection before re-creating it with the correct security protocol selected.

Insufficient Wireless Coverage

Insufficient wireless coverage can refer to a network in which there are users too far from the nearest access point to connect reliably to the network. The term can also refer to an access point that is overwhelmed with traffic. Both of these conditions can potentially cause degraded network performance and dropped connections. The solutions in both cases are typically the same as for signal loss due to attenuation, discussed earlier: move the WAP, add a WAP, or replace the antenna.

Captive Portal Issues

As noted in Chapter 18, "Network Hardening," a *captive portal* is a web page through which new users must pass before they can access a wireless network. Found mostly on public-facing websites, captive portals typically require users to identify themselves and agree to an acceptable use policy before they are permitted access to the wireless network.

Some users might be puzzled by the appearance of the captive portal and think that they are being improperly redirected to another website. In other cases, networks protected by captive portals impose a throttle on the throughput to prevent users from monopolizing the network's bandwidth. This too might confuse users, leading them to request technical support.

Client Disassociation Issues

Client disassociation is a sudden, unplanned disconnection from a wireless network. This can occur for many reasons, several of which have been discussed in this chapter, such as attenuation, interference, and excessive traffic. However, client disassociation can also be the result of a deliberate act, intended as the opening salvo of a denial-of-service attack.

By transmitting altered Wi-Fi management frames, attackers can forcibly disassociate a client device from its current wireless network and then associate it with the attackers' own, for whatever nefarious ends they have in mind. The solution for this type of attack is to use a Wi-Fi implementation that supports the IEEE 802.11w standard for protected management frames.

CERTMIKE EXAM ESSENTIALS

▶ Technicians working with wireless networks should begin their troubleshooting processes with attention to the basic specifications and limitations used to design the network. These include throughput, the network's actual realized transmission rate; speed, the network's theoretical maximum transmission rate; and distance, the strength of the network signal as it arrives from the access point.

▶ Wireless networks have many more variables to consider as possible causes of a communication problem. However, a lot of these variables manifest themselves in the same way, with slow transmission rates and sudden disassociations. Some of the common issues that can cause these problems are interference due to channel overlap and signal loss caused by attenuation.

▶ For a client device to connect to a wireless network, both the device and the access point must be configured to use the same SSID, encryption protocol, and passphrase. Without all three, there can be no network connection.

Practice Question 1

Alice recently received a promotion to the vice presidency she had been working toward for years. She has just moved into her new office in the executive wing, down the corridor from her old one and past the big glass doors. However, since moving, Alice's access to the wireless network with her laptop has been spotty at best. It's either slow or it intermittently drops the connection entirely, forcing her to reconnect. She never had these problems in her old office. Which of the following could possibly be the cause of her problem? (Select all possible answers.)

A. Alice's laptop is using the wrong encryption passphrase.

B. Alice's new office is farther away from the access point.

C. The access point is using an omnidirectional antenna.

D. The big glass doors are causing signal interference.

Practice Question 2

Ralph is the wireless network administrator for a law firm that has its offices on one floor of an old mansion with many small rooms. The network has an IEEE 802.11g access point located at the approximate center of the floor. Laptops and other devices in most of the rooms connect to the network at 54 Mbps, but the computers in one particular room rarely connect at speeds above 11 Mbps. Which of the following might be the cause of the problem?

A. The computers in the problem room are experiencing an SSID mismatch.

B. The computers in the problem room have low RSSI values, due to excessive distance from the access point.

C. The computers in the problem room are using a different encryption protocol than the access point.

D. The computers in the problem room have IEEE 802.11a network adapters, not 802.11g.

Practice Question 1 Explanation

A. is incorrect because a wrong encryption passphrase would prevent the laptop from connecting to the network at all.

B. is correct because greater distance from the access point can result in more signal loss due to attenuation, resulting in the intermittent connectivity that Alice is experiencing.

C. is incorrect because an omnidirectional antenna emits signals in every direction, which would not account for Alice's intermittent connectivity.

D. is correct because interference from the intervening glass wall can cause signal loss, resulting in the intermittent connectivity that Alice is experiencing.

Correct Answer: B and D

Practice Question 2 Explanations

A. is incorrect because an SSID mismatch would not cause the computers to connect at a slower speed. However, it would cause them to connect to a different network.

B. is correct because as wireless devices move farther away from the access point, their signals attenuate, their received signal strength indicators (RSSIs) go down, and the maximum speed of their connections drops.

C. is incorrect because wireless devices using an encryption protocol different from that of the access point would not connect at a slower speed; they wouldn't connect at all.

D. is incorrect because computers with 802.11a adapters cannot connect to an 802.11g network at any speed. 802.11a calls for the 5 GHz frequency band, whereas 802.11g uses 2.4 GHz.

Correct Answer: B

CHAPTER 25

Troubleshooting Network Issues

Objective 5.5: Given a scenario, troubleshoot general networking issues.

This chapter examines some of the network problems that troubleshooters routinely face. The Network+ exam expects candidates to be familiar with these issues and know how to address them.

In this chapter, you'll learn everything you need to know about Network+ objective 5.5, including the following topics:

▶ Considerations
▶ Common issues

CONSIDERATIONS

Troubleshooters are often faced with problems that might have multiple causes, and it can sometimes be difficult to know where to start. When that is the case, there are several elements that troubleshooters should consider first, because they are the areas where many common problems originate.

Device Configuration Review

Whatever the symptoms of the problem, starting with the configuration of the device experiencing the issue is usually a good idea. Depending on the nature of the problem, troubleshooters should consider checking the network adapter's TCP/IP configuration settings and the system's event logs. There are also the obvious solutions, such as whether the network cable is plugged in. If the problem involves network communications, it can be helpful to review the configurations of the intermediate systems—that is, the routers, switches, and other devices on the path to the destination.

Routing Tables

When troubleshooting a problem with packets not getting to their destination, checking routing tables is one way of narrowing down the location of the fault if there is one. Begin by making sure that the routing table on the problem workstation is properly configured with a default gateway address. Then, examine the tables on the network's internal routers to see what path the packets are taking internally. If the packets are reaching the Internet, then the matter is likely to be out of the local troubleshooter's hands. However, it is still possible to use the `traceroute` (or `tracert`) tool to track the path of the packets to their destination.

Interface Status

When troubleshooting a network performance issue, checking the network interface status can provide significant diagnostic information. The status should indicate the speed of the network connection and whether it is running in half or full duplex. If a workstation's network adapter is negotiating a lower than normal speed with the switch, or if it is running in half duplex when it should be full, the troubleshooter's next task is to find out why that is. This usually involves examining the switchport's interface and possibly configuring the interfaces manually.

VLAN Assignment

A VLAN is essentially a virtualized subnet realized inside a switch, so a workstation plugged into a switchport with an incorrect *VLAN assignment* (or just plugged into the wrong port) is connected to the wrong network. For trouble calls in which a user can connect to the network but can't find their familiar servers and printers, checking VLAN assignments should be on the troubleshooting checklist.

Network Performance Baselines

As mentioned in Chapter 13, "Network Availability," it is a good practice for administrators to record baseline readings of key network communication metrics at regular intervals. This is so that future troubleshooters have a history of documented readings that they can compare to the current conditions. When users report that the network seems slow, for example, a baseline comparison can confirm to the troubleshooter that there actually is a slowdown. In addition, the baseline readings give the troubleshooter a way to confirm whether a solution has been successful.

COMMON ISSUES

Troubleshooters might have to deal with a wide variety of issues, but there are some that occur over and over, such as those described in this section.

Collisions

A *collision* occurs on a cabled network when two hosts on a shared medium transmit packets at the same time. The packets collide and both are lost. The two senders must then wait a random interval and retransmit their packets. This was a normal and common occurrence on Ethernet networks back when they used hubs and ran in half duplex.

Today, nearly all Ethernet networks are connected by switches and run in full duplex, so every host has a dedicated link to the switch and can transmit and receive data at the same time. As a result, if a significant number of collisions are occurring on a full-duplex Ethernet network, there could well be something seriously wrong. One possible cause is a switch with ports negotiating half-duplex connections for some reason. Another possibility is that a cable segment is too long, causing late collisions. Both of these conditions can cause a significant performance reduction.

Broadcast Storm

As described in Chapter 11, "Switching," *broadcast storms* are an indication that there are switching loops on the network. The loops are the result of using redundant switches to create fault-tolerant paths through the network. Switches forward broadcast messages out through all of their ports. When a switching loop is present on the network, the switches start receiving duplicate copies of every broadcast message, which they start duplicating themselves. In a moment, the network is flooded with broadcasts that the host interfaces all have to receive and process. To prevent switching loops and the resulting broadcast storms, most enterprise switches use the Spanning Tree Protocol (STP), which enables the switches to hold the redundant paths as inactive standbys until they are needed.

Duplicate MAC Address

Every network interface must have a unique MAC address. On cabled networks, Ethernet adapters have their MAC addresses hard-coded, so the presence of duplicate MAC addresses on a cabled network is usually not an accident. On virtual networks, the MAC addresses of virtual machines' network interfaces are configurable, but the hypervisor manager can usually detect a duplicate MAC address immediately and display an error message.

Therefore, duplicate MAC addresses could well indicate that a MAC spoofing attack is in progress by someone trying to impersonate another host. Troubleshooters can attempt to locate the duplicate by finding the switchports receiving traffic from that MAC address.

Duplicate IP Address

As with MAC addresses, the IP addresses on a network must be unique. If there are hosts with duplicate IP addresses on the network, they will function only intermittently or not at all. Most operating systems test the uniqueness of their IP addresses (at least on the local network) by generating an ARP request broadcast to see if any other host with that same address replies. If one does, an error message typically appears and no access to the network is possible.

As a result of the ARP test, the host with the duplicate address has the MAC address of the other host in its ARP table. Troubleshooters can use that MAC address to track down the switchport to which the duplicate host is connected.

Multicast Flooding

Switches need information about the network to function properly. They use their incoming traffic to compile a table of the MAC addresses associated with their ports. However, if a switch receives traffic destined for a MAC address it doesn't know, the switch floods it out through all of its ports. Multicasts are one-to-many transmissions sent to the members of a designated multicast group. A switch properly configured for multicasts has the ports for the individual group members associated with the multicast address. If a switch is not properly set up for the multicasts, then the transmissions are flooded to all of the hosts on the network. Multicasts are often used for applications such as live video feeds that consist of a lot of traffic, so a *multicast flood* can conceivably degrade the network's performance significantly. A network traffic analysis can help troubleshooters identify where the multicast transmissions are going, and the *IGMP snooping* feature allows switches to listen in on the Internet Group Messaging Protocol (IGMP) traffic and use the information to add the multicast group members to their tables.

Asymmetrical Routing

There are benefits to having redundant routes through an internetwork, especially fault tolerance in the event that one router connection fails. One of the results, however, is a phenomenon called *asymmetrical routing*, which is when traffic takes one router path from the source system to its destination and a different router path from its destination back to the source. This can affect network performance if the two router paths are running at different speeds, and it also interferes with the fault tolerance of the design. If both router paths are needed to support regular traffic, then a router failure will interrupt the connection to the destination. Asymmetrical routing can be difficult to detect and can require careful configuration of the routing tables to prevent.

Switching Loops

As noted earlier, *switching loops* occur as the result of a network design that includes redundant switches for fault tolerance purposes. Redundant switches enable the network to tolerate a switch or cable failure without a loss of connectivity. However, switches connected to two other switches are going to send duplicate packets to each one, resulting in a switching loop. The Spanning Tree Protocol (STP) enables the switches on a network segment to select one designated port. The nondesignated ports are blocked from traffic, eliminating the switching loops, until a port is needed to take on the role of the designated port.

Routing Loops

A *routing loop* occurs when two routers have contradictory information in their routing tables. Each of the two routers has an entry for a particular destination network in its routing table. However, the Next Hop field in each router contains the address of the other router, so packets begin bouncing back and forth between the two routers until their Time to Live (TTL) values reach zero and the packets are discarded.

The `traceroute` (or `tracert`) command can disclose the presence of a routing loop in a display like the following. Resolving the problem will require modifications to the routing tables, either manually or through some adjustment of the routing protocols.

```
Tracing route to 173.146.124.1 over a maximum of 30 hops:
1    <10 ms     1 ms  <10 ms   192.168.2.99
2    101 ms   110 ms    98 ms   131.107.67.1
3    123 ms   112 ms   114 ms   131.107.88.26
4    136 ms   130 ms   133 ms   157.54.116.5
5    146 ms   129 ms   133 ms   157.54.5.1
6    136 ms   130 ms   133 ms   157.54.116.5
7    146 ms   129 ms   133 ms   157.54.5.1
8    136 ms   130 ms   133 ms   157.54.116.5
9    146 ms   129 ms   133 ms   157.54.5.1
10   136 ms   130 ms   133 ms   157.54.116.5
11   146 ms   129 ms   133 ms   157.54.5.1
```

Rogue DHCP Server

As explained in Chapter 6, "Network Services," Dynamic Host Configuration Protocol (DHCP) servers provide network clients with IP addresses and other TCP/IP configuration settings. A *rogue DHCP server* is an unauthorized server deployed on the network to provide clients with falsified settings. Apart from the denial of service, attackers can use DHCP to point clients to their own DNS server, instead of the authorized one. By loading their DNS server with false information, the attackers can direct clients to fraudulent web servers and perform phishing attacks.

Tracking down a rogue DHCP server is possible using the information it supplies to clients. Running the `ipconfig /all` command on an afflicted Windows system displays the IP address of its DHCP server, as follows:

```
Description . . . . . . . . . . . : Intel(R) Dual Band Wireless-AC 8265
Physical Address. . . . . . . . . : E4-70-B9-42-09-D2
```

```
DHCP Enabled. . . . . . . . . . . : Yes
Autoconfiguration Enabled . . . . : Yes
Link-local IPv6 Address . . . . . : fe80::9863:dbd5:70c9:a5aa%14(Preferred)
IPv4 Address. . . . . . . . . . . : 192.168.122.21(Preferred)
Subnet Mask . . . . . . . . . . . : 255.255.255.0
Lease Obtained. . . . . . . . . . : Thursday, January 12, 2023 2:27:07 AM
Lease Expires . . . . . . . . . . : Thursday, January 26, 2023 6:20:48 AM
Default Gateway . . . . . . . . . : 192.168.122.1
DHCP Server . . . . . . . . . . . : 192.168.122.1
DHCPv6 IAID . . . . . . . . . . . : 98857144
DHCPv6 Client DUID. . . . . . . . : 00-01-00-02-21-B2-B8-75-54-E1-AD-D5-96-16
DNS Servers . . . . . . . . . . . : 192.168.12.127
NetBIOS over Tcpip. . . . . . . . : Enabled
```

Running `ipconfig /release` and then `ipconfig /renew` on the affected client causes the system to generate new traffic to the rogue DHCP server, which adds its MAC address to the computer's ARP table. The `arp -g` command displays the table containing the DHCP server's MAC address, which the troubleshooter can then use to find the switch-port providing the server's network connection and disable it.

There is also a feature provided on some switches called *DHCP snooping* that allows administrators to designate certain switchports for use by DHCP servers. When a rogue DHCP server connects to an undesignated port, all DHCP traffic arriving on that port is silently discarded.

DHCP Scope Exhaustion

Dynamic Host Configuration Protocol (DHCP) servers allocate IP addresses to clients from a pool of addresses called a *scope*. A scope has a limited number of addresses, and when the DHCP server allocates all of them, it cannot register new clients until some of the current address leases expire. Attempts by DHCP clients to obtain an address from a server with an exhausted scope will fail, and the clients will configure themselves with a local address that does not provide access to the correct network.

In Windows, the self-configuration process is called *Automatic Private IP Addressing (APIPA)*. APIPA generates addresses on the 169.254.0.0 network with a subnet mask of 255.255.0.0 and no default gateway address. When a troubleshooter finds a host with these address settings on a DHCP network, this is a sure indication that something is wrong with the DHCP process, such as scope exhaustion.

IP Setting Issues

Every interface on a TCP/IP network has IP configuration settings that must be correct for the device to communicate on the network. Depending on how the devices obtain their settings, the chances of incorrect settings occurring vary. On most enterprise networks, devices obtain their IP settings from a DHCP server. If a host has misconfigured IP settings, it is either due to someone manually changing the settings on the host or a misconfiguration of the DHCP server.

If the DHCP server is supplying incorrect settings, then the whole network should be affected, and the troubleshooter should start looking at the DHCP server itself. For an individual host that has misconfigured settings, whether by accident or through tampering, the troubleshooting effort should be directed at the host system itself.

Let's look at four common issues related to IP settings:

Incorrect Gateway   In TCP/IP parlance, a gateway is a router, and the default gateway in an interface's TCP/IP configuration is the router that provides access to other networks. When the default gateway setting is missing or incorrect, the host will be able to access the local network, but not any other networks, including the Internet.

Incorrect Subnet Mask   As noted in Chapter 4, "IP Addressing," the subnet mask associated with an IP address specifies which bits of the address are network bits and which are host bits. If the subnet mask value is incorrect, the host will not be able to connect because it will be looking for a different network, which does not exist.

Incorrect IP Address   On a manually configured IP client, an incorrect IP address could duplicate that of another host on the network, which would generate an error message. It is more likely, however, that the incorrect address would belong on a different network, which would prevent the host from connecting to the current network.

Incorrect DNS Configuration   TCP/IP networks use addresses, not names, to identify systems on a network. The names are for humans. The Domain Name System (DNS) enables a host to resolve the names specified by humans into the IP addresses used by computers. If the DNS server address in the IP settings is incorrect or missing, then name resolution cannot occur, and the host cannot communicate with the network.

Missing Route

In internetwork communications, a missing route means that one of the routers between the source and the destination does not have a routing table entry specifying where to forward the sending system's packets. Therefore, the path ends at that router, the packets go no further, and the router sends an ICMP error message back to the sender. The `traceroute` (or `tracert`) command can sometimes indicate where the path ends, especially if it is on the internal network. A troubleshooter might have to manually add a route to that problem router's table or investigate the state of the routing protocols, if the network is using them. If the missing route is somewhere on the Internet, there is little the troubleshooter can do except report it to the Internet service provider.

Low Optical Link Budget

On a fiber-optic network, the *optical link budget* is the relationship between the strength of sending light source and the minimum signal strength needed at the destination. If the difference between these two values is small, then installers should make every effort to deliver as strong a signal as possible to the destination. Signals on fiber networks attenuate like any others, and many factors can contribute to the signal loss, including overlong cable segments, number of splices, and unclean connections.

Certificate Issues

Certificate errors sometimes appear in browsers when a user attempts to access a server secured with Transport Layer Security (TLS). The error indicates that there is something wrong with the certificate presented by the server, usually one of the following things:

The certificate is expired or not yet valid.   Certificates have expiration dates, after which they should be renewed with the issuing authority.

The certificate was not issued by a trusted authority.   In some cases, certificates are self-issued by the server, which is a common practice during testing and evaluation, but not appropriate for a production server.

The certificate was issued for a different server.   Certificates are issued for particular hostnames. If the certificate for a server specifies a different hostname, then troubleshooters should be suspicious.

In any of these cases, it is possible to bypass the error and proceed to the site using an unsecured connection. Whether it is safe to do so depends on the nature of the site and what the user plans to do there. Always be careful when accepting a certificate error because there is always the possibility that the certificate actually is forged or invalid, meaning that some malicious activity may be taking place.

Hardware Failure

Hardware does fail at times, and there is not much the network troubleshooter can do about it except prepare for that eventuality. That preparation usually involves throwing money at the problem. One way to prepare for hardware failures is to install redundant components in places where continued device operation is critical. Servers with redundant power supplies and fault-tolerant drive arrays, for example, are less likely to suffer service outages than those without those features. Another form of preparation is to enter into service contracts for critical components that guarantee a fast turnaround for repair or replacement.

Host-Based/Network-Based Firewall Settings

Firewalls are configurable filters that allow or deny the passage of traffic to and from specific networks or hosts. When a server is running an application, its host-based firewall must be configured to allow traffic from clients to reach it. The firewall on a web server, for example, must be configured to allow incoming traffic through port 80. If that port is blocked by a firewall rule, then clients cannot access the web server.

When troubleshooting a communication problem in which host-based firewall settings are a possible cause, one of the easiest ways to check that hypothesis is to simply turn off the firewall temporarily. If the problem goes away, then the troubleshooter knows to start looking at the settings of the host-based firewall.

The same principles hold true for network-based firewalls, typically located between an internal network and the Internet or between a screened (or perimeter) subnet and the internal network. Troubleshooters can check the firewall logs to see if any traffic related to a problematic connection was blocked by the firewall. The general rule of least privilege applies to all firewalls; let only the essential traffic through and block everything else. The difference when working with network-based firewalls is that the stakes are far higher since these firewalls are the network's protection against Internet intruders.

Blocked Services, Ports, or Addresses

For network communication to occur, the systems involved must have the correct TCP and UDP ports open so that packets can enter and leave the systems from the right places. Most applications and services open the ports they need during installation, but firewalls—either on the host or on the network—can block those essential ports, rendering the application or service inaccessible from the network. Firewalls can block IP addresses or entire subnets as well. Sometimes, when applying the least privileges principle to a network, administrators inadvertently block essential ports they weren't aware an application needed. As mentioned earlier, when dealing with network communication problems, troubleshooters should always keep firewall rules in mind as potential sources of blockages.

The netstat command can list the open ports on a system, as shown in Chapter 23, "Network Software Tools and Commands." A port scanner can detect open ports on the network. Both are useful tools when trying to troubleshoot a malfunctioning (or nonfunctioning) application.

Incorrect VLAN

As noted earlier in this chapter, an incorrect VLAN assignment is essentially the virtualized equivalent of connecting a device to the wrong network. The device will likely be assigned an incorrect IP address and will be unable to access the user's familiar resources. It is also possible that the device could receive enhanced privileges as a result of connecting to the wrong VLAN. Troubleshooters should check the VLAN configuration at the switch when these *wrong network* situations occur.

DNS Issues

The *Domain Name System (DNS)* resolves server and domain names into IP addresses. If that name resolution process fails to occur, it might appear to the average user as though the network connection is down, but that might not be so. It is only the DNS that is experiencing a problem. A network might have a DNS server on the internal network, or it might use the ISP's DNS server. Either way, the DNS process relies on other servers on the Internet, so when the Internet connection goes down, DNS does as well.

In most cases of DNS issues, the name resolution process is either not working at all or it is returning incorrect information. Troubleshooting a name resolution failure typically starts with checking that the host is configured with the correct DNS server address. If it is, the next step is to check the DNS server the host is configured to use. The DNS service or daemon might not be running on the server, and the troubleshooting process should work its way down the OSI model layers from there. If the server appears to be functioning, then the problem might involve Internet servers that are out of the troubleshooter's control.

If the name resolution process is returning incorrect information, it might be that the DNS resource records have recently been updated, and the revised records are still propagating around the Internet, which might take some time.

NTP Issues

There are many network applications and services that rely on timestamps to synchronize their operations. For these operations to function properly, the systems involved must have synchronized clocks. For example, on a network using Active Directory Domain Services, which relies on a complex exchange of time-sensitive tickets, computers more than five minutes out of synch with the domain controller will not function properly. Certificates are also reliant on timestamps for their dates of validity, and any application that gathers log information from network devices needs the device times to be synchronized if the logs are going to be of any use to troubleshooters.

The *Network Time Protocol (NTP)* allows devices to synchronize their clocks with public time servers on the Internet. Normally, computers have small batteries to keep their internal clocks running, but those batteries can eventually die, which might cause the system clock to reset to a date and time in another century. An NTP-based time service allows the system to periodically set its clock to an accurate time signal. Virtually every operating system has a command or application for configuring the time service. For example, in Windows, the W32tm.exe program can display a status report like the following:

```
Leap Indicator: 0(no warning)
Stratum: 4 (secondary reference - syncd by (S)NTP)
Precision: -6 (15.625ms per tick)
Root Delay: 0.1159744s
Root Dispersion: 0.0540637s
ReferenceId: 0x287706E4 (source IP:  40.119.6.228)
Last Successful Sync Time: 1/28/2023 9:59:35 PM
Source: time.windows.com,0x8
Poll Interval: 10 (1024s)
```

If the time service is not running or if it is set to synchronize with an invalid source, there are other commands to specify the name of a time server and other settings.

BYOD Challenges

Bring-your-own-device (BYOD) policies, as mentioned in Chapter 14, "Organizational Documents and Policies," are common on enterprise networks today, meaning that employees are allowed to use their own personal smartphones, tablets, and other devices to access network resources. To the company management, this is a boon because it saves them from having to buy new devices for everyone. To IT technicians and troubleshooters, however, it is a nightmare. Users have different devices with different operating systems, some new and some old, and IT people must provide support for all of them. Most problematic, in many cases, is that IT must configure the devices to be secure enough to work with potentially sensitive network data.

Licensed Feature Issues

Many software products today are available in multiple versions with various feature sets and corresponding prices. In many cases, the application is complete, even in its most basic version, and purchasing an additional license just unlocks the corresponding features. IT personnel responsible for pre-sales evaluations of software products should be aware of each product's feature tiers. In addition, many software products today are sold on a subscription basis that requires regular renewals. Keeping track of the renewal dates for multiple products and multiple users is another task added to the IT department's list.

Network Performance Issues

A trouble call reporting that the network is slow is not usually a top priority issue for the IT department. It's an isolated, subjective report that might just be a transient issue that will pass in a few minutes. However, when everyone on the network starts reporting a slow-down, IT takes notice. Unfortunately, it can be difficult to know where to start with this type of issue.

Networks typically suffer performance issues because of a bottleneck, a single component or process that is causing the entire network to slow down, just as an accident in one lane of a highway affects the traffic for miles. That bottleneck could be anywhere on the network, so troubleshooters have to start using the tools and techniques described in this book to narrow down its location. Examining logs and comparing current metrics with established baseline readings can be a good place to start.

CERTMIKE EXAM ESSENTIALS

▶ When network troubleshooters approach a problem, it is often a good idea to review some of the basic considerations that can indicate possible causes, such as the problem device's configuration settings, its routing table entries, its VLAN assignment, and the status of its network interface. Comparing the network's current performance metrics to baseline readings taken earlier is also a good starting point.

▶ Some of the common network infrastructure issues that troubleshooters frequently encounter on enterprise networks include switching and routing loops, which can cause traffic to circulate endlessly throughout the network; multicast floods and asymmetrical routing, which can degrade network performance; and incorrect firewall settings and VLAN assignments, which can prevent users from accessing the network resources they need.

Practice Question 1

Ralph is working the IT helpdesk when he receives a call from a user who reports that they can see their colleagues' computers on the local network but they cannot access the Internet. Ralph proceeds to the user's office, opens a command prompt, and runs `ipconfig /all` on their Windows workstation. The results of the command are as follows:

```
Windows IP Configuration

    Host Name . . . . . . . . . . . . : Client12
    Primary Dns Suffix . . . . . . . :
    Node Type . . . . . . . . . . . : Hybrid
    IP Routing Enabled. . . . . . . : No
    WINS Proxy Enabled. . . . . . . : No

Ethernet adapter Local Area Connection:

    Connection-specific DNS Suffix . :
    Description . . . . . . . . . . . : PCIe Family Controller
    Physical Address. . . . . . . . : 60-EB-59-93-5E-E5
    DHCP Enabled. . . . . . . . . . : No
    Autoconfiguration Enabled . . . . : Yes
    Link-local IPv6 Address . . . . . : fe80::c955:c944:acdd:3fcb%2
    IPv4 Address. . . . . . . . . . : 192.168.4.24
    Subnet Mask . . . . . . . . . . : 255.255.255.0
    Lease Obtained. . . . . . . . . : Monday, October 23, 2022
6:23:47 PM
    Lease Expires . . . . . . . . . : Saturday, November 18, 2022
9:49:24 PM
    Default Gateway . . . . . . . . : 192.168.6.99
    DHCPv6 IAID . . . . . . . . . . : 241232745
```

```
        DHCPv6 Client DUID. . . . . . . . : 00-01-00-01-18-10-22-0D-60-EB-
        69-93-5E-E5

        DNS Servers . . . . . . . . . . . : 202.86.11.114

        NetBIOS over Tcpip. . . . . . . . : Enabled
```

Based on the information provided by `ipconfig`, which of the following is the most likely explanation for the user's problem?

A. The address specified in the DNS Servers setting is on a different network from the IPv4 Address setting.
B. The Subnet Mask setting is incorrect.
C. The Default Gateway setting contains an address on another network.
D. The network interface does not have DHCP enabled.

Practice Question 2

Alice is capturing network traffic samples as part of an ongoing project to document performance baselines for future reference and troubleshooting. As she examines one traffic sample, Alice notices that it contains a great deal of multicast traffic that appears to be flooding the network, but she does not know why. After investigating further, she learns that there is a live video stream on the network being transmitted as multicasts, but it is only intended for a select group of users, not for everyone. However, since the multicast traffic is currently flooding the network, all of the hosts must receive and process the packets, possibly resulting in a performance degradation or even a denial of service. Which of the following techniques can Alice use to prevent the multicast traffic from being processed by the unintended hosts most easily?

A. Firewall configuration
B. Flow control
C. IGMP snooping
D. Asymmetric routing

Practice Question 1 Explanation

A. is incorrect because, unlike the default gateway, the DNS server does not have to be on the local network, so the address shown in the `ipconfig` display can be correct.
B. is incorrect because, if the Subnet Mask setting were incorrect, the computer would have no network access at all, not the partial access it has now.
C. is correct because the Default Gateway setting must contain the address of a router on the local network that provides access to other networks, including the Internet. Ralph's client, therefore, should have a Default Gateway address on the 192.168.4.0 network, but the system is using an address on the 192.18.6.0 network, which is not local. As a result, the user can only access systems on the 192.168.4.0 network.
D. is incorrect because it is not necessary for a computer to use DHCP to access the Internet.

Correct Answer: C

Practice Question 2 Explanation

A. is incorrect because while it would be possible to configure the firewalls of the individual systems to block the multicasts, it would be a time-consuming and labor-intensive solution.
B. is incorrect because flow control only affects the speed at which transmitting systems send packets containing TCP segments.
C. is correct because Internet Group Management Protocol (IGMP) snooping is a switching technique that prevents hosts from receiving multicast packets when they are not members of the multicast group. The multicast traffic still appears on the network, but only the members of the group will receive and process the packets.
D. is incorrect because asymmetric routing only affects the paths that packets take through an internetwork. It does not regulate multicast traffic.

Correct Answer: C

Index